Springer Texts in Education

More information about this series at http://www.springer.com/series/13812

Daniel Churchill

Digital Resources for Learning

Springer

Daniel Churchill
Division of Information and Technology
  Studies, Faculty of Education
The University of Hong Kong
Hong Kong
Hong Kong

ISSN 2366-7672 ISSN 2366-7980 (electronic)
Springer Texts in Education
ISBN 978-981-10-3775-7 ISBN 978-981-10-3776-4 (eBook)
DOI 10.1007/978-981-10-3776-4

Library of Congress Control Number: 2017930941

© Springer Nature Singapore Pte Ltd. 2017
This work is subject to copyright. All rights are reserved by the Publisher, whether the whole or part of the material is concerned, specifically the rights of translation, reprinting, reuse of illustrations, recitation, broadcasting, reproduction on microfilms or in any other physical way, and transmission or information storage and retrieval, electronic adaptation, computer software, or by similar or dissimilar methodology now known or hereafter developed.
The use of general descriptive names, registered names, trademarks, service marks, etc. in this publication does not imply, even in the absence of a specific statement, that such names are exempt from the relevant protective laws and regulations and therefore free for general use.
The publisher, the authors and the editors are safe to assume that the advice and information in this book are believed to be true and accurate at the date of publication. Neither the publisher nor the authors or the editors give a warranty, express or implied, with respect to the material contained herein or for any errors or omissions that may have been made. The publisher remains neutral with regard to jurisdictional claims in published maps and institutional affiliations.

Printed on acid-free paper

This Springer imprint is published by Springer Nature
The registered company is Springer Nature Singapore Pte Ltd.
The registered company address is: 152 Beach Road, #21-01/04 Gateway East, Singapore 189721, Singapore

Foreword

This volume addresses the many issues involved in planning, designing, configuring, and making effective use of digital resources to support learning and instruction. These issues have arisen in part due to new and powerful digital devices and technologies (Spector 2015; Spector et al. 2014). Both online learning and mobile learning have increased dramatically in the last ten years due to the possibilities that new digital technologies have made possible. A natural question has been repeatedly raised with regard to how to make the best use of these new technologies (Bereiter and Scarmadalia 2003; Spector and Anderson 2000). Answers have ranged from changing instructional approaches to developing specific applications for specific needs (i.e., still more technology; Moore 2013). Integrating informal learning experiences with formal experiences has also been raised as a way to make good use of some of these technologies (Sampson et al. 2014). Still other suggestions include eliminating classes structured around traditional disciplinary boundaries (e.g., biology, history, literature, and physics) and creating learning centers around various topical areas or problems that cut across multiple disciplines, such as environmental problem solving, stabilizing economic and social situations, designing buildings and bridges, integrating technology into learning, and so many more real-world problems (Rosen et al. 2015).

In terms of the digital technologies available to support learning and instruction, it is the best of times, and even more powerful technologies will surely follow (e.g., affordable wearable devices, dynamic feedback to support complex problem solving, and recommendation engines to support individualized and personalized learning). One only needs to read the various *Horizon Reports* published by the New Media Consortium (see www.nmc.org) to understand how quickly digital technologies are emerging and the many affordances they now make possible. It is the best of times for instructional designers and educators in terms of available digital technologies.

In terms of planning for the effective use of new technologies, it is the worst of times, especially given the rapid pace of technology emergence into mainstream living, learning, and working. As soon as teachers are trained in the effective use of one device or platform, along comes a more powerful device or platform. Moreover, given the wide variety of digital technologies now available, it is difficult to choose which one best suits a particular need or requirement. There are ever more open repositories of digital resources and learning objects from which to choose from. More challenging is matching a resource to a need—finding an appropriate resource to achieve effective learning outcomes. Needs range from access to relevant content, information, and data to ascertain how information, data, and content can or should be presented and represented to support specific learning goals and objectives. In addition, there is an even more challenging need to integrate digital resources in meaningful ways into learning activities that include practice exercises, collaborative problem solving, and the exploration of related issues and problems. Pre-service teachers need to be trained, and in-service teachers require ongoing professional development if success in making the effective use of new technologies is to be achieved on a large scale. Moreover, unlike the previous generation of computer-assisted learning and instruction, mobile devices and social networking need to be considered in terms of how they can best be used to support learning and instruction. It is the worst of times in terms of educational technology planning and implementation.

This volume should prove useful in guiding educators and instructional designers through these challenging times. Hopefully, the lessons learned will pertain to the learning much more than to the technologies mentioned and described in various cases and studies. The mantra I have adopted to guide me through these challenging times is as follows: technologies change; technologies change what people do; technologies change what people can do, should do, and will eventually do; and technologies can change what people want to avoid doing.

What this book is about is changing learning and instruction to make the best use of digital technologies. A framework for thinking about different kinds of technologies is presented along with a variety of issues and discussion for each of those categories. In that sense, this book is about the learning that can be attained by effective use of technologies, with the understanding that the technologies will surely change and the framework presented in this volume is likely to evolve with changing technologies and pedagogies.

J. Michael Spector
Professor
Department of Learning Technologies
College of Information
University of North Texas
Denton, USA

References

Bereiter, C., & Scardamalia, M. (2003). Learning to work creatively with knowledge. In E. De Corte, L. Verschaffel, N. Entwistle, & J. van Merriënboer (Eds.), *Powerful learning environments: Unravelling basic components and dimensions* (pp. 55–68). Bingley, UK: Emerald Publishing. Retrieved from http://ikit.org/fulltext/inresslearning.pdf

Moore, M. G. (Ed.). (2013). *Handbook of distance education* (3rd ed.). New York, NY: Routledge.
Rosen, Y., Ferrara, S., & Mosharraf, M. (Eds.). (2015). *Handbook of research on technology tools for real-world skill development*. Hershey, PA; IGI Global.
Sampson, D. G., Ifenthaler, D., Spector, J. M., & Isaias, P. (Eds.). (2014). *Digital systems for open access to formal and informal learning*. New York, NY: Springer.
Spector, J. M. (Ed.). (2015). *The SAGE Encyclopedia of educational technology*. Thousand Oaks, CA: Sage Publications.
Spector, J. M., & Anderson, T. M. (Eds.). (2000). *Integrated and holistic perspectives on learning, instruction and technology: Understanding complexity*. Dordrecht: Kluwer Academic Press.
Spector, J. M., Merrill, M. D., Elen, J., & Bishop, M. J. (Eds.) (2014). *Handbook of research on educational communications and technology* (4th ed.). New York, NY: Springer.

Preface

The central questions this book is addressing are, what are the effective digital resources for contemporary teaching and learning? and How such resources can be designed, developed, classified, used, and reused?

Countries around the world have been transforming and modernizing due to cultural, political, social, scientific, economical, and other conditions created by emerging technologies. Technological development has been rapid; however, this, to a large extent, also has been too fast for educational institutions to fully understand and create timely responses. Governments around the world are investing in education and support of educational modernization, and initiatives of their education authorities emerge to focus on the transformation of pedagogical practices away from traditional teacher-centered to modern learning-centered approaches empowered by the contemporary technological developments and practices. For traditional, teaching-centered educational practices, the goals of teaching are to transfer curriculum content to learners, prepare learners to score highly on examinations, and develop knowledge in a specific discipline that they would use and practice throughout their life. These are no longer holding the ground, and societies for today and the future need people who have deep conceptual foundations of disciplinary knowledge required for them to make sense of developments and solve problems and, at the same time, be prepared for lifelong learning and challenges that emerge in front of all of us now and in the future.

However, one of the key problems for drives to modernize education in line with the technological development is somehow limited ability of many educators and education policy-makers to transform their own traditional expectations, understanding, and mind-sets of what is teaching and learning, and how technology plays important roles in that process. It is strongly emerging, as recognized by the authorities and researchers, that changes are essential in (a) what we teach, that is, in the curriculum design; (b) how we teach, that is, in the pedagogy; and (c) how we evaluate learning, that is, in assessment, as essential conditions for effective technology integrations. These, in turn, impose a need for changes in the resources we design and use in teaching and learning, including those digital resources for learning. We need to think differently about the design and use of digital resources for learning than it has been done so far in the context of traditional teaching and learning. Speed and form of learning achieved in the traditional educational practices simply are no longer sufficient to enable individuals and societies to be in line with developments and demands. In this sense, an organizing idea of this book is that there is an unavoidable transformation of teaching and learning, influenced by broader changes and needs of contemporary societies, and this imposes a demand for rethinking what are effective digital (and non-digital) resources for learning. In a nutshell, this book is not only about digital resources for learning (which are seen as one of the tools for changes), but also an attempt to promote the modernization of teaching and learning.

> **Important**
> One of the key problems for drives to modernize education is somehow a limited ability of many educators and education policy-makers to transform traditional expectations, understanding, and mind-set of what is teaching and learning, and how technology plays important roles in that process.

There has been widespread absence of understandings of what are effective digital resources for contemporary learning, their connection to a curriculum, and their design and learning uses. Often, technologies and digital resources are taken simply as instructional medium for the transfer of explicit information to passive learners, or as specific media types, such as digital videos, animations, simulations, and slide presentations. Before articulating effective design and strategy use of resources for contemporary and modern teaching and learning practice, we need to have a curriculum approach that will enable these. Once more, the goal of education should be that learners accumulate lifelong lasting knowledge foundation (conceptual knowledge primarily) and skills needed to utilize these in dealing with challenges successfully (e.g., in continuous learning, problem solving, design, and innovation). There is a need for the curriculum to embrace a new approach, not the traditional one focusing on information and a single dimension of what will learners know, but a multidimensional approach that integrates all aspects of knowledge content, knowledge use, and emerging literacies and skills. Traditional curriculum models such as Bloom's Taxonomy (see Bloom et al. 1956) and even variations and revisions such as those proposed by Anderson et al. (2001) and Krathwohl (2002) might not sufficiently address the needs of such a need. Without an appropriate curriculum in place that emphasizes important components, there will not be any change in traditional teaching and learning for twenty-first century education. The proposed curriculum model for modern education in this book emphasizes three components or directions:

- *Knowledge content dimension*—where, in addition to declarative and procedural knowledge, more attention is given to the development of conceptual knowledge shaping disciplinary specific thinking and decision making (theoretical thinking);
- *Knowledge use dimension*—disposition to make intellectual uses of knowledge content to solve problem(s), continuously learn, and create innovation; and

- *New literacies and skills dimension*—which creates conditions for effective participation in intellectual activities and engagements, and use of modern tools in the contemporary world.

Hence, the three components are emphasized, and this proposed approach to the curriculum design is called the '3D curriculum.' The traditional classroom practices are insufficient to achieve curriculum outcomes integrating these three dimensions. The traditional practices focus primarily on the content knowledge dimension, while knowledge use is given attention to a limited extent. However, even in this context of the learning of curriculum knowledge content, the traditional practices are limited, as they are effective mostly with the learning of declarative and procedural aspects of content knowledge, while the development of conceptual knowledge is left to happen spontaneously. Traditional teachers naively equate knowledge with information to be transferred, and mostly are unaware, or lack understanding of the importance and meaning of conceptual knowledge. Information transfer can hardly achieve conceptual knowledge, and intellectually challenging activities are essential for deep thinking, generalizing, abstracting, and conceptual changes to occur. Traditional practices need to be replaced by 'learning-centered' practices that focus on activities engaging learners in knowledge content development, knowledge use, and the development of new literacies and skills. Activities must be central to learning, and teachers' primary roles should be the design and facilitation of such experiences for learners.

How do digital resources for learning fit in with this proposition? Digital resources for learning are representations of the curriculum knowledge content (declarative, procedural, or conceptual) that, at best, are designed to be effectively useful within learning activities. This central proposition will be unpacked in this book in the chapters that follow. Currently, there is absence of literature that provides any useful classification of digital resources for learning. This book is changing such a situation by providing an in-depth discussion of different forms of digital resources for learning, expanding the traditional conception of digital resources as information containers, and includes categories supporting the 3D curriculum, enabling knowledge use, as well as the development of new literacies and skills. Digital resources for learning are discussed and classified into a distinctive taxonomy in this book, including five definite types corresponding to different forms of curriculum content knowledge (declarative, procedural, and conceptual), as follows: presentation resources, information displays, conceptual representations, practice resources, and data displays. Each of these types of digital resources is discussed separately in various chapters of this book. It is emphasized that their design should enable effective learning within learning activities where, in addition to the learning of knowledge content enabled by these resources, knowledge use and the development of new literacies and skills are achieved. Particular emphasis in this book is given to conceptual representation as a special form of digital resource designed to support conceptual knowledge development.

> **Important**
> There is a need for the curriculum to embrace a new approach, not the traditional one focusing on information and a single dimension of what will learners know, but a multidimensional approach that integrates all aspects of knowledge content, knowledge use, and emerging literacies and skills.

Traditionally, digital resources for learning have been designed as a replacement to a teacher in a context of information transfer, thus mostly supporting traditional educational practices. The main idea there is that there are representations in the world which correspond to representation in our minds, and learning involves copying external into internal representations. At least, that has been the case with most of the learning objects, computer-based courseware, computer-based tutorials, computer-managed instruction, and even many of the most contemporary produced MOOCs. At best, such resources can support the learning of declarative and procedural knowledge; however, their effectiveness for the development of conceptual knowledge is limited, and if concept learning occurs, it is accidental rather than intentional. In the ideas presented in this book, only presentation resources are suitable for such traditional purposes. A design approach underlining the development of such traditional resources is known as the 'instructional design,' and an instructional designer's task is to articulate the best possible approach to information transfer through the application of affordances of representational media and determine how content is to be presented to learners through a specific medium (technology in our context). Norman (1988) defines affordances as 'the perceived and actual properties of the thing, primarily those fundamental properties that determine just how the thing could possibly be used' (p. 9). For Barnes (2000), a teacher's use of new technology in teaching and learning is carried out with a belief that this technology will afford learning in some way. Similarly, designers of digital resources for learning will design these resources by leveraging affordances of representational technology with the belief that these will support learning. Key affordance of representational design for learning are affordances of visualization and interactivity. Various aspects of these affordances are unpacked in this book.

In the past, there have been several widely used instructional design models, and the most popular among them remains ADDIE (Analyze, Design, Develop, Implement, Evaluate), the systematic design of instruction model developed by Dick and Carey (1978, 1985, 1990, 1996). It is understood that the instructional design emerged as early as in the 1940s from a military organization's practices of designing systematic instruction. Underlining it is the instructivist tradition of what constitutes learning. Instructivism is based on behaviorist learning theory, and it refers to a teacher-directed, carefully developed, instructional planning, sequencing, and delivery, with the purpose of transfer of curriculum content information to passive learners. For a learner, there is little space for active self-discovery, knowledge construction, and reflection. Thus, the central focus of instructivism is on transfer of the curriculum contents (with the aid of media as it is the case with digital resources), rather than on learning activities, as it should be in the context of pedagogical practices supporting modern education. Since these initial days, the instructional design has changed very little, even though that, in particular over the last 20 years, we have gone through significant development in technology and the transformation of teaching and learning. The same old thinking about teaching as a transmission of curriculum information from a teacher, or a source, to a passive learner continues to be dominant when decisions about how learning technologies are to be designed and used are determined by many designers, publishers, and educators.

> **Important**
> Design of digital resources for learning must focus on how people learn with the utility of such materials in their learning activities. These activities engage learners to work on tasks and experience processes of knowledge construction and use, while developing new literacies at the same time.

Even though, more recently, the visual and interactive capabilities and affordances of education technology have progressed significantly with the development of powerful processing and video display architecture, mobile technologies, and software tools, very little advancement has been done overall in the way how digital resources for learning are conceptualized, designed, and used.

There is an urgent need to define possibilities and articulate strategies that can be useful to teachers, designers, publishers, and researchers in their drive to modernize education in line with the contemporary developments. We need to think of a suitable design and structure of digital resources that would support declarative, procedural, and conceptual knowledge developments, as well as activities where knowledge is used, and where new literacies and skills for today and the future are developed. Instead of relying on instructional design as an underlining idea for the design of digital resources for learning, we need to start adopting and using what in this book is called 'learning design.'

Learning design places central emphasis upon a learning activity that creates experience and opportunity for learners to construct and use knowledge and, at the same time, develop literacies and other skills for twenty-first century participation. Digital resources for learning, in their most effective format, are tools used in these learning activities; they are not a replacement to a teacher, and they do not explicitly teach and transfer curriculum content. Rather, these enable, facilitate, and mediate learning activities and empower learners. This thinking brings about the fact that the central role of a teacher is no longer planning of instructional sequences; rather, it is the design of learning activities, that is, the learning design. Recently, learning design has been explored in the context of contemporary pedagogies such as constructivist learning environments (e.g., Cetin-Dindar 2016; Kwan and Wong 2015), problem-based learning and problem solving (e.g., Jonassen 2011; Savery 2015), engaged learning (e.g., Pipere 2016), active learning (e.g., Chiu 2016;

Chiu & Cheng 2016; Lee et al. 2016), and conceptual change approaches (e.g., Azevedo 2015; Deck et al. 2016; McNeil 2015). Underlining these is a set of foundational learning theories and models, such as the following:

- *Constructivist learning environment* (Jonassen 1999). In this view, learning should be arranged around activities and occur in an environment that supports knowledge construction, as opposed to knowledge transmission. Knowledge construction is a process where students individually construct their understanding of the content of the curriculum based on exploration, social engagement, testing of understandings, and consideration of multiple perspectives.
- *Problem solving* (Jonassen 2000). For Jonassen, learning is most effective when it occurs in the context of activity that engages students to solve ill-structured, authentic, complex, and dynamic problems. These types of problems differ significantly from logical, well-structured problems with a single solution. These types of problems include dilemmas, case studies, strategic decision making, and design, all of which require learners to engage in deep thinking, examination of multiple possibilities, deployment of multiple theoretical perspectives, uses of tools, creation of artefacts, and exploration of possible solutions. Students learn by solving complex problems rather than by absorbing ready-made rules, information, and procedures.
- *Engaged learning* (Dwyer et al. 1985–1998). Dwyer, Ringstaff, and Sandholtz conducted a longitudinal study to investigate the most effective adoption of Apple technology in a student-centered learning environment (i.e., The Apple Classroom of Tomorrow). These scholars argue that technology must serve as a tool for learning, which supports engagement in activities, collaboration, and deep learning. Central to their work is the concept of 'engaged learning,' which is critical in making students more active in their learning and uses of technology.
- *Problem-based learning* (PBL) (Savery and Duffy 1995). Savery and Duffy propose PBL as an optimal design model for student-centered learning. Similar to those above, PBL builds upon constructivist philosophy and contends that learning is a process of knowledge construction and social co-construction. One of the features of PBL is that students actively work on activities which are authentic to the environment in which they would be naturally used. That is, students construct knowledge in contexts which reassemble those in which they would use that knowledge. Creativity, critical thinking, metacognition, social negotiation, and collaboration are all perceived as a critical component of a PBL process. One of the key characteristics of PBL is that teachers should not primarily be concerned with the knowledge students construct, but should focus, more attention to metacognitive processes (awareness of one's own thinking and learning).
- *Rich environments for active learning* (Grabinger and Dunlap 1997). Similar to Savery and Duffy, Grabinger and Dunlap propose PBL as a highly effective educational intervention. However, in their approach, further attention is given to the context of the environment in which PBL occurs, considering the further

aspects of components and complexities that such an activity requires. In particular, emphasis is placed upon making students more responsible, willing to provide initiatives, reflective, and collaborative in the context of dynamic, authentic, and generative learning. This approach also emphasizes the importance of the development of lifelong learning skills (one of the important skills for twenty-first century learning).

- *Technology-based learning environments and conceptual change* (Vosniadou et al. 1995). In this view, the central role of technology is to support students' conceptual changes and concept learning rather than simple knowledge/information transfer. Students construct mental models and other internal representations via attempts to explain the external world. Students often bring prior misconceptions to learning situations. Therefore, learning activities ought to be designed to correct such misconceptions. Technology will scaffold not only the presentation of effective external representations of conceptual knowledge, but also the externalization of internal representations so that teachers can gain insight into students' knowledge and understanding. Taking a more constructivist perspective, technology resources will serve the role of mediator in learning activities.
- *Interactive learning environments* (Harper and Hedberg 1997; Oliver 1999). In order to serve the complexity required for learning, Oliver proposes that a learning module must contain resources, tasks, and support. For full learning to take place, a task must engage students to make purpose-specific use of resources. The teacher's role is to support learning. These integrated components will lead to interactivity essential for learning to occur. Harper and Hedberg strongly emphasize a constructivist philosophy and argue that technology itself should provide an environment where learners can interact with tools and each other. Similar to Jonassen (2000), Hedberg supports problem-based approaches as the most effective educational intervention.

> **Important**
> This book is providing an in-depth discussion of different forms of digital resources for learning, expanding the traditional conception of digital resources as information containers, and includes categories supporting the 3D curriculum, enabling knowledge use, as well as the development of new literacies and skills.

- *Collaborative knowledge building* (Bereiter and Scardamalia, in press). Knowledge building is a theoretical construct developed by Bereiter and Scardamalia to provide interpretation of what is required in the context of collaborative learning activity. Personal knowledge is seen as an internal, unobservable phenomenon and the only way to support learning and understand what is taking place, and to deal with the so-called public knowledge (which represent what a community of learners know). This public knowledge is

available to students to work on, expand, and modify through discourse, negotiation, and collective synthesis of ideas. Digital resource for learning should serve as the representation of the public knowledge.
- *Situated learning* (Brown et al. 1989). Brown and colleagues build upon the activity theory perspective to emphasize the central role of an activity in learning. An activity is where conceptual knowledge is developed and used. It is argued that this situation produces learning and cognition. Thus, activity, resources, and learning should not be considered as separate from a learning design. Learning is a process of enculturation where students become familiarized with the uses of cognitive tools in the context of working on an authentic activity. Both activity and how these tools are used are specific to a culture of practice. Concepts are not only situated in an activity, but also are progressively developed through it, shaped by emerging meaning, culture, and social engagement. In Vygotsky's terms, concepts have history, both personal and cultural. A concept can only be understood and learnt at a personal level through their uses within an activity. Active tool uses and an interaction between these resources and activity lead to an increased and ever-changing understanding of both, the activity and the context of tool use, and the tool itself. Tool use might differ between different communities of practice, so learning how to use a tool specific to a particular community is a process of enculturation. How a tool is used reflects how the specific community sees the world. Concepts also have their own history and are a product of sociocultural developments and experience of members of a community of practice. Thus, Brown and colleagues strongly suggest that activity, concept, and culture are interdependent, in that 'the culture and the use of a tool determine the way practitioners see the world, and the way the world appears to them determines the culture's understanding of the world and of the tools... To learn to use tools as practitioners use them, a student, like an apprentice, must enter that community and its culture' (p. 33). Hence, learning is a process of enculturation, where students learn to use a domain's conceptual tools in an authentic activity, and digital resources for learning should serve as such tools.
- *Inquiry-based learning supported by technology.* Work under this general idea includes practically oriented frameworks and design guidelines for building technology-based learning modules, such as the Quest Atlantis (Barab et al. 2005), MicroLessons (Divaharan and Wong 2003), ActiveLessons (Churchill 2006), and WebQuest (Dodge 1995). Similar to the previously discussed theoretical work, this approach elevates the importance of learning activity as critical for an effective educational intervention. Learning begins with an inquiry or a problem (supported with a multimedia presentation) being presented to students in an interesting way. The learners are then assigned to a task(s), provided with a template to assist them in the completion of the task(s), directed to Web-based and other resources to assist them, and collaborative tools such as discussion platforms. Most often, students use digital resources in completing

their tasks and are directed to submit outcomes via electronic means. As a design model, these approaches make a significant step in directing teachers to move away from the traditional, content-driven, teacher-centered use of technology.

> **Important**
> A learning activity and development and uses of conceptual knowledge should emerge as central to teaching and learning. Digital resources alone are not sufficient for full achievement of learning outcomes; rather, a learning activity is the mandatory condition.

What can be observed from all these ideas is that a learning activity and development and uses of conceptual knowledge should emerge as central to teaching and learning. Later on, in this book, an entire chapter will be dedicated to the discussion of an activity-based learning, with more specific emphasis on the activity-theoretical perspective (e.g., Engeström 1987). Overall, the proposed approach to digital resources for learning in this book strongly aligns with contemporary theories and research and is a strategy for transforming traditional teacher-centered teaching to a learning-centered paradigm. Articulating a learning design upon these theoretical ideas leads us to an important conclusion that digital resources alone are not sufficient for the achievement of learning outcomes; rather, a learning activity is the mandatory condition in this context. In this book, a specific learning design model is introduced. That model is called the 'RASE'; on the basis that it includes four key components: resources (R), activity (A), support (S), and evaluation (E). Design of a learning experience should focus on an activity (e.g., problem solving, projects, and inquiries) that engages learning in knowledge construction through intellectual uses of resources serving as mediating tools (inducing digital resourced for learning). A teacher's role during the implementation of a learning design is that of a facilitator supporting learners, although this should gradually fade out to allow learners to take more responsibilities and develop skills for supporting their own (lifelong) learning. Outcomes of an activity produced by learners must be formatively evaluated, and recommendations for improvements integrated in their final learning outcomes. Although the move called 'learning analytics' is attempting to automate evaluation, for now, and likely in the future, this will not be effective through technology alone, and the involvement of teachers and communities of learners is essential for effective evaluation.

In this book, particular attention is given to two affordances of contemporary representational technologies: affordances for (a) visualization of information, data, and ideas through the design and arrangements of colors, lines, shapes, images, symbols, etc.; and (b) interactivity as a means for providing learning with tools for manipulation and exploration of information, data, or ideas through the use of sliders, buttons, clickable areas, text inputs, etc. It is argued that these affordances empower the design of digital resources for learning, maximizing representation through multimodalities, and, in particular, making possible for complex concepts to be represented in a format that can be effectively useful in the context of learning activities. Furthermore, this book examines the design and delivery of digital resources for learning via mobile technologies. In the final chapter, emerging representational and interactive technologies are explored, and some proposals on how these might influence digital resources for learning are provided. The chapters include activities carefully selected and designed to facilitate the understanding and learning of ideas presented in this book. Throughout the book, numerous examples of digital resources for learning, mostly designed by the author, are provided and discussed. The author hopes that these will be useful and inspirational to teachers, publishers, and designers of educational resources and that the ideas presented will lead to positive changes in teaching and learning practice, as well as to open possibilities for effective research questions to be explored.

Hong Kong   Daniel Churchill

References

Anderson, L. W., Krathwohl, D. R., Airasian, P. W., Cruikshank, K. A., Mayer, R. E., Pintrich, P. R., et al. (2001). *A taxonomy for learning, teaching, and assessing: A revision of Bloom's taxonomy of educational objectives*. New York, NY: Longman.

Azevedo, R. (2015). Defining and measuring engagement and learning in science: Conceptual, theoretical, methodological, and analytical issues. *Educational Psychologist, 50*(1), 84–94.

Barab, S., Thomas, M., Dodge, T., Carteaux, R., & Tuzun, H. (2005). Making learning fun: Quest Atlantis, a game without guns. *ETR&D, 53*(1), 86–107.

Barnes, S. (2000). What does electronic conferencing afford distance education? *Distance Education, 21*(2), 236–247.

Bereiter, C., & Scardamalia, M. (in press). Learning to work creatively with knowledge. In E. De Corte, L. Verschaffel, N. Entwistle, & J. van Merriënboer (Eds.), *Unravelling basic components and dimensions of powerful learning environments*. EARLI Advances in Learning and Instruction Series. Retrieved from http://ikit.org/fulltext/inresslearning.pdf

Bloom, B. S., Engelhart, M. D., Furst, E. J., Hill, W. H., & Krathwohl, D. R. (1956). *Taxonomy of educational objectives: The classification of educational goals*. New York, NY: David McKay Company.

Brown, J. S., Collins, A., & Duguid, P. (1989). Situated cognition and the culture of learning. *Educational Research, 18*(1), 32–42.

Cetin-Dindar, A. (2016). Student motivation in constructivist learning environment. *Eurasia Journal of Mathematics, Science & Technology Education, 12*(2), 233–247.

Chiu, P. H. P. (2016). A technology-enriched active learning space for a new gateway education programme in Hong Kong: A platform for nurturing student innovations. *Journal of Learning Spaces, 5*(1), 52–60.

Chiu, P. H. P., & Cheng, S. H. (2016). Effects of active learning classrooms on student learning: A two-year empirical investigation on student perceptions and academic performance. *Higher Education Research & Development*, 1–11, 269–279.

Churchill, D. (2006). Student-centered learning design: Key components, technology role and frameworks for integration. *Synergy, 4*(1), 18–28.

Deck, S. M., Platt, P. A., & McCord, L. (2016). Engaged teaching-learning: Outcome evaluation for social work students in a graduate-level service learning research course. *Advances in Social Work, 16*(2), 233–248.

Dick, W., & Carey, L. M. (1978, 1985, 1990, 1996). *The systematic design of instruction.* Glenview, IL: Harper Collins Publishers.

Divaharan, S., & Wong, P. (2003). Student-centered learning: Microlessons. In S. C. Tan (Ed.). *Teaching and learning with technology: an Asia-pacific perspective* (pp. 182–198). Singapore: Prentice Hall.

Dodge, B. (1995). *Some thoughts about WebQuests.* Retrieved from http://webquest.sdsu.edu/about_webquests.html

Dwyer, D. C., Ringstaff, C, & Sandholtz, J. H. (1985–1998). *Apple classroom of tomorrow.* Cupertino, CA: Apple Computer Inc. Retrieved from http://www.apple.com/education/k12/leadership/acot/library.html

Engeström, Y. (1987). *Learning by expanding.* Helsinki: Orienta-konsultit.

Grabinger, R. S, Dunlap, J. C. (1997). Rich environments for active learning: A definition. *Research in Learning and Teaching, 3*(2), 5–34.

Harper, B., & Hedberg, J. (1997). *Creating motivating interactive learning environments: A constructivist view.* Retrieved from http://www.ascilite.org.au/conferences/perth97/papers/Harper/Harper.html

Jonassen, D. (1999). Designing constructivist learning environments. In C. M. Reigeluth (Ed.). *Instructional design theories and models: A new paradigm of Instructional Theory* (Vol. 2, pp. 215–239). Hillsdale, NJ: Lawrence Erlbaum Associates.

Jonassen, D. (2000). Towards design theory of problem solving. *ETR&D, 48(4),* 63–85.

Jonassen, D. (2011). *Learning to solve problems: A handbook for designing problem-solving learning environments.* New York: NY: Routledge.

Krathwohl, D. R. (2002). A revision of Bloom's Taxonomy: An overview. *Theory into Practice, 41*(4), 212–218.

Kwan, Y. W., & Wong, A. F. (2015). Effects of the constructivist learning environment on students' critical thinking ability: Cognitive and motivational variables as mediators. *International Journal of Educational Research, 70,* 68–79.

Lee, C. B., Chai, C. S., Tsai, C. C., & Hong, H. Y. (2016). Using knowledge building to foster conceptual change. *Journal of Education and Training Studies, 4*(8), 116–125.

McNeil, S. (2015). Visualizing mental models: Understanding cognitive change to support teaching and learning of multimedia design and development. *Educational Technology Research and Development, 63*(1), 73–96.

Norman, D.A. (1988). The psychology of everyday things. New York: Basic Books.

Oliver, R. (1999). Exploring strategies for on-line teaching and learning. *Distance Education, 20*(2), 240–254.

Pipere, A. (2016). Engaged learning: Primary teachers' beliefs and performance-related self-perception. *Acta Paedagogica Vilnensia, 14*(14), 100–112.

Savery, J. R. (2015). *Overview of problem-based learning. Definitions and distinctions.* Retrieved from https://docs.lib.purdue.edu/cgi/viewcontent.cgi?article=1002&context=ijpbl

Savery, J. R., & Duffy, T. M. (1995). Problem based learning: An instructional model and its constructivist framework. *Educational Technology, 35*(5), 31–38.

Vosniadou, S., De Corte, E., & Mandl, H. (1995). *Technology-based learning environments.* Heidelberg: Springer-Verlag.

Contents

1	**Educational Reforms, Learning-Centred Education and Digital Resources for Learning**...	1
	1.1 Introduction to Digital Resources for Learning...............	1
	1.2 Digital Resources and Learning-Centred Education..........	4
	1.3 Classification of Digital Resources for Learning.............	10
	References..	17
2	**Information Display Resources**...	19
	2.1 What Is an Information Display Resource?...................	19
	2.2 A Single Interactive Screen for Display of Information	22
	2.3 Examples of Interactive and Visual Information Displays.......	26
	2.4 Designing an Information Display Digital Resources for Learning?...	31
	References..	35
3	**Concept Representation Resources**..	37
	3.1 What Is a Concept Representation?...........................	37
	3.2 What Is a Concept?..	39
	3.3 Concept Learning...	42
	3.4 Designing and Developing a Concept Representation Resource..	47
	3.4.1 Identify/Determine a Concept for the Design..........	47
	3.4.2 Specify Concept's Particulars	48
	3.4.3 Design a Storyboard Specifying How a Concept's Content Will Be Represented	48
	3.4.4 Develop a Prototype of the Concept Representation Resource and Evaluate It...........................	50
	3.4.5 Develop the Final Concept Representation Resource....	51
	3.5 Examples of Concept Representation Resources...............	53
	3.5.1 Maximizing Content Presentable in a Minimal Screen Space: Machining Parameters	53
	3.5.2 Concept Representation Resources in Non-conceptual Domain: Tenses and Four Tones....................	54

		3.5.3	Difficult to Visualize Domains: Algebra Blocks and Multiplication of Fractions	56
		3.5.4	Teaching Young Learners to Generalize: Drying Rate	58
		3.5.5	Simulations and Concept Learning	59
	3.6	A Study of Design of Concept Representation Resources		59
		3.6.1	The Study of Presentation Design	61
		3.6.2	Recommendations for Presentation Design	65
		3.6.3	An Example of a Concept Representations Resource Design Reflecting the Recommendations	68
		3.6.4	Call for Further Empirical Studies	69
	References			71
4	**Presentation Resources**			75
	4.1	What Is a Presentation Resource?		75
	4.2	An Instructional Presentation Resource		77
	4.3	Presentation Resource for Self-learning		80
		4.3.1	Video Presentation	81
		4.3.2	E-Book Presentation	81
		4.3.3	Computer-Based Instructional Presentation	82
		4.3.4	Learning Object	82
	4.4	Theoretical Perspectives of Uses of Visuals and Interactive Representations in Instruction		90
	References			102
5	**Practice Resources**			105
	5.1	What Is a Practice Resource?		105
	5.2	Drill & Practice Resources		106
	5.3	Procedure and Practice Resources		109
	References			114
6	**Data Display Resources**			117
	6.1	What Is a Data Display Resource?		117
	6.2	Examples of Data Display Resource Designed Specifically for Learning Purposes		121
	6.3	Designing Data Display Resources		126
7	**Using Digital Resources for Learning in a Learning Activity**			133
	7.1	An Idea of a Learning Design		133
	7.2	A Concept of a Human Activity		135
	7.3	A Learning Activity and a Learning Design		136
	7.4	Learning Resources and Tool Mediation		140
	7.5	Learning Design Model and Uses of Digital Resources for Learning		142
		7.5.1	Resources	144
		7.5.2	Learning Activity	144

		7.5.3	Support	150
		7.5.4	Evaluation	150
	7.6	An Example of Digital Resource for Learning Used Within an Activity		151
	References			157
8	**Repository of Digital Resources for Learning**			**159**
	8.1	Repository of Digital Resources for Learning		159
	8.2	Web 2.0 Paradigm and the Social Web		161
	8.3	An Example of a System Based on Web 2.0 Ideas that Can Serve as a Model for a Repository of Digital Resources for Learning		164
	8.4	What Is Useful from RISAL in Relation to a Repository of Digital Resources for Learning Presented in This Book?		171
	References			174
9	**Mobile Technologies and Digital Resources for Learning**			**175**
	9.1	Introduction to Mobile Learning		175
	9.2	Affordances of Mobile Technology		177
	9.3	Digital Resources for Small Screens of Mobile Devices		180
	9.4	Design for Learning Uses		188
	9.5	iPads and other Tables in Education		202
	9.6	A Case of Design of an App Resource: From a Small-Screen Mobile Device to a Tablet Version		208
		9.6.1	Development of a Resource for Mobile Learning	209
		9.6.2	Development of iMobilese for iPod Delivery	212
		9.6.3	Tablet Version of iMobilese Digital Resource for Learning	220
	References			222
10	**Emerging Possibilities for Design of Digital Resources for Learning**			**227**
	10.1	New and Emerging Developments		227
		10.1.1	Emerging Representation Technologies	228
		10.1.2	New Forms of Interactivity	232
		10.1.3	Other Relevant Technological Developments	234
	10.2	Emerging Developments and Digital Resources for Learning?		237
	10.3	Summary of Main Ideas from This Book		240
	References			243

Educational Reforms, Learning-Centred Education and Digital Resources for Learning

Learning Outcomes:

- Describe what is a digital resource for learning;
- Discuss key ideas that underline digital resources for learning as presented in this book;
- Describe the main role of digital resources in learning-centred activities; and
- Classify digital resources for learning into different forms according to a classification based on declarative-procedural-conceptual curriculum content knowledge forms.

1.1 Introduction to Digital Resources for Learning

The central question this book is attempting to address is what are effective digital resources for today's teaching and learning, and how such resources can be designed, developed, used, reused and managed. In the book, we will explore forms of digital media for teaching and learning. More specifically, the purposes of the book are as follows:

- The book is a useful guide for the development of digital resources for learning.
- The book presents a set of practical recommendations for the uses of these resources in educational activities. Thus, the book is a useful reference material for teachers in identifying, using and reusing digital resources for learning in their teaching.

- The book is a valuable resource for those teachers who wish to conceptualize digital resources for their own teaching.
- The book is useful reference material for digital media publishers and designers of educational resources as it provides a unique perspective and approach to the conceptualization, design, development and deployment of digital resources for learning.
- The book is a useful guide for researchers investigating learning issues surrounding design, development and use of digital resources for learning.

There has been a wide spread absence of understandings of what are digital resources for learning, their connection to a curriculum, and their learning uses and management. Often, technologies and digital resources are taken simply as instructional medium for the transfer of explicit information to passive learners. Even the most contemporary initiatives such as MOOC[1] and Flipped Classroom, continue to deploy information technologies and digital resources in a way that reflects such outdated practice.

Digital resources for learning are best described as technology-based multimedia content specifically designed for educational (and training) purposes. There are a lot of digital resources on the Internet and other sources, designed for various purposes, such as to provide news information, marketing or entertainment. However, digital resources for learning are designed with specific intention to be used for learning rather than for any other information purposes. Therefore, their design includes a focus on how people learn with the utility of such media in their activities, and how such resources can be designed, developed and managed for that specific purpose.

> **Important**
> Digital resources for learning are best described as technology-based multimedia content specifically designed for education and training purposes.

Here are some brief examples of what might be effective digital resources for learning:

- Learners are presented to an interactive representation that permits the manipulation of parameters and exploration of relationships, e.g., changing some parameters that cause pollution and observing effect on climate change, or changing parameters related to the migration of a population and observing the impact on regional economies.

---

[1] A massive open online course (MOOC) is a contemporary approach to the development of online courses aimed at wide participation and open access via the Internet. A number of top universities in the world provide MOOC courses for free to prospective students and others interested to learn specific topics. The educational quality of many of MOOCs is questionable as there is absence of any useful learning design strategy to guide their development.

> **Important**
> Digital resources for learning are designed based on focus on how people learn with the utility of such media in their activities, and how such resources can be designed, developed and managed for that specific purpose.

- Data, information and ideas are presented mathematically, e.g., selecting start and target destination on the map and manipulating the acceleration of a vehicle to obtain information about its velocity and displacement, or increasing the number of vehicles in Europe and obtaining mathematical or statistical representations of the amount of certain pollutants in the air.
- Data, information and ideas are expressed in non-mathematical ways, e.g., manipulating changes in social welfare regulations and obtaining statements of opinions from people across Europe.
- Representations are manipulated graphically, e.g., dropping an icon of an electric coal power station on the map and observing the change in global warming over some areas of China.
- Data, information and ideas are represented and structured in information networks and pop-up displays, e.g., rolling a mouse pointer over a city to access information about its population, selecting two of more cities and obtaining information about the distance between them; dragging a slider along a time line and accessing some historical information relevant to different countries.
- Data are accessed by dragging an icon of a thermometer or a barometer and collecting data about weather conditions in different locations on a map. In this approach, learners could collect some real-life data about a phenomenon if this digital resource is linked to some meteorological data source. Data could be randomized to ensure that different learners or teams access different quantities and various representations of these, but remain unified within a method of solving a specific problem at the center of a learning activity set for them.

These examples illustrate how interactive and visual affordances of contemporary representational technologies can be leveraged to provide resources that can be used in learning (within activities). Contemporary authoring tools (e.g., Adobe Flash, HTML5 and MIT App Inventor) allow a designer to bring interactivity and visualization together into a digital resource for learning that, for example, allows the manipulation of parameters and relationships, or access to data and information.

> **Important**
> Activities are not built-in or integral parts of the design of digital resources for learning, rather, these are planned by teachers based on intended learning outcomes. The most effective digital resources for learning are tools that mediate learning activities.

The most effective digital resources for learning are those designed for use (and reuse) in the context of learning-centered activities.[2] In this context, and for this book, activities are not built-in or integral parts of digital resources for learning. Rather, activities are planned by individual teachers based on the intended learning outcomes of their curriculum. This proposition is the central cornerstone of the ideas presented in this book—the most effective digital resources for learning are tools that mediate learning activities.

In this book, the author places central emphasis upon an activity that creates an experience and an opportunity for learners to (a) construct and (b) use knowledge and, at the same time, (c) develop New Literacies and other generic skills for 21st century participation. Digital resources for learning are tools used in these activities. This thinking brings about that the central role of a teacher is no longer planning of instructional sequences; rather, it is the design of activities, that is, learning design.[3]

> **Important**
> A learning activity must provide an experience and an opportunity for learners to (a) construct and (b) use knowledge and, at the same time, (c) develop New Literacies and other generic skills for 21st century participation.

The author hopes that this book will provide a unique strategy to advance digital learning, not just teaching in schools, universities and other formal education contexts, but also in the contexts of consumer and corporate training, professional development and private tutoring. The approach to the classification of digital resources for learning presented in this book is a unique strategy, which has never been explored before commercially or within a large educational system.

1.2 Digital Resources and Learning-Centred Education

Education in the contemporary world requires that teachers transform their traditional pedagogical practices, and become learning designers, that is, to embrace learning-centered pedagogy. Some aspects of teacher-centered practice are contrasted to learning-centered practice in Table 1.1.

---

[2]Learning-centered activities are designed to engage students in working on tasks and experience processes of knowledge construction and use. An example of an activity is a troubleshooting task, a design task or a case study. Later charters will provide more in-depth discussion of activity and examples, as well as how digital resources for learning are used to mediate activities.

[3]Learning Design refers to a strategy for teachers' instructional planning based on learning-centered pedagogy.

Table 1.1 Some aspects of teacher-centered and learning-centered practice

Focus of teacher-centered	Focus of learning-centered
• Learning of facts and declarative knowledge	• Learning of conceptual knowledge
• Memorizing information	• Working with information
• Teacher is central to learning	• Activity is central to learning
• Passing the test/exam and achieving the grade	• Applying knowledge, theoretical thinking and demonstrating generic skills
• Drilling of right answers and routines	• Problem-solving, design, project work and inquiries
• Learning to pass exams	• Learning how to learn
• Focus on information presentation to passive leanings	• Focus on how learning occurs within an activity
• Technology as a media channel	• Technology as intellectual partner in learning
• Learning from resources and technology	• Learning with resources and technology

Transition to learning-centered practices is essential for reforms of education in-line with the needs and demands of the 21st century. The following are some of the key requirements for this transition:

- Overall approaches to teaching practice need to change away from the instructivist and teaching-centered towards learning-centered. We need to ensure that our graduates are competent lifelong learners, knowledge workers and creative innovators, not just walking libraries with information passed to them through instruction. Such goals cannot be achieved through traditional teaching and learning practices.
- Curricula need to be written explicitly to encounter three forms of knowledge including (a) declarative, (b) procedural knowledge, and most importantly (c) conceptual. Furthermore, curricula must be explicit about how these forms of knowledge should be used in the context of specific courses. Uses can range from (a) recalling, (b) explaining, (c) applying, to (d) innovating. Traditional models are based on information transfer and reproduction, while today this is not sufficient for education. Societies need graduates who are able to construct and work with knowledge, not just know a lot.
- As the world is becoming more technologically sophisticated, there is a growing need to learn more disciplinary knowledge. While we need to teach more to learners, the time available remains the same. The challenge, therefore, is how to teach more in shorter time—not just curriculum content, but also knowledge use skill, as well as other knowledge and skills required for modern day living, working, learning and socializing.
- At the same time, education must consider knowledge and skills essential for today's and tomorrow's generations to be effective participants in society. These are New Literacies and other generic skills and practices, such as, creativity,

Fig. 1.1 New literacies for 21st century's information society

problem solving, thinking skills, lifelong learning, and collaboration skills. Shorter time for teaching disciplinary knowledge content might be needed in order to allow new literacies and knowledge uses to enter the curriculum in any effective way. In this context, we need to seriously rethink about the forms of educational content and their uses (activities), how to teach more in a shorter time and yet at greater depth of understanding, and how to minimize material but maximize learning through effective design and uses of resources. Figure 1.1 presents various aspects of New Literacies that are more specifically related to today's information society.

There is a need for a practical framework and a guiding model for teachers how to best utilize digital resources for learning and achieve learning outcomes of the multidimensional curriculum.[4] Such a framework is to serve as a powerful intervention, aligning education professionals to transform traditional practices and promote a learning-centered culture. This framework is elaborated in the later parts of this book. The book proposes such a framework in the later chapters. How do digital resources for learning, as presented in this book, assist transition to learning-centered education? Here are some key issues to consider:

- Digital resources for learning should be designed according to the three types of curriculum knowledge content, that is, these resources can not only be designed to support the learning of declarative and procedural knowledge, rather, and more importantly, digital resources for learning can be designed to support the development of fundamental concepts that contribute to an essential base of disciplinary and cross-disciplinary knowledge.

> **Important**
> Digital resources alone are not sufficient for full achievement of learning outcomes. In addition to Resources, when developing a learning design, teachers need to consider Activity, Support and Evaluation (RASE).

- Digital resources for learning should be designed in a way that supports activities where knowledge is created and used, not just for the transfer of knowledge content. In this context, digital resources for learning can serve as tools that mediate activities where learning occurs, and shape learners' thinking and decision-making. In other words, digital resources for learning can be practically useable knowledge representations within activities where learners engage in (a) analytical processes to generalize and abstract concepts and ideas based on affordances of digital resources for learning, and (b) the application of any cognitive residue emerging in that processes.
- Digital resources for learning should be designed to support activities leading to development of New Literacies. In this sense, digital resources for learning should not simply present information in a convenient manner. Rather, these should require learners to apply their literacies, such as visual, media and critical literacy in order to extract meaning. Furthermore, digital resources for learning should be designed to support activities that facilitate New Literacy practices

---

[4]The multidimensional curriculum focuses on three dimensions: (a) *knowledge content*—declarative, conceptual and procedural, (b) *knowledge use*—recalling, explaining, applying and innovating, and (c) *new literacies* as essential practices in knowledge creation and uses with the deployment of emerging technologies and practices.

and developments, such as those related to the productive utility of emerging technologies in developing digital essays.
- Digital resources for learning can be designed to allow presentation maximizing the amount of content, often in a small and temporally limited screen space through the use of effective visual, other multimodalities, and interactivity.

> **Important**
> Teachers should play a key role in the design of learning-centered activities and the facilitation of learning, rather than being transmitters of ready-made knowledge to passive learners.

Traditional thinking about digital resources for learning as a replacement to teachers and books is not helpful at all for today's education. Instructional multimedia, computer-based tutorials, computer-managed instruction, programmed instruction, reusable learning objects etc., all assume that learning occurs when learners are studying information on the screen of a computer device, and reinforce remembering that the same content through an interactive drill and practice questions or similar reinforcement mechanisms. Actually, it is not evident if such an approach has ever been effective except in scenarios where teachers were not available to students at all, such as in distance learning programs, cooperate training where a company's offices are distributed all over the world and require just-in-time information, or in a case where customers receive a computer based package together with a product they purchased (e.g., an interactive tutorial how to use fire safety equipment). However, such an understanding of the role of digital resources as an information container presenting information in a convenient way for remembering, appears to be wide spread even in the context of formal education and training. In this context, (a) teachers should be playing central roles in the design of learning activities and facilitation of learning, rather than just being transmitters of ready-made knowledge to passive learners, and (b) where students should be engaged and learn through experiences and opportunities created by these activities. It is somehow disturbing to witness that even top scientific journals are continuing to promote the understanding that technology is just a medium for the transfer of information to passive learners. For example, the image in the article by Kellogg (2013), published in the top-ranked journal *Nature*, depicts a computer as a surrogate teacher, and students sitting in rows, passively watching, reading and listening to the content being displayed, and occasionally answering questions posed by a machine.

Therefore, there is a significant need for this book to contribute to the transformation of a wide misunderstanding of the roles of digital resources for learning in the context of formal education, primarily at schools, but also in higher education and corporate training. Digital resources for learning, at least in the context of formal education, must serve different purposes than being the media for the transfer of explicit curriculum content and information. These resources should in

1.2 Digital Resources and Learning-Centred Education

no way be seen as a replacement to teachers or other resources, either digital (e.g., web sites or e-books) and traditional (e.g., books).

So what roles should these digital resources for learning serve? Here are some of the important points:

- Digital resources for learning should supplement, not replace, a teacher.
- Digital resources for learning should supplement other resources, including the traditional resources, not necessary to replace them, and
- Digital resources for learning should supplement and mediate activities where learning is to occur, not replace activities or be activities on their own.

Activity 1.1

What is a digital resource for learning? You will find that there are a number of repositories of resources for learning (often called learning objects) available on the Internet. The following are some examples of those:

- *Merlot (Multimedia Educational Resources for Learning and Online Teaching) at* https://www.merlot.org/
- *Open Learning Initiative at Carnegie Mellon University* http://oli.cmu.edu/
- *MIT Open Courseware at* http://ocw.mit.edu/
- *Cal Poly Pomona Multimedia Learning Objects* https://elearning.cpp.edu/learning-objects/objects.php
- *The Orange Grove Florida's Open Educational Resources Repository* https://www.floridashines.org/orange-grove

Explore these repositories and attend to the following:

- *Which one of these collections contains most useful resources? How useful are these collections? What criteria you used to determine what might be the best resource?*
- *How are resources organized in these collections (e.g., by disciplines, or types)?*
- *What is the difference between a digital resource for learning and a learning object?*
- *How can resources from these collections be used in teaching and learning?*
- *Identify one good example of what a digital resource for learning might be.*

1.3 Classification of Digital Resources for Learning

As it is understood by now, digital resources for learning are technology-based representational media specifically designed for educational purposes. This is a very important definition as it separates digital resources designed with a specific purpose to facilitate learning, from all other available digital media on the Internet and elsewhere, that has been designed for different purposes (e.g., entertainment, news, digital art, commerce or marketing).

> **Important**
> The most effective digital resources for learning are designed to be used and reused as mediating tools in learning-centered activates.

Digital resources for learning have often been classified according to media types. Thus, the literature and practitioners refer to digital videos, interactive multimedia, e-books, web pages, simulations and other forms of technology-based media as forms of digital resources for learning. This approach to the classification of digital resources for learning is less than useful in the context of planning, designing, developing, using and reusing digital resources for learning. An alternative classification might provide a useful framework to support teachers and designers of digital resources for learning.

Rather than classifying digital resources for learning according to the media and other formats (e.g., educational videos, animation, simulation, web pages, multimedia, or podcasts), a more effective approach is to consider forms of curriculum content knowledge, and what kinds of digital resources may be the most effective to represent each of these forms. Disciplinary curriculum content must include multiple knowledge forms, not just declarative and procedural knowledge, but also, most importantly, conceptual knowledge. Conceptual knowledge is what forms one's foundation of intellectually activity and theoretical thinking within and across disciplines. Without an appropriate level of conceptual knowledge, it would not be possible for an individual learner to effectively think in a discipline, solve problems and learn further. Hence, a curriculum must include conceptual in addition to declarative and procedural knowledge. Thus, this book reflects an attempt to articulate and present a classification of digital learning resources that is aligned with an effective approach to curriculum design. Potentially useful classification would lead to a more acceptable definition of learning resources, and will promote generally a more aligned understanding of what digital resources for learning may be. Better understanding of this could lead to improved standards and quality indicators for the design of educationally useful and reusable digital material and activities for their utility. At the same time, appropriate classification could lead to the development of a strategy that provides support to people involved in the reuse of these resources. Having a classification that synthesizes a variety of forms of digital learning resources would also support different pedagogical models while

1.3 Classification of Digital Resources for Learning

Table 1.2 Classification of digital resources for learning according to curriculum knowledge content forms primarily intended to represent

Types of resources	Curriculum content		
	Declarative	Procedural	Conceptual
Information display resource	X		
Presentation resource	X		
Practice resource		X	
Concept representation resource			X
Data display resource			X

providing a variety of education material that might be designed and reused for the purpose of achieving diverse curriculum outcomes.

Therefore, in the context of this book, the question is what kind of digital learning resources can support different forms of curriculum knowledge? What kind of digital learning resources can be designed to represent declarative, procedures and conceptual knowledge from a disciplinary curriculum content? In the context of these questions, this book proposes a classification that contains five distinct types of digital resources for learning, each of which is designed to represent a specific form of content/curriculum knowledge (see Table 1.2). This classification classifies digital resources for learning into five fundamental types including: information display resources, presentation resources, practice resources, conceptual representation resources and data display resources.[5] A brief introduction to each of these types is given in this section of the chapter. Later chapters will provide in-depth discussions of each of these types of digital resources for learning.

Here is a brief description of each of the types of digital resources for learning discussed in this book. More detailed discussion about each of these types will follow in the later sessions.

- *Information Display Resources*—These digital resources for learning display information in a variety of modes,[6] use various organizers and innovative interfaces to facilitate information presentation and uses. These are not specifically designed to instruct about some of the content we want learners to remember, as is more of the case with the design of presentation resources (see the next category). Rather, these are creative and effective ways to organize and present information that can be used in learning (e.g., comparison table, a

---

[5]In the author's previous work, a term learning object was discussed as an adequate representation of digital resources for learning (Churchill 2007). However, due to extensive debates and unresolved differences in the literature of what a learning object is, this term has been abounded in this book, and a substitute term of digital resources for learning is adopted. See Chap. 4 for discussion of learning objects as a specific form of digital resources for learning.

[6]Modes of representations can be textual, graphical, pictorial, auditory, animated, special effect, etc., and when several modes are mixed or mashed into a single representation, the terms 'multiple representation,' and sometimes 'multimodal text' are used for such resources.

concept map with pop-up information, a case story about some event, and even an e-book and a digital version of a journal article). In learning, learners are using information to assist their completion of an activity, for example, extracting information from an interactive periodic table, or a trigonometric table to solve a certain problem-based task. Contemporary digital technologies allow easy creation and the presentation of information, such as scanning a text or taking a photograph with a mobile device. However, in this case, we are not talking only about how information can be digitized and delivered via technology. We are concerned with a strategy of how information can be presented in the most effective way supported by the affordances of contemporary representation technologies so that it can find effective use in activities leading to learning.

The simple example of an information object presented in Fig. 1.2 contains textual and visual information about native and non-native animals found in Australia. Information about animals is accessed by rolling a mouse pointer over the text comprising the name of an animal and through decisions which include the dragging of an animal's name into a corresponding area indicating the animal's origin. The initial story line about Australian native animals was converted through content analysis into an interactive representation that allows learners to explore this information space within the context of some learning activity. The essence of the story was preserved in the information object; however, long lines of texts have been reduced in order to shorten key statements that are delivered to a learner randomly.

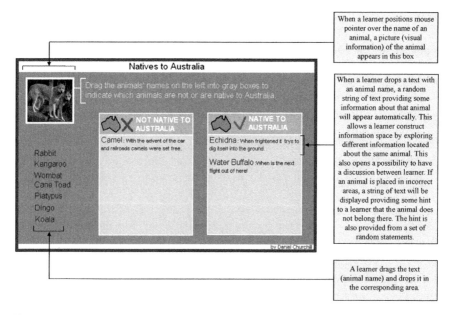

Fig. 1.2 An example of an information display resource

- *Presentation Resources*—These resources are designed to present certain information with the purpose of instructing learners and often expecting them to remember and/or understand the content presented. With the difference from the information display resource, these resources explicitly present specific declarative curriculum content (e.g., PowerPoint presentation slides, a recorded computer screen activity with audio or annotated explanations, a recorded lecture with a voice-over and slides, a computer based tutorial). Often, these are designed with an assumption that information can be passed from a resource or a teacher to a student through a medium rather than serving the purpose of an activity that leads to learning. For learning-centered practice, an activity is essential for learning to happen, therefore, any resource should be designed to support it. Resources not designed for such purposes explicitly, and might still be used within an activity when carefully integrated to mediate it. Figure 1.3 presents an example of a screen of presentation resources. This resource allows a learner to view different slides, read content and listen to voice over explanations recorded by a teacher.
- *Practice Resources*—These digital resources for learning are designed to allow a learner to practice certain procedures, often repetitively, providing some form of feedback leading to an increase in understanding and performance (e.g., a drill and practice question item, educational game, a puzzle). Presentation objects can have such resources integrated in their structure to provide reinforcement and/or practice tools for learners. This is usually the case with more comprehensive computer-based instructional packages. However, having these as separated resources will have the benefits of allowing them to be reused in a variety of other digital resources for learning, in a variety of learning-related situations and for different purposes related to the completion of an activity. Figure 1.4 presents an example of a practice item. A learner is presented with a

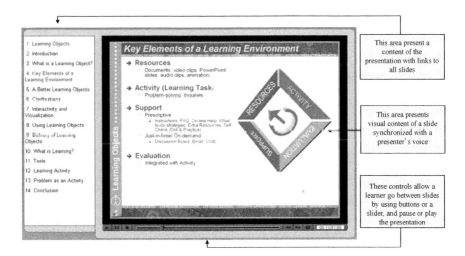

Fig. 1.3 An example of a presentation resource

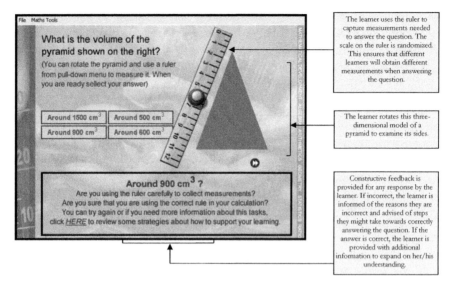

Fig. 1.4 An example of a practice resource

question to approximate the area of a pyramid displayed in the resource. Then, the learner rotates the polyhedral and uses the provided interactive ruler to measure its sides and calculate the answer. In this way, a learner practices a procedure of obtaining measurements and calculating the volume of a pyramid. The size of object and answers are randomized, so every time the practice resources are presented from the beginning, different configurations of the parameters of the question will be presented. Feedback is provided based on the learner's answer.

- *Concept Representation Resource*—This book holds this form of digital resources for learning as the most important category for learning-centered activities. These are designed to represent disciplinary concepts from a curriculum, their properties, parameters and relationships that underline generalizations to be made or articulated by learners in their learning-centered activities. For example, a concept of velocity, inflation, reaction time, or right-angled triangles can all be used to assist learners to complete some learning activity (e.g., a problem to be solved), and through this activity, some conceptual change in learners' knowledge should occur.

An example of a conceptual representation resource, "Exploring Trigonometry", is presented in Fig. 1.5. This resource is an interactive representation of a key concept from trigonometry: a trigonometric circle. A subject matter expert, a mathematics teacher in this case, identified this concept as one of the key concepts in the mathematics curriculum knowledge content. Learners can input different values for angle x and observe changes in the values of sine and cosine as they conduct an inquiry. The changes in the values of sine and cosine are presented in multiple representation formats:

1.3 Classification of Digital Resources for Learning

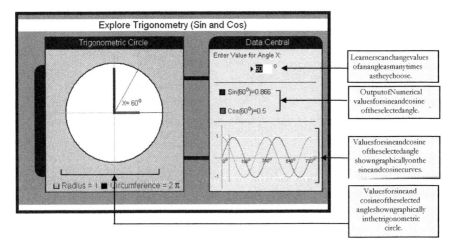

Fig. 1.5 An example of a conceptual representation resource

- Numerically, as numbers between 0 and 1;
- Visually, as projections of an arm of an angle along the x-axis (for value of cosines) and along the y-ordinate (for value of sine x) of a trigonometric circle (a circle with radius one unit long); and
- As points along the sine and cosine lines on the graph.

- *Data Display Resources*—These digital resources for learning are displays of data that can be used as mediating tools in activities leading to learning. Usually, there are two elements of such resources: data records or some logic for articulation or capture of data, and an interface used to retrieve that data. Some analytical functionalities can be included for more effective and useful presentation and processing of data. Usually, a scenario, not just an interface, is designed to allow learners to gain some experiences of, not just accessing and manipulating data, but also collecting that data in an authentic context, e.g., by using simulations of data measurement tools and instruments to capture data from an environment.

Figure 1.6 shows a screen from a "Water Experiment" data display resource. This digital resource for learning allows learners to collect data on factors affecting the quality of water of the imaginary lake presented in the scenario. This data can be used in a problem-solving activity that directs learners to act as an environmentalist, investigate a problem situation (e.g., algae infestation) and propose a solution to a problem in the form of a report to an environment protection agency.

Another way to consider classification of digital learning resources is as those designed to represent data, information or knowledge representations. That is, certain learning objects can be designed to represent each of these forms, such as

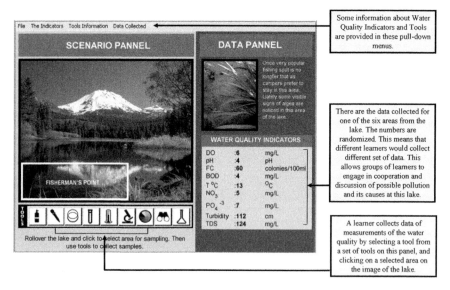

Fig. 1.6 An example of a data display representation

conceptual representations are designed to represent knowledge, information and presentation resources represent information and data displays represent data. Nevertheless, in the context of a formal education curriculum, it is much more appropriate to adopt declarative-procedural-conceptual knowledge classification as a way of classifying digital learning resources. This can significantly support later management and the reuse of digital resources for learning.

A digital resource for learning of one format might result in other knowledge forms than those initially planned by designers, e.g., a presentation resource might result in conceptual knowledge changes if used in an activity for this purpose. However, a digital resource for learning should initially always be designed to represent a specific form of curriculum content, and this is a strategy for the effective articulation of a systematic collection of digital resources to cover a certain curriculum discipline.

Education authorities such as Ministries of Education should assist education publishers to articulate and develop digital learning resources in a way that can support classroom teachers in their everyday instructional planning and teaching. Teachers are not to be replaced with digital learning resources. Contrary, they are empowered with these digital resources to more effectively design, develop and implement learning-centered activities. The teacher's role in this sense is that of a facilitator; someone who is at the center of learning design, rather than on the periphery of a classroom. To achieve the maximum outcome for education, there is a need for a concerted effort to identify systematic collections of digital learning resources for different disciplines. Developing isolated digital learning resources for a specific topic, while omitting other parts of a curriculum should not be an option for the maximum effect on education to be achieved through a digital media resource strategy. The connection that teachers and students build between these resources is an important dimension in overall learning within disciplines.

Further chapters in this book will discuss each of the forms of digital learning resources in more details, provide illustrative examples and suggest activities for readers.

> **Activity 1.2**
> *Design a single PowerPoint, Keynote or Prezi slide to tell us everything you want us to know about what a digital resource for learning is, and how such resources are classified. Try to provide links to some examples of resources you identified in your Individual Task 1.1. Attend to these conditions:*
>
> - *You can create only a single slide to tell us the maximum of what you want us to know about digital resources for learning.*
> - *You should not have any sentences; rather tell us about a digital resource for learning with images, diagrams and other graphical representations.*
> - *Use text only for labels, hints and pointers.*

References

Churchill, D. (2007). Towards a useful classification of learning objects. *Education Technology Research and Development, 55*(5), 479–497.

Kellogg, S. (2013). Online learning: How to make a MOOC. *Nature, 499*(18 July), 369–371. Retrieved from http://www.nature.com/nature/journal/v499/n7458/full/nj7458-369a.html

Information Display Resources

Learning Outcomes:

- Emphasize visuals and interactivity as the key features of contemporary information design;
- Describe how visual and interactive affordances of technology support design if information display;
- Describe different types of Information Displays; and
- Design information display digital resources for learning.

2.1 What Is an Information Display Resource?

An information display digital resource for learning is a digital media that presents certain information in an organized manner, often through visual and interactive affordances of representational technologies. We might also refer to these as *infographics* for learning. The purpose of that information is to be used in the contexts of learning activities to, for example, stimulate thinking, provide essential information, illustrated cases, stories and examples, provide technical information in an organized and easy to understand manner, and present informational material in an effective way for learners to use as required by their learning activities. An information display is primarily a strategy for designing and presenting educationally-useful information through visuals and interactivities that contemporary digital representational technologies afford, and in a way that can be effectively utilized as a mediating tool for learning.

> **Important**
> An information display is a strategy for the design and presentation of educationally-useful information that can be effectively utilized as a mediating tool in a learning activity.

Information is everywhere around us, and we come into contact with it daily through, for example, newspapers, books, television programs, billboards, Internet sites, posters, signs and messages, mobile devices and interaction with people and the environment. How well we can understand information, and how effectively we can reuse it to mediate our activities, depends in the first place on how effectively that information is represented, organized and arranged for purposes of informing a specific targeted audience. Parameters that define target audiences might include, for example, age, level information and media literacy (or literacy in general), language, culture, nationality, religion, disabilities, motivation, physiological characteristics, disabilities, etc. There are those aspects of cognitive abilities of a human to intellectually work with information which appear common across all of us, such as the ability to more easily and quickly use visual information, and give attention to details based on perception (unless we are dealing with individuals with specific disabilities impairing their visual abilities). Scanning with our eyes over a display of visual information can occur in no time. For example, as Tufte (1997) argues, a human eye can identify a single black pixel on a screen display amongst a million of white pixels within seconds. Tufte writes:

> Our eyes can make a remarkable number of distinctions within a small area. With the use of very light grid lines, it is easy to locate 625 points in one square inch or, equivalently, 100 points in one square centimetre... The resolving power of the eye enables it to differentiate to 0.1 mm where provoked to do so. (pp. 160–162)

However, giving attention to messages embedded in that screen is not always well-developed for learners today because visual literacy is hardly noted in a curriculum in schools, unlike reading and writing traditional text. Although in early childhood and primary school education, children are frequently engaged with consuming and producing visuals, very quickly, this fades out, and the predominant mode of communication and expression through education tends to become traditional text (e.g., reading articles, writing essays and presenting arguments as lines and pages of linearly distributed text. This needs to change and students need to learn to effectively work with and produce visual and other multimodal information, not just in the context of their daily information activities, such as in communication and social networking, but also in the context of their school-related information work. The development of visual literacy, in addition to other new literacies, is a much needed change in education. Educators need to give attention not only to the traditional literacy of reading writing, speaking and listening, but also to emerging new literacies including, for example, visual literacy, digital literacy, critical literacy, media literacy, etc. This is, in particular, important because

2.1 What Is an Information Display Resource?

emerging representational formats are beginning to dominate our information-related activities and uses of technologies. Students in schools need to learn how to engage with these formats, not only to consume information, but also to represent their knowledge and ideas in visual and interactive ways.

Contemporary representational technologies can afford for a large quantity of information to be effectively structured and presented in small screen spaces. The use of visuals (composed for example of lines, shapes, color, images, symbols, signs, animations, videos, etc.), and other modalities such as audio and special effects, screen arrangement and interface design possibilities, as well as interactivity are made possible by contemporary representational technologies (e.g., sliders, clickable area, drag & drop, and text inputs), to create innovative possibilities for the design of information. Here are some possibilities for the design of information displays in visual format:

- Illustrations;
- Timelines;
- Cartesian coordinates;
- Photorealistic images;
- Paintings and drawings;
- Caricatures and cartoons;
- Charts such as pie, bar, line, area, scatterplot, histogram, box plot, spectrograms;
- Radar chart, spider net charts, Gantt charts;
- Flowchart, Toulmin map, funnel map, bridge diagram, temple diagram;
- Argument slide, V-diagram;
- Cycle diagrams, Venn diagrams, Sakey;
- Mindmaps, cluster maps, concept maps, semantic networks;
- Maps of territories (abstract and real), data maps, tree map, cone tree maps, metromaps, pathways, continuums;
- Motion formats such digital stories, animation and video content;
- Tables such as classification tables, contrast and comparison tables, matrixes;
- Symbols, signs and icons;
- 3-dimensional object and spatial representations;
- Panoramic images;
- Wordly Cloud Tags;
- Virtual reality representations; and
- Augmented reality representations.

Activity 2.1
Visualization of information has been used in various disciplines as a means of packing and presenting large quantities and complexity of information. Such is the case, for example, in journalism, information science, business and marketing, sciences, engineering and medicine. Examine the periodic table of images in this link below, and explore various possibilities:

http://www.visual-literacy.org/periodic_table/periodic_table.html
Also, you can read this article that discusses the periodic table of visuals:
http://www.visual-literacy.org/periodic_table/periodic_table.pdf
Furthermore, the following web site shows 50 examples of various visual information displays:
http://www.hongkiat.com/blog/50-informative-and-well-designed-infographics/
Review these examples and draw your own conclusion about:

- *Which one is the best information display according to your opinion?*
- *What makes an information display effective?*
- *What makes an information display ineffective?*

Some more interesting examples of visuals: http://infographicworld.com/

Activity 2.2
Designing visual information is not a matter of just copying textual information into a visual format. It can be a very complex and intellectually demanding task. Here is a task for you to illustrate this complexity.

In 1984, linguist Thomas A. Sebeok was commissioned by the Office of Nuclear Waste Isolation and a group of other institutions to create a sign that could be read 10,000 years from now, indicating the danger of any excavation on the nuclear waste storage at the Yucca Mountain.

Your task is to draw such a sign. This is relatively complex task as you must consider a variety of ill-defined parameters in order to articulate your visual representation that could be read so far in the future.

(Source: http://www.washtimes.com/upi-breaking/20041109-030639-4304r.htm)

2.2 A Single Interactive Screen for Display of Information

Effective organization and the presentation of information can be achieved through a digital resource by the way of using visuals and other multiples forms of modalities (or modes). Modalities such as sound, text, color, lines, shapes, sizes of objects, pictures, animation, videos, symbols and icons can be all used to communicate information. An important consideration is when a specific modality is the most effective for the purpose of mediation of learning. In some cases, certain

2.2 A Single Interactive Screen for Display of Information

modalities might appear attractive to designers, but actual results can be achieved in different, simpler, and more effective ways. For example, would a video information be more effective than a simpler presentation of that information through few key frames (images) with captions? Or, would presenting information as an animation be more effective than a static diagram that uses arrows to illustrate movements? Moreover, these can be carefully combined in an innovative communication piece, making complex information much easier to understand. So, the main questions here are: (a) how visuals and other modalities can be arranged in an effective information display, (b) which modality is the best for a specific purpose, and (c) how modalities supplement each other to represent information. Combining these visual and multimodal possibilities with interactive affordance of contemporary representational technologies, makes possible to design this particular form of digital resource for learning.

Important
Visuals allow the design of representations that communicate not just information, but also meanings, feelings, moods, giving unique atmospheres to the informational space, while enabling large quantities of information to be presented simultaneously, through visual elements such as symbols, icons, colors, lines, shapes, photographs, highlights, format, etc.

Activity 2.3
Here some interesting tools on the Internet that can be utilized to develop information displays.

- *Maps*—e.g., http://www.ontheroad.to/
- *MindMaps*—e.g., http://www.mindmeister.com/
- *Diagrams*—e.g., http://www.smartdraw.com/
- *Flowcharts*—e.g., http://flowchart.com/ *and* http://www.slickplan.com/
- *Timelines*—e.g., http://www.preceden.com/ *and* http://www.timetoast.com/
- *Cartoons*—e.g., http://www.toondoo.com/

Review these tools and pay attention to how they afford the design of information displays. Note your observation in a separated display that you create by using one of these tools.

The author of this book holds that the most powerful modality for all forms of digital resources for learning are those presented in visual form. Visuals allow the design of representations that communicate not just information, but also meanings, feelings, moods, giving unique atmospheres to the informational space, while enabling large quantities of information to be presented simultaneously, through visual elements such as symbols, icons, colors, lines, shapes, photographs, highlights, format, etc. The human eye has a remarkable power to give attention to visual information, while the human mind has a similar remarkable power to cognitively work with such information.

The most effective digital resources for learning activities might be those that integrate all informational content of a resource in a single screen presentable via a device. This is contrary to most of the current designs which use various forms of structuring, segmenting and presenting information in a series of screens, long scrollable page, menu items, chapters or sections, often overloading cognitive capacity with unnecessary screen complexity, navigation elements and more than one curriculum focus (e.g., declarative and procedural knowledge). Visual and interactive affordances of contemporary representational media and technologies enable a much better design, allowing for a large amount of information to be presented via a small screen space, and even in cases when mobile technologies are used for delivery. In the design, all extraneous and unnecessary content and other information should not be included in order to empower a learner to fully dedicate his or her cognitive load onto the content. This is an important issue that this book will discuss in the later parts in more details.

We need to keep in mind that in the context of teaching, rules are different comparing to, for example, someone browsing a web site for interesting information or news, viewing a billboard, watching a television program or reading a newspaper. A higher level of cognitive engagement is often required from learners for learning to occur. However, learning in the context of information displays, does not mean that learners simply consume and remember content. Critical issues here are how information can be designed to effectively mediate learning activities, and how the intended purpose of that information relates to tasks being completed by learners. A concept of 'mediation' is important here. A mediator is something or someone that influences/mediates decision-making and thinking, that is, it refers to learners utilizing digital resources as mediating tools in their activity so that they gain intended learning outcomes. In this context, learning is not simply a process of internalizing external information presented in a digital learning resource. Rather, learning is a direct product of an experience where information is applied and used as a mediation tool in completing a learning activity. The internalization of properties of external mediating tools—not the memorizing of content—and experiences of working on an activity leads to learning. Through learning, the features of information should become part of the learners' thinking process. We might think that learning has occurred when internalized properties of tools are begging to serve as internal, cognitive or psychological mediating tools. This is consistently emphasized and repeated in this book, and will be re-examined in the context of different forms of digital resources for learning later on. With careful design, arrangement and creative presentation of interface elements and information, information displays would be able to deliver maximum information in a small screen space, and in a way that facilitates intellectual utility of the features of that information.

2.2 A Single Interactive Screen for Display of Information

> **Important**
> Learning is a direct product of an experience where information is applied and used as a mediation tool in completing a learning activity. Learning is not simply a process of internalizing information presented in a digital learning resource.

This book proposes an approach where designers should almost always design digital learning resources for presentation via a single screen. This should not be seen as granulation of learning content (as classical approaches to digital resources for learning appear to promote), rather, this is an effective strategy of how to maximize a total amount of information to be presented in a minimum screen space, reducing cognitive load expected from a learner for engagement, and requiring less time to extract what is needed to inform actions required by the learning activity, as well as reducing the time needed to be spent glaring at the screen. In simple words, learners do not learn the content of an information display in the way they would do with a presentation resource. Rather, learners interrogate and use features of information to mediate their thinking when working on a learning activity.

> **Activity 2.4**
> *In addition to visuals and multimodalities, interactivity significantly enhances the power of visual displays of information. Large quantities of information can be structured within a small screen space, while users can be engaged in manipulating parameters and configuring what information they want to preview. Here are some general examples you should review to get understanding of how interactivity functions within a visual display of information:*
>
> - *Eddie the Yeti History of Social Media* http://avalaunchmedia.com/history-of-social-media/Main.html
> - *Interactive timeline* http://after64.sbs.com.au/#timeline/en/April-15
> - *Interactive narratives site containing numerous examples* http://www.interactivenarratives.org/. *Search for good examples.*
> - *Visual display of information about various tools that can be used for design* http://www.visual-literacy.org/pages/maps/mapping_tools_radar/radar.html
>
> *What do you conclude about the use of interactivity in design of information displays for learning?*
> *Now, try to complete this task. The following is the Basic Wine Guide information display:*
> http://winefolly.com/tutorial/wine-for-beginners-infographic/
> *Although this display contains an effective arrangement of visuals, it is a static image without any use of interactivity. Your task is to carefully analyze*

> *this display, and describe (draw a sketch and explain) how it can be redesigned to include interactivity for more effective presentation. In other words, redesign it from visual into visual and interactive format.*

2.3 Examples of Interactive and Visual Information Displays

What is characteristic of an information display as a particular kind of digital resource for learning? It is that interactivity and visualization are a critical affordance of contemporary representational technologies that enables the maximum amount of visual and other multimodal information to be presented in a minimal screen space. In this book, particular attention is given to these two affordances of contemporary representational technologies: affordances for (a) visualization of information, data and ideas through the design and arrangements of colors, lines, shapes, images, symbols, etc., and (b) interactivity as a mean for providing learning with tools to manipulation and explore that information, data or ideas through the use of sliders, buttons, clickable areas, text inputs, etc.

> **Important**
> Interactivity is a critical affordance of contemporary representational technologies as it enables the maximum amount of visual and other multimodal information to be presented in a minimal screen space.

The following example in Fig. 2.1 illustrates such a possibility of how a maximum amount of information can be presented in a single interactive display. This is an information display of a revised and digitized version of one of the best examples of a paper-based infographic produced by Charles Joseph Minard in 1869. This original work, is known as 'Carte figurative des pertes successives en hommes de l'Armée Française dans la campagne de Russie 1812–1813', or simply as Minard's map. Minard constructed this infographic to illustrate the adventure of Napoleon and his army during the attempted conquest of Russia in 1812. Minard's purpose was to portray a powerful and a dramatic display to inform, as quickly as possible, the public in France about the disastrous adventure on Napoleon Bonaparte's Army in Russia in 1812 during which more than 400,000 French soldiers died. This resource has become one of the most popular examples for authors writing about visual information, infographics and graphic design (e.g., in Edward Tufte's work on visual explanations, see Tufte 1997).

2.3 Examples of Interactive and Visual Information Displays

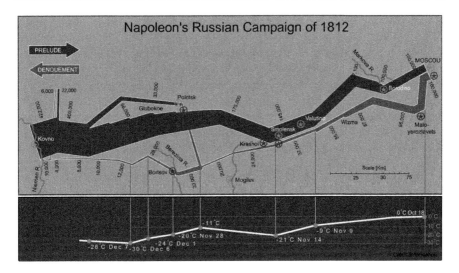

Fig. 2.1 Reworked 'Minard's Map' information display resource

The author of this book redesigned and digitized this example in order to demonstrate the affordances of contemporary representational technologies, which enable even more powerful ways of organizing and presenting information through, for example, the uses of sharper shapes and lines, contrasting colors that carry certain meanings, interactive elements such as pop-up areas containing further information, etc. This information display shows advancement and retreat paths of the French army from the then Russian border until Moscow and vice versa. The paths are represented as lines of different thickness. Thickness corresponds to the number of troops at any given point, showing the troop numbers ranging from 412,000 on the point where the French army entered Russia, down to 10,000 at the point where the army left Russia. The advancement line is presented in blue color and the retreat line in red (color giving a special tone). The paths are plotted over a map that corresponds to geographical locations at specific dates where the army came across various rivers and major towns, and engaged in significant battles.

Information presented can lead learners as a user of this information, to connect, contrast and compare different pieces of information (e.g., advancement and retreat pathways). Use of appropriate colours, in particular, provides meta-information that assists learners to pay attention to specific information pieces (e.g., brighter standing out colours of advancement and retreat paths of the French army), and committing certain cognitive processes (e.g., comparing the blue against the red pathway of the army). It might be said that meta-information provides leads to cognitive interactions with information.

Colour is one distinct element that separates current computer-based representations from those in the past. Such outcomes can be achieved today even through print materials. What distinguishes contemporary technology-based representational media is interactivity. With interactivity, various areas on the display can be configured to correspond to various forms of user interactions, such as, when the user rolls over a mouse pointer over a specific area, or when a user clicks, right-clicks or double-clicks over a specific area on the display (or when a user places a finger, or uses two or more fingers simultaneously in a finger-driven, multi-touch interactive screen of a device). New collages of information can be displayed based on these interactions, while pointers to further information from other sources can be presented through hyperlinks. In the case of Minard's map, once a user places a mouse point over one of the stars corresponding to city names, certain details about that node will be provided. If the user clicks on that star, more information about a specific event will be displayed.

With the aid of contemporary technology, Minard's Map has been redesigned in a way that new representational and interactive affordances have enhanced its communication capacity. How to use this information display resource in teaching and learning? Traditional approaches would be to give it to learners to study, and then provide them with a worksheet, a test or other form of assignment to reinforce and examine the content remembering and understanding. However, according to a learning-centred approach, learners will be presented with an engaging activity. For example, a learning activity might give learners a task where they are assumed to be a newspaper journalist tasked to write a report about the French military campaign in Russia. Alternatively, learners might be asked to design a multimedia presentation to show what happened in this war. Minard's map is then provided as a source of information they can use to assist them in completing the activity. A learner can cognitively interact, explore and interrogate information presented in this single display of information by:

- Contrasting advancement and retreat of the French Army represented in the red and blue coloured pathways;
- Examining key geographic locations, cities and rivers, and key events that took places there;
- Examining weather conditions at different dates and link these to key battles, troop losses and events taking place at different locations; and
- Reading about specific events and previewing some artefacts from that period.

What is important to understand in this particular context, the activity is not about remembering information from this resource. Engaging in using this information display within an activity is not about memorizing historical facts, rather at the center is learning to work with historical data, engage analytically with information and deeply think about and understand courses and issues affective to the particular historical circumstance.

In addition to what is achieved with the original paper-based representation developed by Minard all the way back in 1869, design features of the new technology-based representation allow:

2.3 Examples of Interactive and Visual Information Displays

- Clarity and emphasis of information through the uses of sharp and contrasting colours, e.g., colours of advancement and retreat lines of the French Army, emphasized temperature lines, and coloured stars on the key geographic locations in bright colours to capture attention;
- Structuring of information in panels and pop-up displays enables related groups of information to be presented within specific screen areas;
- Use of interactivity to trigger the display of information, e.g., a roll-over hot-spot area on the display will show one piece of information, while clicking on that hot-spot area, would provide further information; and
- Use of in-build capability of the display technology to zoom on specific areas of the screen for better preview.

> **Important**
> Visualization and interactivity are the key affordances of contemporary representational technologies and an important strategy for the design of digital resources for learning.

So, going back to how can this information display can be used in learning, certainly, our idea is not just to give this to learners and instruct them to learn from it by consuming and remembering the content displayed. We would not go very far with this approach. According to the idea of the learning-centred approach continuously emphasized in this book, there should be an activity that learners are to work on.

This example demonstrates how a large amount of information can be structured and presented in a small screen space with the aid of visuals, and where interactivity allows the organization and retrieval of that information within a single display. By this stage, this book has emphasized the importance of an activity as an essential component in learning-centred teaching. These ideas will become much clearer later in this module. At this stage, the author hopes that each reader considers visualization and interactivity as the key affordances of contemporary representational technologies and as important part of a strategy for the design of digital resources for learning. Overall, it is argued that an effective digital resource for learning is an interactive and visual representation designed to serve as a mediating tool in a learning activity.

The second example of an information display is as a specific form of digital resource for learning, as presented in Fig. 2.2. It again shows how interactivity and visualization allow for a large quantity of information to be presented in a single information display digital resource for learning. This digital resource for learning displays information related to 'Machining' in a Mechanical Engineering area of study. It displays information related to 'Chip Control' of chips breaking of a metal work piece during the 'Turning Machining' process. Information is displayed based on a combination of two parameters controlled by a learner. The configuration of

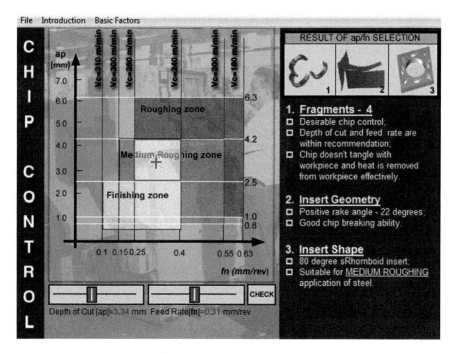

Fig. 2.2 'Chip Control' information display resource

parameters is presented graphically on an X-Y graph depicting different zones of possible configurations, and the outcome of such configurations displays specific visual and textual information. This information is useful within learning activities that require engineering learners to explore and apply concepts of machining parameters and Computer Numeric Programming.

One distinct difference with the previous example is how interactivity functions in this information display resource. In the first example, chunks of information beyond the initial screen display are displayed based on interactions with interactive screen areas. If a mouse is positioned over an interactive screen area, some additional information will be displayed, and if that area is clicked on, some further information will be displayed. In the second example, underlining mathematical regularities drive the display of information. A learner manipulates two sliders to change the values of 'Depth of Cut' and 'Feed Rate,' and depending on the combination of these two values and underlying mathematical processing, certain visual and textual information are displayed (information about 'Fragments', 'Insert Geometry' and 'Insert Shape').

Figure 2.3 shows the third example that further demonstrates the use of interactivity to manipulate information and display chunks of it based on a learner's choices. In this example, titled 'Resistor Colour Code', a new form of interactivity to this chapter is used to configure the information displayed. There is a set of four pull-down lists of items to select. These will configure a band of colours on the

2.3 Examples of Interactive and Visual Information Displays

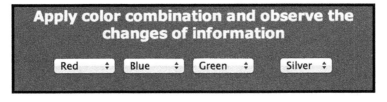

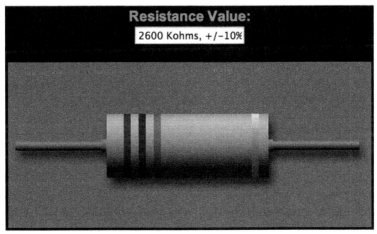

Fig. 2.3 'Resistor Colour Code' information display resource (developed based on the script from book "JavaScript™ Bible" by Goodman 2001)

displayed 'Resistor' and based on that combination display 'Resistance Value'. What is unique to this information display resource is that no textual information is used to display the main content, rather visuals (colour bands) and numerical (value of resistance) are used. It is important to consider that now days capabilities of representational technologies allow information to be presented in non-textual, and yet powerful ways.

2.4 Designing an Information Display Digital Resources for Learning?

Each separate design of an information display, as well as that of other forms of digital resources for learning, is innovation in itself. In the absence of any strong design rules and grammar, designers are left to engage their own creativity and technical skills to develop information displays. To design an information display, it is necessary that a designer is able to think creatively and innovatively about how specific information can be presented in an educationally useful format. At the same time, the designer must understand the content to be presented (or be able to work closely with a content/subject matter expert) and conduct appropriate analysis of that content in order to develop pieces of information, that like a puzzle, which can be arranged through some rules in a final information display.

Unlike in the case of text that has well-defined grammatical rules, and is navigated from left to right, top down (unless in other specific languages) design of information displays are not informed by any specific rules, that is, the rules for navigation and 'grammar' of such design are non-existent. So-called Gestalt Theory,[1] offers some advice on the display and arrangement of information, including recommendations such as proximity, continuation, similarity, figure and ground, closure and symmetry. Furthermore, Theories of Multimedia Learning developed by Mayer (2001), offer a number of principles which might be applied in this context (e.g., the concurrent use of text and visual, modality and redundancy principles). Otherwise, there are no fixed set of rules for design, and designers have almost full and complete freedom in approaching the task in creative and innovative ways.

Let us use the following simple example in Fig. 2.4 to illustrate key issues in the design of an information display resource. This resource includes information regarding possible approaches to dealing with human activities and phenomena affecting our environment, such as of Global Warming, Acid Rain and Ozone Depletion. Information is structured, classified and arranged in diagrams that display further information once a learner clicks on various components. Visuals in the background provides some information regarding the air pollutants such as traffic and factories, while further visual information is displayed within the presentation of each of the additional information for specific components of the diagram. Learners will be able to contrast and compare different methods of keeping the air clean and access various pieces of information related to different options.

This information display is designed in the following way:

- Identification of the main topic for the information display (Keeping the Air Clean).
- Collection of information to be included in this information display. In this stage, we need to ensure that all relevant sources of information (and/or data) are considered, and that all required information are collected. In certain cases, it might be possible to include dynamic information that emerges and is collected from a database, either internally built in the resource, or externally via the Internet. For example, an approach called 'mashing' or 'mashup' enables the development of information displays based on information and/or data collected from certain sources on the Internet.[2]
- Separation of information in groups. In this stage, content analysis of the information is conducted, and the information is separated into the smallest possible chunks or units. In the case of our example, information is about each

---

[1]See http://graphicdesign.spokanefalls.edu/tutorials/process/gestaltprinciples/gestaltprinc.htm for explanation of key some key Gestalt principle.

[2]See https://en.wikipedia.org/wiki/Mashup_(web_application_hybrid) for explanation of Mashups.

2.4 Designing an Information Display Digital Resources for Learning?

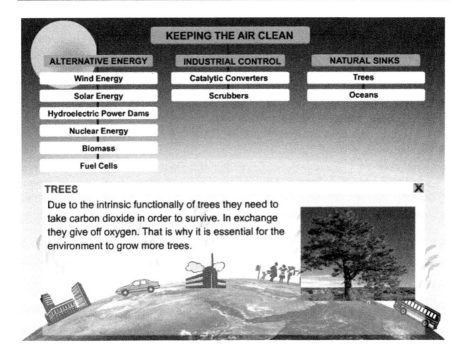

Fig. 2.4 'Keeping the Air Clean' information display

of the possible methods of keeping the air clean (e.g., solar energy, catalytic converters or fuel cells).
- Exploring possibilities for the organization of information units in some form of network, matrix, flow, mathematical logic, relation, etc.:

  - Analyse common properties of each of the information units. Something belongs with something else, or something is dependent on something else. Can information be structured according to these properties?
  - Is it possible to arrange information units in a temporal space (e.g., a timeline), representation of a real or imaginary space, or a map (e.g., geographical map)? See Fig. 2.1 for an information display organized according to this rule.
  Is there any underlining mathematical relationship between information units and/or their properties? Can this information be organized according to this relationship? See Fig. 2.2 for an information display organized according to this rule.
  - Is it possible to arrange information units according to certain classification format, a chart, or a network of certain properties? This is the case with the 'Keeping the Air Clean' information display in Fig. 2.3.

- Determining the most effective way of how each of the units of information can be presented in the most consistent and effective way (e.g., as text, numbers, pictures, graphical elements such as lines and shapes and their thickness and color, sounds, movement, animation, video, 3D model, and transitions). Give priority to presenting information in visual ways.
- Storyboarding the main interface of the information display, and storyboard an example of the information unit. If required, evaluate your design, e.g., by showing it to your client and/or a subject matter expert, as secure consensus for further development.
- Designing the main interface. Keep in mind important design specifications, such as screen size for the final display, method of delivery (e.g., a mobile device), and possible interactions (e.g., finger driven). In the case of the featured example in Fig. 2.3, this interface consists of a background informational screen that visually shows some major sources of air pollution, and a foreground classification diagram that presents strategies for keeping the air clean, classified into three main groups (alternative energy, industrial control, and natural sources). Design areas for titles, navigation elements, manipulation/control of information elements, presentation of information, labels, and help messages.
- Developing a prototype. Configure interactivity and navigation in the visual display, and make at least a few areas functional. Evaluate your prototype, e.g., by trying it out with some representatives of real users (learners and teachers) and/or reviewing it by your client and a subject matter expert.
- Finalizing the information display and make it available for learning uses (e.g., deposit it in a repository of learning resources, publish it on the Internet, or make it available through Google Play Store, App Store, etc.).

Activity 2.5
Analyze the following text and develop an information display based on its information. Your information display must be presented on a single screen, utilizing multimodalities. Follow-up the procedure described in Sect. 2.3.
[Modified based on the Annenberg Foundation (2016)]

In the deep space, the temperature is a chilly -260 °C. Closer to the Sun, temperatures reach thousands of degrees. What makes the Earth's climate so livable? Separating Earth from the extreme climate of outer space is an 800-km-thick cocoon of gases called the atmosphere. The Earth's atmosphere is made up primarily of nitrogen and oxygen, but also includes carbon dioxide, ozone, and other gases. These keep us warm and protect us from the direct effects of the Sun's radiation.

The atmosphere is made up of several layers including the troposphere (closest to Earth), stratosphere, mesosphere, ionosphere, and exosphere. Most of the clouds are found in the **troposphere** which extends up to 16 km above the Earth's surface.

It also includes a number of other gases such as water vapor, carbon dioxide, methane, and nitrous oxide. These gases help retain heat, a portion of which is then radiated back to warm the surface of Earth.

Above the troposphere is the **stratosphere**, which also includes the ozone layer, and extends from about 16 to 48 km above the surface of the Earth. Ozone molecules in this layer, absorb ultraviolet radiation from the Sun and protect us from its harmful effects, and that is why this layer is so important for us. A further 48–80 km above the surface of the Earth is the **mesosphere**, which is the coldest part of the atmosphere. Above it is the layer called the **ionosphere** or the **thermosphere,** which extends about 80–290 km from the surface of the Earth, and where temperatures can reach up to couple or more thousand degrees Celsius. Beyond this is the **exosphere**, extending up to 800 km; it is the outermost layer of the atmosphere, the transition zone into space.

References

Annenberg Foundation. (2016). *The atmosphere.* Retrieved from https://www.learner.org/exhibits/weather/atmosphere.html)

Goodman, D. (2001). *JavaScript™ Bible.* New York, NY: Hungry Minds Inc.

Mayer, R. (2001). *Multimedia learning.* New York, NY: Cambridge University Press.

Tufte, E. (1997). *Visual explanations.* Cheshire, CT: Graphics Press.

3 Concept Representation Resources

Learning Outcomes:

- Describe a concept representation as a special form of digital resources for learning;
- Appreciate complexity and importance of concept knowledge in overall disciplinary knowledge;
- Understand the challenges of concept teaching and propose and activity as a solution for effective learning;
- Analyse own concept knowledge and resources to identify a concept's properties, parameters, relationships and related sub-concepts;
- Design a concept representation based on own knowledge of a specific concept; and
- Apply design for presentation recommendations to the design of a concept representation.

3.1 What Is a Concept Representation?

A concept representation resource is a particular kind of digital resource for learning designed to support the learning of disciplinary concepts. Such representation allows a learner to manipulate properties, parameters and relationships, and explore relevant information related to a concept. Properties, parameters and relationships are displayed in depictive and descriptive ways with variety of modes or representations such as textual, numerical, pictorial, graphical, animated, auditory, video, special effect etc. Properties are manipulated with interactive elements such as sliders, text entrees, hot-spots and buttons.

A simple example of a concept representation resource is presented in Fig. 3.1. This concept resource represents a right-angled triangle and its associated properties, parameters and relationships (a concept of a right triangle). It allows a learner to manipulate parameters including base and height of the triangle by dragging corresponding sliders. Manipulating either of the two parameters of the triangle (base or height) by dragging the sliders will result in an immediate update of the display (changes in properties), that is, the triangle will be redrawn in a corresponding size, and the numerical information regarding dependent parameters (such as the value of the hypotenuse) will be updated. These changes are driven by certain relations, which learners will explore during their learning activity.

This resource can be reused for different activities and with different groups of students. For example, lower grade students could use it to explore the properties of a right-angled triangle, while more senior students might explore concepts such as Pythagorean theorems and basic trigonometric functions (sine and cosine) in the contexts of their activities.

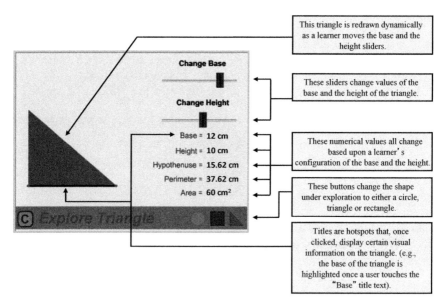

Fig. 3.1 "Explore Triangle" concept representation resource (from Churchill and Hedberg 2008b)

3.2 What Is a Concept?

> **Important**
> A concept is a complex and genuine act of thought, and a psychological or intellectual tool that forms a basis for our cognitive activities. As a disciple-specific tool, framework or a schema it underlines theoretical thinking.

The intention of this chapter is not to be drawn too deeply into a philosophical discussion of what a concept might be. However, it is worth noting some issues. This is a very complex discussion that has not reached a conclusion since the time of Plato and Aristotle, although some of the best-known names in psychology, philosophy and education, such as Kant (1922), Piaget (1972a, b), Vygotsky (1962), Dewey (1910), Bruner (1960) and Gagne (1971), explored it. Existence of concepts in someone's head cannot be really proven empirically, although neuroscientists are attempting to do so based on various emerging possibilities brought about by new biometric technologies (e.g., Functional Neuroimaging). The construct of a concept has been largely explored by psychologists and philosophers with interest in the forms of knowledge and how these develop in individuals' cognition, as well as those who subscribe to theories of cognitive, information sciences or neurosciences (e.g., Bruner et al. 1967; Dewey 1902, 1997; Gagne and Driscoll 1988; Hartnack 1968; Hjørland 2009; Lawrence and Margolis 1999; Li et al. 2015; Piaget 1972a, b, 1990; Stock 2010; Traill 2008; Turner 1975). A concept is broadly understood as a form of knowledge that enables an individual to comprehend new information and learn, communicate and understand language, and engage in specific disciplinary thinking, decision making, problem solving, generalizing, reflecting, making inferences and forming and reconstructing personal theories. There are various interpretations in the literature, such as, a concept is a fundamental unit of cognition, a node-in network in a knowledge schema, patterns of synaptic connections, a system for classifying objects into categories, or a psychological tool for thinking. For example, Vygotsky and his followers define a concept as a complex and genuine act of thought, and a psychological or intellectual tool that forms a basis for our cognitive activities (e.g., Vygotsky 1978; Ivarsson et al. 2002; Kozulin 1990; Sierpinska 1993). For Engeström (1987) "individual consciousness is formed under the influence of knowledge accumulated by society and objectified in the world of things created by humanity" (p. 36). A concept is, therefore, understood as a socio-cultural phenomenon developed by humans in their attempt to interpret the nature and ways of conquering it. Pursuing a different line of thought, Merrill et al. (1992) describe a concept as "a set of specific objects, symbols, or events which are grouped together on the basis of shared characteristics and which can be references by a particular name or a symbol". Such a view is in contrast with Vygotsky's perspective of concepts as psychological tools, and more in line with what Jonassen (2006) labels as *Aristotelian position* that assumes concepts are representations of classes of objects, symbols, or events grouped together based on common properties or attributes. However, in all these, a concept is a form of knowledge that is not simply declarative.

In this book, we like to think of a concept as a disciple-specific act of thought, framework or a schema for theoretical thinking. It is essentially socio-cultural, that is, a concept is a representation of knowledge accumulated by humanity, and not just as something that might exist independently in one's own mind. Applications, generalizations, reflections and abstractions based on a concept lead to the formation of concept knowledge, which then serves as internal disciplinary tools for theoretical thinking, or a psychological tool. Disciplined specific concept knowledge are the foundation of one's theoretical thinking and his/her ability to intellectually operate within that discipline (e.g., solve problems or conduct a research in the way that scientists do).

Concept knowledge contains both, declarative and procedural knowledge reconstructed from experiences and integrated in an internal tool for thinking. This knowledge can only be exhibited through our activities such as problem solving, designing, innovating, decision and inference making, but not simply by asking a learner to use words and describe a concept learnt.[1] We know that performing these activities requires knowledge that simply is not only declarative, but also procedural, and involves applications of some higher forms of cognitive activity and strategies rather than simply recalling facts and definitions (e.g., mental modelling, cognitive simulation, cognitive visualization and imagination).

Furthermore, we need distinguish between everyday concrete concept knowledge, which is developed spontaneously through experiences, life, growth, games and social interaction with parents, relatives and friends, and those more abstract concept knowledge formally developed over time through formal education and learning (formal or scientific concepts). For Kant, some concepts originate in the mind itself through various processes such as comparing mental images, abstraction and reflection based on these (he calls these priori concepts). Inevitably, there is a relationship between these informal and formal concepts, and knowledge and learning of them, affecting knowledge and learning and re-learning for the others, once their developmental trajectories somehow intersect.[2,3] However, how formal concept knowledge is developed is based on organized, systematic, intentional, planned, and educator-managed learning designs that represents the interpretation of curriculum requirements into a set of learning and teaching actions.

---

[1]To evaluate concept knowledge, the literature suggests techniques such as think aloud problem solving and concept mapping (see Jonassen 2006).

[2]Learning of formal concept knowledge does not start in a vacuum. It builds upon student's concept developmental levels and prior knowledge, which might include, formal conceptions, spontaneous conceptions and misconceptions.

[3]Vygotsky in "Language and Thought" wrote about how every day and scientific concept knowledge develop, and how their developmental trajectories intersect.

> **Important**
> A concept representation resource is a particular kind of a digital learning resource designed to support the teaching and learning of disciplinary concepts.

From a different perspective, concepts develop over prolonged periods of time, passing through certain stages. Most studies appear to explore student misconceptions of specific concepts rather than the generic process of concept development. To gain a better understanding of that process, we can draw on the theoretical perspective of Vygotsky (1962) and those who subscribe to it (e.g., Berger 2004a, b; Blunden 2011; Scott 1997; Sierpinska 1993; Wellings 2003). For Berger (2004a), "Vygotsky's theory around the genesis of concepts is a theory around the genesis of intellectual operations such as generalization of objects and situations, identification of features of objects, their comparison and discrimination (that is, their abstraction), and the synthesis of thoughts" (p. 3). Therefore, a concept is an act of thought. According to the Vygotskian perspective, concepts develop through pre-conceptual stages, including syncretic heaps (characterized by subjective grouping of unrelated objects by chance), complexes (grouping of objects in the mind, not only by subjective impression, but by bonds that actually exist, in forming associations, collections, chains, and pseudo-concepts) and, finally, socially and culturally accepted scientific concepts (Berger 2004a, b; Blunden 2011). For Vygotsky (1962), "a concept is not an isolated, ossified, and changeless formation, but an active part of the intellectual process, constantly engaged in service of communication, understanding and problem solving", and the process of concept appropriation "is not a quantitative overgrowth of the lower associative activity, but a qualitatively" new activity mediated by signs (e.g., language, symbols, and internal images) (p. 109). Both social interaction and interaction with spontaneous concepts are seen as critical in scientific concept formation.

Concepts in a school curriculum (or any other education or training curriculum), are there because they are determined by experts in the fields over time.[4] We include concepts such as force, ratio, energy, landforms, trade, freedom, velocity, vector, polygon, evolution, cell, inflation, poverty, acid rain, adjective, idiom, revolution, human rights, magnetic field etc. in a curriculum given our up-to-date progressively developed understanding of disciplines' concept tools. These concepts all have socio-cultural histories, some emerging years ago and undergoing public revisions since then. They are articulated through human attempts to interpret and deal with nature and their own self, and emerge as a tool in this process (e.g., Activity Theory perspective). For example, a force, philosophers in ancient time, such as Aristotle and Archimedes, used this concept in the study of stationary and moving objects and

---

[4]There are other factors determining curriculum content such as expectations of society, industry requirements, education policy-making, pedagogical content knowledge, philosophy of education, etc. [see Tyler (1949)].

simple machines. At that time, they were not able to completely understand the force of friction, and consequently held the belief that a constant force is required to maintain constant motion. These misunderstandings were mostly corrected by others including Galileo, and later by Sir Isaac Newton who formulated *Laws of Motion*. By the 20th century, Albert Einstein had developed the *Theory of Relativity* providing and insight into forces on objects with increasing momenta nearing the speed of light, and the forces produced by gravitation and inertia. More recently, quantum mechanics and particle physics have resulted in a Standard Model to describe the forces between particles smaller than atoms. So, it can be understood, a concept of force has been under continuous development since ancient times.

Activity 3.1
Think of any concept. For example, what is your concept of 'Heat?' Can you write a sentence to explain what 'Heat' is? Read this sentence and think whether you really understand what 'Heat' is? How easy it would be for others to understand the content of your sentence? Would words in your sentence be sufficient for them to understand the concept?

Most likely, your definition of the everyday concept of 'Heat' associates you with certain other concepts, such as warmth, sun, summer, candle, matches, blanket, bath, or weather. However, let's now think about the scientific concept of 'Heat' and what it might include. This might significantly differ, and yet, in some ways overlap with your everyday conception. Would everyday conception lead you to form a misconception of the scientific concept? Think about that.

But let's do something else. Think of the scientific concept of 'Heat'; consult the literature and people if needed, list down all associated sub-concepts, properties, parameters and relationships, and use a mind-mapping tool of your choice (e.g., Mind42 or Mind Meister) to create a mind map containing and linking all these. Discuss your map with your colleagues, class peers, a teacher, etc. How does mind-mapping help you to articulate your understanding, expose your misconception and think about the concept?

3.3 Concept Learning

The literature underlines the importance of concept knowledge and refers to evidence that incomplete concept knowledge and misconceptions seriously impede learning (see Mayer 2002; Singer et al. 2012; Smith et al. 1993; Vosniadou 1994). However, concept learning has been challenging for teachers and students, as it requires deep cognitive engagement, and individual preconceptions and misconceptions tend to present obstacles. It is widely held that concepts develop from fragmented, piecemeal, and highly contextualized naïve theories, misconceptions, and incorrect beliefs at the level of a single idea, flawed mental models representing an interrelated set of concepts, and/or the incorrect assignment of core concepts to laterally or ontologically inappropriate categories (e.g., Chi 2008; diSessa 2008).

> **Important**
> A purpose of concept learning should be the gradual approximation of sociocultural and individual concept knowledge and development of intellectual disposition to engage and apply that knowledge in theoretical thinking.

Merrill et al. (1992) suggest students might develop misconceptions, and that instruction should be designed such that this is prevented, and that a concept learnt by learners is the same to that held by a teacher (or as intended by a designer of an instructional product). Merrill et al. (1992), present an instructional design model that arguably can be applied to optimize concept learning. A concept representation is promoted as an object that supports instruction, usually to depict and describe examples, illustrating attributes of a concept to be learnt. For Merrill et al. (1992), learners learn a concept through pattern recognition; that is, by recognizing (a) how a concept structurally relates to other concepts, and (b) how attributes of a concept relate to each other and link to prior knowledge. Two cognitive processes involved in pattern recognition are generalization and discrimination. Merrill and his colleagues' ideas influenced other instructional design models such as Cisco's Reusable Learning Object strategy (Cisco Systems 2001). For Cisco Systems, a concept is "a group of objects, symbols, ideas, or events that are defined by a single word or term, share common features, and vary on irrelevant features" (p. 16). Numerous other instructional design researchers and practitioners subscribed to this classical view that concept learning involves internalizing external concepts (e.g., Canelos et al. 1982; Carrier et al. 1985; Gagné 1966, 1968; Hicken et al. 1992; Jonassen 1978, 1986; Merrill 1983, 1987; Merrill et al. 1977, 1979, 1992; Montague 1983; Newby et al. 1995; Tennyson 1978; Tennyson and Buttrey 1980; Tessmer and Driscoll 1986). However, Jonassen in his later writings (see Jonassen 2006), rightly criticizes and challenges this thinking, and argues that concepts can only be learnt in context of their intellectual uses that lead to conceptual changes and the development of personal theories. Therefore, instruction should lead students to engage in the intellectual uses of concepts though experiences designed and facilitated by teachers (learning designs).

Provision of certain models is believed to have a positive effect on concept learning (see Ivarsson et al. 2002). Dawson (2004) in his book "Mind and machines" writes that a model is an artefact that can be mapped on to a phenomenon that is difficult to understand. Furthermore, Dawson writes, by examining the model a learner can increase understanding of a phenomenon (concept) modeled, and although a model can imitate a phenomenon, it most often does not reassemble it, that is, it is a representation of a phenomenon rather than a copy or an identical replica. However, Dawson adds, a property common to all models, appears to be the notion of 'predictive utility'. A model is used to generate predictions that can be used to test a theory and, thus, it might provide an easier and faster route to learning. Similarly, others have suggested models as effective tools for concept learning, and their educational use has been described as model-centred learning and instruction (see Dawson 2004; Gibbons 2008; Lesh and Doerr 2003; Mayer 1989; Norman 1983; Seel 2003). For example, Lesh and Doerr (2003) define a model as "a concept system consisting of elements, relations, operations, and rules governing interactions" (p. 10). Such models can be used for constructing, communicating, describing, or experimenting with a system (see Johnson and Lesh 2003).

> **Important**
> Concepts can only be learnt in context of their intellectual uses that lead to concept changes and the development of personal theories.

Engaging students to use technology to develop concept knowledge has been explored in the context of cognitive tools (Lajoie and Derry 2000), mindtools (Chu et al. 2010; Jonassen and Reeves 1996; Jonassen 1996; Jonassen and Carr 2000), and technologies of the mind (Pae 1985; Salomon et al. 1991). Examples of cognitive tools include computer-based tools such as system modeling applications, e.g., Stela and Interactive Physics; knowledge organizing tools, e.g., database software, knowledge construction tools e.g., Knowledge Forum; and idea processing tools, e.g., Mind Manager and Axon. According to Jonassen (2006) and Chai and Quek (2003), cognitive tools are used to engage students in exploring and analysing how variables interact in a manner that can be defined mathematically or in terms of other properties, identifying relationships between categories of relevant information, and linking relationships within and between concepts. For Jonassen (2006), cognitive tools have been "adapted or developed to function as intellectual partners with the learner in order to engage and facilitate critical thinking and higher order learning" (p. 9). After being presented with a problem or inquiry that includes the particular phenomenon to be examined, students build a representation to help them to understand it and/or develop solutions. Using cognitive tools, learners create artefacts, representations, or external models representing their thinking while engaged in the knowledge-construction process. These tools support knowledge construction by enabling learners to learn *with* rather than *from* technology, generating questions and predicting outcomes, creating meaningful data structures and generating hypotheses, and enhancing such skills as collaboration, communication, metacognition, and resource organization (e.g., Chai and Quek 2003; Jonassen 2006; Jonassen and Reeves 1996). Interpersonal engagement is critical in this type of learning.

However, in the context of this book, we are exploring the design and uses of representations that are already designed, and made available for learners as tools in their learning activity. De Jong and Joolingen (1998) in their paper "Scientific discovery learning with computer simulations of concept domains" specify a number of possibilities including hypertext environments, concept mapping environments, interactive representations (simulations), and modelling environments. Today's technology adds an important advantage of enabling the design of concept representation resources and models in interactive multimedia format (see Churchill 2013; De Jong et al. 1998; Fraser 1999; Johnson and Lesh 2003; Norman 1983; van Someren et al. 1998). It is suggested that these concept representations support learning through the activation of certain cognitive processes such as reflection, mind modelling, abstraction, reconceptization and linking between internal representations (e.g., Churchill 2008; Seel 2003; Mayer 2003). The gradual *interiorization*, or *appropriation* (the term used by such scholars as Vygotsky (1978), Davydov (1999), Sierpinska (1993) and Kozulin (1990), of the features of concept representations through their intellectual uses in such operations as generalization, identification, comparison, discrimination, and synthesis of thoughts within a learning activity will lead to deeper disciplinary concept knowledge. If a psychological tool for theoretical thinking involving a concept is absent, a representation of that concept (concept representation resource) might be supplied externally. This might be one way how technology can provide an intellectual partnership in order to support disciplinary thinking and activities.

It is important to note that even the most appealing concept representation resource might not be effective unless it is appropriately integrated in educational activities. Pedagogical effective use of a concept representation resource must be driven by an activity (Churchill and Hedberg 2008a). For Foo et al. (2005), an activity design (learning design) should be a central concern for a teacher engaged in instructional planning. Mayer et al. (2003) suggest that an activity should present learners with a conceptually demanding question that requires deep intellectual engagement (theoretical thinking). In this context, a concept representation resource design must be informed by possible learning uses, and allow learning to happen in the process of concept changes and development of personal theories based on that experience. Concept learning, in most cases, is not possible simply through declarative knowledge presentations and traditional instruction. Such a strategy is likely to result in misconceptions, incomplete conception, and temporary remembering of certain definitions or other information, or no learning at all. Effective concept learning requires activities that include generalization, abstraction, and the building of personal theories, reconceptization and application of concept knowledge. Digital resources for learning are only one component in a learning design. It is an activity that creates context for these resources to be deployed and used. In many cases, digital resources for learning are effective, but there are numerous situations where other forms of resources alone or together with digital ones, will prove to be more effective for concept learning. Digital resources for learning might also play other roles in learning activities such as providing support and remediation.

Finally, in conclusion of this difficult discussion, concept learning is not simply mapping or copying of external content, models, and representations of someone's knowledge into learners' mind. A concept needs to be deconstructed (e.g., through analysis of its properties, relationships and parameters), and reconstructed in the mind (e.g., through generalization and abstraction) in order for concept learning to happen.

A concept representation is a representation of a concept, not a copy or a replica. A purpose of concept learning should be the gradual approximation of sociocultural and individual concept knowledge and development of intellectual disposition to engage and apply that knowledge in theoretical thinking. Therefore, when we discuss an idea of a concept in the context of this book, we consider it to be a specific form of sociocultural knowledge, not as a something that strictly exists in and is copied across minds. Concept learning should result in conceptual knowledge; a tool that supports theoretical thinking, or a psychological tool. However, concept learning is often a prolonged process of gradual approximation of learners' thinking and concept knowledge on one side, and concepts specified by the curriculum and determined in the context of their socio-cultural development within a discipline on the other. This is to say that concept knowledge has its own personal development trajectory that intersects with sociocultural trajectory in the context of formal education.

Most of the design and research work of the author of this book focuses on concept representation resources. Previously, the author referred to such digital learning resources as 'concept models', however, this term has been abounded in this book. The author holds that this kind of resources are critical for learning, and that education media designers should dedicate much more attention to them, especially in the context of emerging mobile representational technologies that allow access to resources at anytime and anywhere. A special form of intellectual partnership with technology might be achieved when learners' concept knowledge is supported by externally supplied concept representations. This book gives strong attention to these kinds of resources, elevating their importance for learning at all levels. Ultimately, education should, instead of filing in learners with information, empower these learners to develop their own concept tools for their intellectual activities within disciplines and beyond.

> **Activity 3.2**
> *How are concepts learnt by learners? How do you learn a concept? Let's recall your experience in Activity 3.1. How did mind-mapping help you to learn the concept of 'Heat?' Think about this, and discuss your ideas with your peers. Try to develop your claim about how concepts are learnt based on your own experience. However, how do you know that the concept you learnt is not actually a misconception? Reflective learning practice is critical for concept learning. What you are asked in this case, is to reflect back on your own conceptual knowledge and examine it with aid of your mind-map. However, most effectively, reflections occur in the context of some intellectual use of a concept, that is, some problem to solve or other task requiring that conceptual knowledge to be examined, refined, tested etc. So, describe a task, inquiry or a problem solving where learners might use their concept of 'Heat' in a reflective way.*

3.4 Designing and Developing a Concept Representation Resource

A concept representation is developed through the following stages:

- Identify/Determine a concept for design.
- Specify concept's particulars.
- Design a storyboard specifying how a concept content will be represented:
  - Determine context for the concept representation;
  - Determine functional areas of the screen;
  - Determine modes of representation; and
  - Determine interactive elements.
- Develop a prototype of the concept representation resource and evaluate it.
- Develop the final concept representation resource.

We will illustrate these phases through an example of a concept representation resource designed to facilitate the learning of the concept of Velocity.

3.4.1 Identify/Determine a Concept for the Design

A process of design of a concept model begins with the curriculum analysis and identification of a concept(s) to be represented through a concept representation resource(s). It is assumed that the best outcome can be achieved by systematic analysis of a curriculum, identification of concepts and the relationship that exists between these, rather than by identifying based on some criteria of a single concept for development. Relationships will define groups and sub-groups that include sets of concepts. For example, a group/topic of mechanics might contain various concepts such as: density, gravity, space, time, displacement, motion, position, direction, velocity, acceleration, mass, momentum, force, energy, torque, conservation law, and power. Some of these concepts can be grouped together (in a single or multiple groups) when determining final concept representation resources to be developed, e.g., velocity, time, displacement and acceleration, or acceleration, mass and force.

We might take the first example of a group of concepts (velocity, time, displacements and acceleration) and include it in several concept representation resources, with the main focus changing from the concept of velocity to acceleration and displacement. So, one concept representation can be designed with the main focus on velocity, and another separate concept representation can be developed with the main focus on acceleration, for example.

In practice, many educators decide on a concept based on their experience and opinion, rather than through any systematic analysis of curriculum content. Some educators are guided by thinking about importance of certain concepts over other concepts, or selecting those concepts that are difficult for students to understand, or due to personal theory that a particular concept can be effectively taught through the use of representational technologies. That is the reason why we might find that there are numerous concept representations based on the same set of specific concepts, while there are other concepts that have not been included at all. What determines an educators' decision are his or her private theories about issues such as what is learning, how his or her students learn, technology, roles of a teacher, and assessment (see Churchill 2005).

3.4.2 Specify Concept's Particulars

The next step in the process is to determine and specify particulars including related concepts, properties, parameters, relationships and information. The following particulars presented in the completed planning form should be determined and specified (see Table 3.1).

3.4.3 Design a Storyboard Specifying How a Concept's Content Will Be Represented

A storyboard, in the formal sense, is a blueprint for the development of the final product, a quality assurance document, a design specifications document, project team management tool and a tool for managing client-developer relationship and issues. As a formal document, a storyboard specifies all particulars in sufficient details to enable a project manager to coordinate the process, and the development team to develop the media required, and integrate these in a final product or a prototype. Depending on a kind of digital learning resource, sometimes, a preliminary set of flowcharts might be needed in addition to storyboards, but in the case of a concept representation resource, this might not be always needed.

However, this book is not so much concerned about formal multimedia development project management and processes, although all of these ideas from this book do apply in that context as well. The purpose of the book is to provide a useful guide and empower educators to understand, select and engage in the design of resources for their own practice. In the informal sense, a storyboard can be a tool to assist a designer (e.g., an educator) to articulate ideas and arrive at a sketch of an intended final product before commencing any development, or before passing that storyboard to others with suitable technical skills for development. Thus, this can be an informal and rough sketch of a possible content presentation and interface screen design. The final product will evolve through further processes (prototyping, evaluation and development of the final product).

3.4 Designing and Developing a Concept Representation Resource

Table 3.1 Concept representation planning form

Concept representation planning tool
Name of a concept representation resource:
Velocity
Main concept(s):
Velocity
Related concept(s):
Acceleration
Displacement
Time
Properties:
Velocity, acceleration and displacement are vectors and they have +ve and −ve values indicating intensities and directions
Dynamic parameters:
Acceleration changes based on learner interaction between values of −1 to 1 m/s^2
Relationships:
Velocity changes in value from −100 to 100 m/s based on acceleration
Displacement changes between −20 to 20 km depending on velocity and time
Information:
Direction, how fast an object moves and effect of acceleration are shown as an animation (e.g., a car on the move)
Value of velocity is displayed numerically and at the same time represented on a velocity-time graph
Value of acceleration is displayed numerically
Displacements are shown in 'km' and shown on displacement-time graph

Important
Discipline specific concept knowledge are the foundation of one's theoretical thinking and his/her ability to intellectually operate within that discipline (e.g., solve problems or conduct a research in the way that scientists do).

When conceptualizing a storyboard, a designer will consider the following particulars:

- *General treatment and context for the concept representation*—In our example, the context will be that a learner changes the acceleration of a moving vehicle. Such a realistic context might not be always required, however, in some cases of concept resources, it can be useful to enable learners to relate a new concept to prior knowledge and experience.

- *Determine functional areas of the screen*—A screen of a concept resource might contain various functional areas, such as the functional areas where interactive elements are arranged, and functional areas where certain information is constantly displayed. In the case of our example, the screen is divided into four functional areas: v-t graph and d-t graph areas showing changes in velocity and displacement over time; a screen showing an animation that simulates movement of a vehicle on a road; and an area where numerical information about parameters, and interactive controls are displayed.
- *Determine modes of representation*—A designer must make a decision how to represent the relevant information. In our example, the movement of a vehicle is shown as an animation of a car moving along a road the value of velocity is presented as a car speedometer as well as a point on a line of v-t graph; acceleration is shown as a number between -1 and 1; and displacement is presented as a point on a line of a d-t graph.
- *Determine interactive elements*—A designer needs to make the decision how a learner will manipulate the dynamic parameter. Various possibilities exist for interaction, such as, sliders, text entry boxes, buttons, and clickable hot-spots. Emerging mobile technology also allows for finger driven interaction. There are even more innovative possibilities nowadays that allow interactions through gestures and body movement (e.g., Kinect or Myo). In our example, the dynamic parameter is acceleration, which is controlled by a learner with a slider that can be moved between maximum and minimum values.

3.4.4 Develop a Prototype of the Concept Representation Resource and Evaluate It

Until this stage, we see that these activities of the design can be comfortably carried out by educators. No technical skills are actually required, as all the work so far has included conceptualizing and sketching ideas. So, how to proceed further from this point on? The next step is to produce a prototype. In the formal sense, a prototype of software product is an important project management and client management tool. It provides a glimpse of what the final product will look like, including examples of screen design, interface elements and media. Once these are understood as acceptable by the project team and a client, and in some cases tested with real users, the production of a final product will proceed with the required amendments in place.

In case of collaboration between an educator and a developer (a multimedia designer, and in some cases a programmer supported by a graphics artist), a storyboard serves as a tool to clearly communicate requirements, ideas and expectations of that educator. Usually, an educator will meet with these professionals, and explain what he or she wants to have in the concept representation resources under development.

In case of holistic work by an individual educator who is able to carry on all of these technical activities, the development of a prototype might proceed without any storyboard being previously developed. In this case, an educator-as-designer would use the multimedia authoring tool as an aid in conceptualizations and planning, that is storyboarding and, at the same time, using the emerging design as a prototype.

In all of these scenarios, a prototype might be a useful tool to test ideas, obtain real users' feedback, and prevent spending time developing what might later not be accepted by a client or real users. The process of evaluating a prototype might be exceptionally useful to help a designer to further refine ideas through feedback from users. Several aspects are evaluated in such a scenario, including some of the following:

- Interface;
- Screen design;
- Suitability of content; and
- Effectiveness of presentation for learning uses.

3.4.5 Develop the Final Concept Representation Resource

The final step in the process is to develop the concept representation resource. This is technical task to execute what has been formalized though storyboarding and prototype development and evaluation. In the case of the Velocity example, the final concept representation resource is shown in Fig. 3.2.

When developing concept representation resources, specific delivery technology should be kept in mind. Nature of interaction and screen parameters strongly influence the design. For example, if we design a resource for an iPod, we need to keep in mind that this technology supports finger-driven interaction. The screen size is smaller than an iPad. Delivery technology also influences the kind of development approach used. For example, developing a resource for delivery via a computer might be effective with Adobe Flash. However, such a resource would not be functional on either iOS or Android based devices. HTML5 might possibly overcome this problem, and allow a resource to be deployed across multiple platforms.

Finally, once a resource is developed, it needs to be made available for accessing real users (teachers and students). This can be achieved in a number of ways. A resource can be delivered via course spaces such as those designed within Moodle or Blackboard Learning Management System (LMS) technologies. In such systems, a resource is uploaded in a space dedicated to a specific course. However, from an institutional perspective, this has limited impact because such resources are 'buried' in specific courses and students and teachers other than members of that course cannot access them at all. Since, there might be a need for an institution to

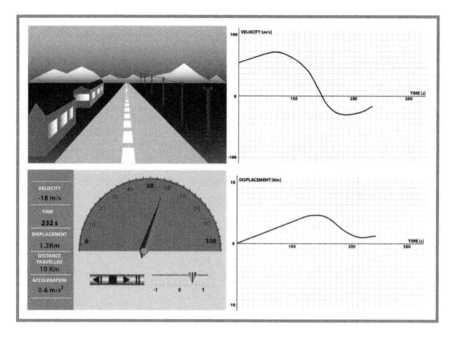

Fig. 3.2 'Velocity' concept representation resource

deploy a repository system that allows resources to be shared amongst individuals and used across platforms.[5] In addition, common for mobile learning content, resources can be deployed via systems such as App Store (Apple) or Play Story (Android). Furthermore, platforms such as Apple iTunesU allow for some content to be delivered to learners globally or within a subscribing institution.

> **Activity 3.3**
> *Let's go back to your concept of 'Heat' and a corresponding mind-map you developed. Examine this concept again and draw a sketch on paper of a conceptual resource that would allow a learner to examine this concept's properties, parameters and relationships, and refine your own misconception. Think about your Activity 3.2, and note how might your design support concept learning in the context of inquiry or problem solving you proposed.*

---

[5]More about repositories will be discussed in Chap. 8.

3.5 Examples of Concept Representation Resources

In this section of the chapter, a number of examples of concept representation resources developed by the author and his students are features. Each new design of a concept representation resource is an innovation in itself. There is no prescribed grammar of visual language, and the designers of such resources are required to be creative and innovative when developing each new representation. Therefore, these examples are just a few cases of concept representation resources and design possibilities.

3.5.1 Maximizing Content Presentable in a Minimal Screen Space: Machining Parameters

The concept representation resource presented in Fig. 3.3 was developed by the author and his colleague at a technical education institute in Singapore. The resource presents parameters, relationships and properties of concepts related to machining parameters in a precision engineering course. In particular, the resource represents content related to the 'Turning Machining' process. The resource has been used within an activity that requires students to consider a client's request for the machining of a certain work piece according to specifications presented in a supplied technical drawing. The final outcome is to develop a proposal for a client outlining the required machining time, and based on it, the most competitive cost for producing the work piece according to specified requirements. The teacher would also create an atmosphere where different groups of students work on this

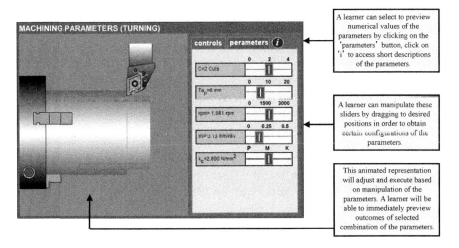

Fig. 3.3 'Machining Parameter (Turning)' concept representation resource (developed with a teacher from a technical education institute in Singapore)

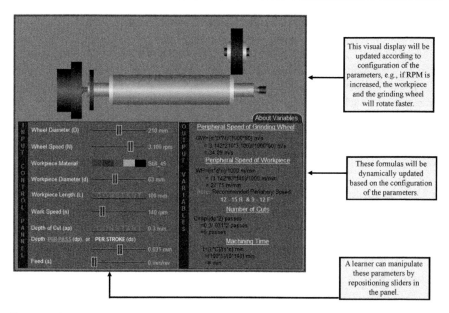

Fig. 3.4 'Machining Parameter (Grinding)' concept representation resource (developed with a teacher from a technical education institute in Singapore)

activity and compete for the most appropriate cost for the production based on optimization of the machining parameters.

The main purpose of this concept presentation is to allow learners to study fundamental concepts which they need for later understanding of computer numeric programming (CNC) and the use of real turning machines. What is interesting for this resource is that a huge amount of curriculum content is embedded in a single screen display. According to the colleague responsible for teaching that specific course, the concept representation resource includes content traditionally presented in more than 60 pages of a textbook used for his class, and equivalent to almost three months of teaching under traditional arrangements. The teacher involved in the design and use of this representation with his students highly appreciated this kind of material, and was motivated to continue collaboration with the author to develop an additional two resources for Milling and Grinding machining parameters. Figure 3.4 shows a screen from the Grinding machining parameters resource.

3.5.2 Concept Representation Resources in Non-conceptual Domain: Tenses and Four Tones

This book argues that curriculum content should include concept, as well as procedural and declarative knowledge, and emphasizes the use of all these forms of knowledge. Although this thinking that curriculum content should include concept

3.5 Examples of Concept Representation Resources

knowledge might be more obvious in the context of science, mathematics, technical subjects, and social sciences, almost all domains have certain content that could be learnt through generalizing and abstracting rather than in declarative ways (e.g., by remembering facts and definition). In some subject domains, we might not be using terms and concepts, however, these domains also have certain key content that cannot be simply learnt in a declarative way, and some generalization and abstraction is required. What might more prominently differ between disciplines are specific ways of constructing generalization, e.g., scientific inquiry, content analysis of a literary text, or an investigation and constructing a theorem in mathematics.

For example, the resource in Fig. 3.5 demonstrates how this might work in the context of English language. This concept representation was developed for the use in an English as a second language class. It is a tool that helps learners conceptualize certain rules in language learning (tenses). A learner can input times into the two boxes on the screen and based on this configuration, the scenario will display a grammatically correct sentence in terms of tense and based on a selected verb (e.g., run, eat, sing, study and sing).

Figure 3.6 is an example from a Chinese as second language learning context. As we have already noted, language learning does not have concepts such as those commonly found in sciences, social sciences or mathematics. However, there are those kernels of these disciplines which are not declarative knowledge, rather, these are more abstract and difficult to learn. A teacher of Chinese as second language at a university in Hong Kong told the author that one of the kernels of her subject matter

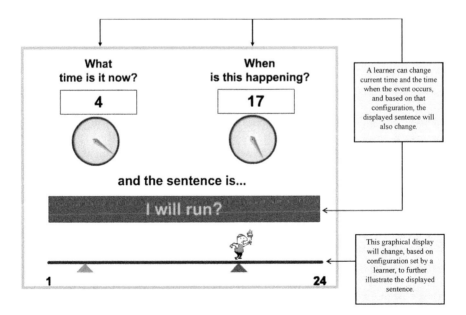

Fig. 3.5 'Multiplication of Fractions' concept representation resource (developed by the author and his student)

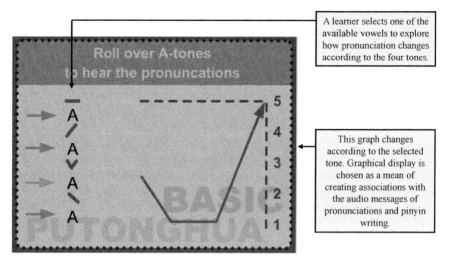

Fig. 3.6 'Four Tones' resources (developed by the author and a Chinese as a second language teacher)

is the four distinct tone intonations. Distinguishing between these tones, and becoming skilled to use them in reading so-called Pinyin, and later in speaking, is a critically important part of learning the Chinese language. The author subsequently worked with this teacher and designed a resource with the focus on the four tones.

3.5.3 Difficult to Visualize Domains: Algebra Blocks and Multiplication of Fractions

Some concept content of domains such as mathematics are difficult to visualize. In mathematics, for example, teachers are accustomed to mathematical expressions, symbols, formal diagrams and graphics, to the extent that prevents them to express their ideas through any different representational systems. However, using more intuitive, simpler and visual representational systems can greatly enhance mathematics learning. One such example is factorizing expressions of a form $x^2 + ax + b$. The concept representation called 'Algebra Blocks' is shown in Fig. 3.7 and designed to help learners understand and perhaps visualize independent factorization of expressions.

Figure 3.8 shows another Mathematics example, a representation of the multiplication of fractions. Multiplication is represented as two sides of a rectangle. Each side represents one whole. The repositioning of sliders will fraction sides, and the final product of the multiplication of two fractions will be represented as a shaded portion of the whole.

3.5 Examples of Concept Representation Resources

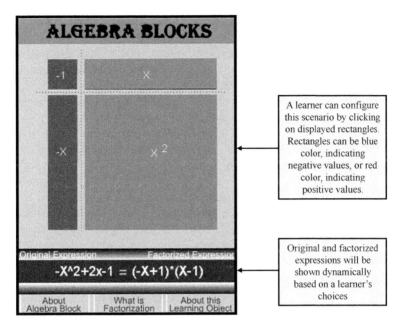

Fig. 3.7 'Algebra Blocks' concept representation resource

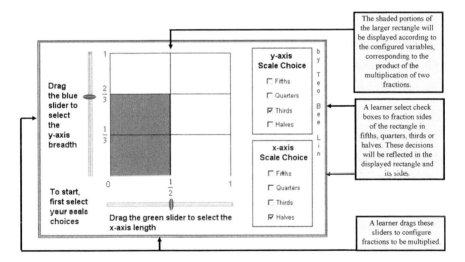

Fig. 3.8 'Multiplication of Fractions' concept representation resource (developed by the author and his student)

3.5.4 Teaching Young Learners to Generalize: Drying Rate

The concept of representation resources presented in Fig. 3.9 was designed with an intention to engage young learners to learn about the processes of generalization and abstraction and in that way, develop their disposition to approach concept representations in a systematic way during their learning. Developing such disposition is a kind of literacy that contemporary education should develop for learners today. Schools teach students from an early age how to read and write, listen and speak, but more attention should be given to viewing and representing the skills required to effectively consume and communicate with emerging representational forms.

This resource is not discipline specific. It is a general representation of something that young learners might encounter in their real life. However, the way they would need to approach this resource in order to understand it, is the same as for any discipline specific concept representation. Young learner's cognitive load is freed from any burden in trying to understand the disciplinary content and, in such a way, they can focus purely on processes, understanding properties and relationships, and subsequent generalizing and abstracting.

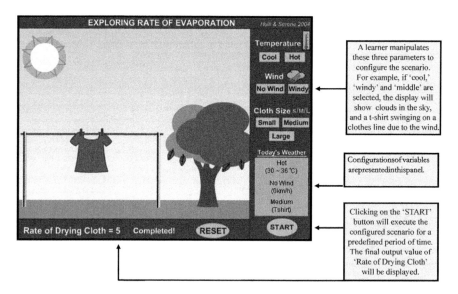

Fig. 3.9 'Draying Rate' representation (developed by the author and his student)

3.5 Examples of Concept Representation Resources

3.5.5 Simulations and Concept Learning

A simulation[6] is a specific form of digital media that might be integrated into a concept representation resource or in a practice resource. It displays a real system, process, event and object, unlike those representations which address more abstract concepts. Often, simulations are designed to enable learners to understand how a corresponding real thing works, practice certain procedures, and experiment. A simulation can be used to represent concept knowledge. However, a simulation might also be used to support procedural learning. When used in a concept representation resource, a simulation can represent a system and its parts and properties, and allow a learner to learn and understand underlining properties, relationships and develop abstract concepts. An example of such concept representation resource is presented in Fig. 3.10.

The upper part of this concept representation resource displays two cross-sections of a centrifugal water pump. A learner can manipulate a set of parameters, and explore how these interact and what they mean (by noting changes in number of impellers and increases in revolutions), and how these affect pressure produced by the pump. The bottom part of the concept representation displays a scenario showing a system where a pump is used to lift water to a certain height for filling reservoir position at the top of a building. A learner can examine relevant parameters and develop an understanding of the relationship. These understandings are then applied in a project (a learning activity) requiring learners to design a water system to be used in a specific building configuration that their teacher set.

Figure 3.11 shows another interesting example of a concept representation resource that contains some real-life elements included in its display. This example from a 'Chemistry' course was designed to help students to understand and learn the concept of 'Reaction Rate'. A learner can manipulate the particle size of a marble to be exposed to a chemical contact/reaction with acid, and examine time taken for the reaction to take place.

3.6 A Study of Design of Concept Representation Resources

Over the last several years, the author has engaged in investigating the aspect of design of concept representation resources (previously called 'concept models'). Two aspects of design were identified and studied: (a) Presentation Design and (b) Design for Learning Uses. Presentation design addresses features and

---

[6]The term 'simulations' should not be used for anything that is visual and interactive. More than anything, a simulation is a kind of media, not specifically a kind of digital resource for learning. For us in this book, the kinds of resources for learning are associated with specific forms of curriculum content knowledge, e.g., procedural or concept knowledge, and various media types that can be integrated into the design of such resources.

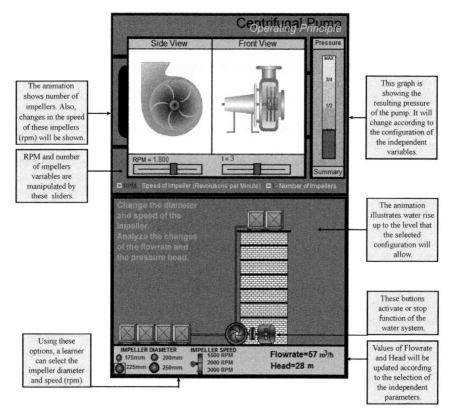

Fig. 3.10 'Centrifugal Water Pump' concept representation resource (developed in collaboration with a teacher teaching 'Mechanical Maintenance' course at a technical education institute in Singapore)

possibilities for arranging various media elements on a screen. Design for learning uses, on the other side, refers to aspects of design that would support later reusability in the context of learning-centered activities such as inquiries and problem-solving. In this section of the chapter, discussion of presentation design will be provided. Discussion of the design for learning uses will be provided later in a different chapter.

A concept representation is an important educational multimedia resource that, when appropriately designed and used, can contribute to improvements in concept learning. Currently, there is a lack of empirically-developed guidelines on how to design technology-based concept representations for educational purposes. Although some guidelines for the design of representations for multimedia learning exist (e.g., Mayer 2001), there are almost no guidelines in relation to the presentation design of concept representation resources and other forms of digital resources for teaching and learning. At the same time, it is important to note that

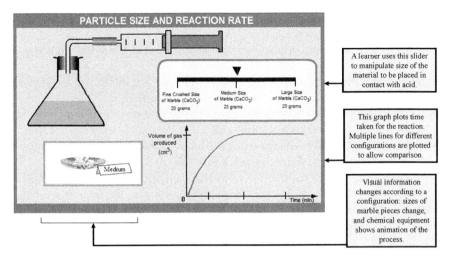

Fig. 3.11 'Particle Size and Reaction Time' concept representation resource (developed by the author's students)

even the most effectively designed concept representation might not be useful unless it is properly designed for integration in learning activities.

The author previously conducted a study of presentation design of concept representation resources. A number of recommendations for presentation design are provided. These are explicated based on a study involving a review of a collection of concept representation resources.

3.6.1 The Study of Presentation Design

The recommendations developed in the study emerged from a review of a collection of 54 concept representations and their design characteristics (Churchill 2014). Five expert reviewers conducted the review. The reviewers were identified and selected based on the following criteria relevant to the objectives of the projects:

- Formal qualification related to areas such as instructional design, e-learning or information technology in education;
- Experience in the design of multimedia content/learning objects;
- Teaching experience in a specific discipline and previous use of learning objects in supporting discipline-specific learning; and
- Willingness to participate in the study as an expert reviewer.

The researcher also attempted to engage reviewers from across educational institutions including a primary and a secondary school, a technical education institute and a university. The reviewers also ranged in respect to their teaching disciplines. The reviewers included:

- A Geography secondary school teacher with a Master Degree in information technology in education qualification;
- An English language primary school teacher with a Graduate Diploma in E-learning Instructional Design qualification;
- An Engineering lecturer from a technical education institute with a Graduate Diploma in E-learning Instructional Design qualification;
- A university professor with expertize in IT in Education (previously worked as an Economics teacher in a school); and
- A university professor with expertize in Multimedia Design (previously worked as a Mathematics and Science teacher in a school).

The expert reviewers independently previewed each of the 54 concept representation resources from the collection provided. The reviews were recorded by using a form created for the purpose of the study. This form is presented in Fig. 3.12. The form was developed in partial consideration of certain issues from the 'cognitive theory of multimedia learning' (Mayer 2001) and based on a discussion between the reviewers. The cognitive theory of multimedia learning provides a set of empirically developed guiding principles for the design of educational multimedia for delivery via computer screens. Issues considered in developing the form were:

- *Multimedia principle*—What is the predominant mode of representation for the essential content of this concept representation (e.g., visual, textual, animation, auditory)?
- *Principles for managing essential processing (navigation)*—Describe characteristic structure and navigation (e.g., single or multiple screen, user-paced or automatic, hierarchical or linear navigation, physically and temporally integration of modes).
- *Principles for managing extraneous processing (interactivity)*—Describe the interactive features used to manipulate the represented concept (e.g., slides, buttons, and clickable hot-spots).
- *Principles for reducing extraneous processing*—How was the extraneous content used (e.g., use of colour to highlight the organization of the essential content)?

For example, a category in the form titled 'Modes of Representation' was influenced by the 'Multimedia Principle,' while the 'Content Structure' category was influenced by the 'Principles for Managing Essential Processing'.

Data from the completed forms were converted to numerical values according to the following schema:

- Scores for Pedagogical Quality (PQ) included: 1 (very low and low quality), 2 (average quality) and 3 (high and very high quality);
- Scores for Multimedia Quality (MMQ) included: 1 (very low and low quality), 2 (average quality) and 3 (high and very high quality);

3.6 A Study of Design of Concept Representation Resources

Review of a Conceptual Representation Resource Form

Reviewer:

Title of the conceptual representation resource under review:

Brief description of the conceptual representation resource:

Pedagogical quality of the conceptual representation resource				
☐ Very low quality	☐ Low quality	☐ Average quality	☐ High quality	☐ Very high quality

Multimedia quality				
☐ Very low quality	☐ Low quality	☐ Average quality	☐ High quality	☐ Very high quality

Interactivity Features						
☐ Text-input boxes	☐ Buttons	☐ Hot spots	☐ Pull-down menu	☐ Roll-over	☐ Sliders	☐ Target area

Content structure		
☐ Single screen	☐ Linear sequence of screens	☐ Hierarchical structure of screens

Screen Display Area		
☐ < 640 by 480	☐ ≥ 640 by 480	☐ ≥ 800 by 600

Modes of representation	
Modes used in the design	The predominant mode
☐ Text [labels and values only]	☐
☐ Text [sentences explaining content]	☐
☐ Visuals – drawings, diagrams and illustrations	☐
☐ Visuals – photographs	☐
☐ Video	☐
☐ Animation	☐
☐ Audio	☐

Any other comment about the conceptual representation resource

Fig. 3.12 Form used in the review of concept representation resources

- Scores for Interactive Features (IF) were obtained by adding the number of unique interactive elements used in the design (range from 1 to 7);
- Scores for Content Structure (CS) included: 1 (single screen), 2 (linear sequence of screens) and 3 (hierarchical structure of screens);
- Scores for Screen Display Area (SDA) included: 1 (less than 640 by 480), 2 (greater or equal to 640 by 480) and 3 (greater or equal to 800 by 600); and
- Scores for Modes of Representation (MR) were obtained by adding the number of different representations used in design, ranging from 1 to 7.

The reviewers were required to provide their independent assessment for 'Pedagogical Quality' and 'Multimedia Quality' respectively. Scores of all the reviewers were added together to obtain the final values (ranging from 5 to 15). In addition, the reviewers were required to indicate the predominant mode of representation for each of the concept representations. The other measures were objective (CS, SDA, MR and IF) and were pre-inserted into the forms for each of the resources in the collection. The data were processed using SPSS statistical analysis software to obtain values for correlations between various measures. Outcomes are shown in Table 3.2.

Interpretation of correlation coefficients was informed by Cohen (1988), who provides the following guidelines for effect sizes: small effect size, $r = 0.1 - 0.23$; medium, $r = 0.24 - 0.36$; large, $r = 0.37$ or larger. In addition, statistical analysis was applied to obtain differences in the means in pedagogical quality between resources with visual as the predominant mode of representations and other resources.

Processing and analysis of data resulted in a set of recommendations for presentation design. The analysis of the data was conducted and conclusions reached in collaboration and discussions with the reviewers. The team discussed contradictions and differences in opinions in order to interpret the data and develop assertions and articulate final recommendations. The team also articulated some general observations about the features of the designs, and some unique aspects of design that hinted at pedagogical quality. The following categories of recommendations were explicated in the study: present information visually, design for interaction, design a holistic scenario, design for a single screen, design for small space, use audio and video only if they are the only option, use of color in moderation, avoid unnecessary decorative elements, design with a single font, and use frames to logically divide the screen area.

Table 3.2 Summary of correlation coefficients and p-values

Measures	r	p
PQ/MMQ	0.079	0.57
PQ/CS	−0.12	0.391
PQ/SDA	−0.017	0.905
PQ/MR	0.132	0.342
PQ/IF	0.454	0.001

3.6.2 Recommendations for Presentation Design

A major aim of this study was to develop recommendations by linking features of design to the perceived pedagogical quality of the concept representation resources. The author's intention at this stage was to provide sufficient description of the recommendations in order to allow readers to examine whether these are useful in their own educational media development practices. The following recommendations emerged:

- *Present information visually*—The study results showed a small correlation between the level of perceived pedagogical quality (as judged by the reviewers) and the quantity of modes of representation ($r = 0.132$, $p = 0.342$). However, when the pedagogical quality of resources with visual as the predominant mode of representations ($N = 41$, $M = 10.24$, $SD = 3.277$) was compared to that of learning with other predominant modes ($N = 13$, $M = 7.62$, $SD = 2.959$), significant differences were observed ($t = 4.6$, $p = 0.013$). These differences were also substantive as indicated by a large effect size ($d = 1.48$). The differences suggested that the content of a concept representation resource should be presented predominantly through visual representations (e.g., photographs, illustrations, diagrams, graphs, colors, icons and symbols). Sometimes, the same information can be presented in a number of modes simultaneously (e.g., as text, visually and via audio). However, results strongly suggested that visuals should be the central mode of representation. Representing the same information through multiple modalities should be carefully managed [see redundancy principle (Mayer 2001)].
- *Design for interaction*—The result of this study showed that there was a large correlation between pedagogical quality and the total number of interactive features used in the designs of the concept representations under review ($r = 0.454$, $p = 0.001$). This suggests that the more interactive features a concept representation has, the higher its pedagogical quality. Relationships and properties should be displayed in interactive ways to allow the user of a concept representation to manipulate parameters and observe outcomes (e.g., by manipulating sliders, clicking on buttons, or inputting text/numbers). Outcomes of the manipulation can be presented in a single mode or in several modes at the same time (e.g., as a number or a graph); however, visuals emerged in this study as the most pedagogically effective representation.
- *Design a holistic scenario*—Design elements should be arranged in such a way that some of the content are integrated into a holistic presentational scenario depicting the concept that is represented. In other words, all areas of the screen need to be integrated into a holistic scenario that supports multimedia representation of a concept. This recommendation emerged from the observation that content structure had a small correlation with pedagogical quality ($r = -0.12$, $p = 0.391$). Distributing content across multiple screens will add complexity to

the development of a concept representation resource without any significant increase in pedagogical quality.

- *Design for a single screen*—A concept representation resource can be designed for presentation in a single screen. Single screen presentation is likely to allow a learner to have a holistic focus on all elements of the required concept knowledge. Further, a single screen is likely to enable a learner to manipulate relationships and properties, and to access the outcomes of this manipulation all in one place. At the same time, a single interactive screen can be easily meshed with other media into structures such as web pages. Content structure had a small correlation with pedagogical quality. The review provided an additional hint that concept representation resources designed on a single screen might be sufficiently effective in terms of the pedagogical quality, and designing for presentations in more than one screen might not have any positive effect on pedagogical quality; rather, this might have a negative effect by causing split-attention and increased 'Cognitive Load' (see Mayer 2001).
- *Design for small space*—The design of a concept representation resource should utilize only the screen space necessary to present all the required information, properties, relationships and interactive elements. From the review, it was observed that most of the concept representation resources were designed in a screen space that does not exceed 640 by 480 pixels. The data from the study did not produce any significant correlation between pedagogical quality and sizes of the screen display area ($r = -0.017$, $p = 0.905$). This recommendation might lead to two important implications. Firstly, a smaller screen area would enable students to concentrate their attention on a smaller space, thus, reducing split-attention. Secondly, a resource designed for a small screen might later serve as a media object that can be embedded into larger screen displays such as in blog posts, instructional products and presentation slides.
- *Use audio, animations and video only if they are the only options*—Audio should only be used if it is effective for a representational purpose or to enhance realism when required (e.g., a specific sound indicating a faulty machine), or to offload cognitive processing from the visual channel [see modality principle (Mayer 2001)]. Similarly, video should only be used when, for example, the manipulation of relationships requires different segments from a video to be presented based on the configuration of parameters. Often, content from a video might be presented as several images of the key frames, with short blocks of text explaining each of the frames [which might support the temporal contiguity principle (Mayer 2001)]. Qualitative observations in the study suggested that the use of video, animations and audio had no effect on pedagogical quality; rather, these only increased the complexity of a concept representation in terms of effort required for learning, as well as in terms of efforts required for development of a concept representation resource.
- *Use color in moderation*—Another qualitative observation suggested that in order to present the content clearly, color should be used in moderation. On the

other hand, quantitative data suggested that there was an insignificant correlation between pedagogical quality and the multimedia quality of a concept representation resource design ($r = 0.079$, $p = 0.57$). Often, color was found in the reviewed cases of concept representation resources to be effective when used as visual content and to connect related information (e.g., connecting a positive numerical value displayed in red with a red bar on a bar graph). Different shades of color can be effectively used, but the use of sharply contrasting colors must be avoided. The focus should be on the simplicity and clarity of presentation and support for learning, rather than on the pursuit of gratuitous artistic and multimedia beautification of the display.

- *Avoid unnecessary decorative elements*—This is another recommendation emerging from understanding that there is no correlation between pedagogical quality and multimedia quality. Unnecessary decorative elements can add complexity to the representation and result in increased extraneous cognitive load (Mayer 2001). They should be used in moderation, or not at all. All elements of the design should serve the purpose of representing a concept (or should facilitate this representation) and allow a student to manipulate its properties and explore relationships. In addition, cartoon-like characters should be avoided unless they serve some representational purpose. Many designers assume that cartoon-like characters will motivate students by making learning fun; however, such graphics are less than productive for learning. For Collins (1996), designers should not assume that fun is a desirable component of presentation, because there is a risk that students might not take such learning seriously; thus, a 'fun' presentation might impede learning. Motivation lies in a learning task that engages a student in the use of a concept representation resource, rather than in the resource itself. A concept representation resource is a strategy for effective representation of educationally useful concepts, and unless its design elements support this representation, they should not be included.
- *Design with a single font*—In order to keep the presentation simple, a single font style should be used (e.g., Arial font in different sizes, shades and styles). The same color fonts can be used to relate pieces of information. Using multiple font types might increase extraneous cognitive load and have a negative effect on learning. Similar to the previous two recommendations, this recommendation is connected to the absence of a correlation between pedagogical quality and multimedia quality.
- *Use frames to logically divide the screen area*—Review of the collection of concept representation resources indicated that frames can be useful in dividing the presentation screen into functional and logical areas and groupings. For example, interactive elements such as sliders and buttons can be grouped together in one area of the display, while another area can be used to display output information. Such areas might support visual attention (as a student focuses attention on one framed area at a time) and positively affect the utility of the essential cognitive load required to process information (Mayer 2001).

3.6.3 An Example of a Concept Representations Resource Design Reflecting the Recommendations

The concept representation resource featured in Fig. 3.13 was designed to support secondary school students' learning of the concept of a volcano. This concept includes issues such as lava types, how they affect the structure of eruptions, and the effects of eruptions on the environment.

A learner can select one of the following types of lava: runny with little water, runny with lots of water, sticky with little water or sticky with lots of water. After selecting the lava type, the learner will be able to explore the structure of an eruption and the effect that it has on the environment. This will allow the learner to compare changes in structure and differences in the effects between different volcanoes and eruption types.

Design features of this concept representation illustrate the usefulness of the recommendations discussed here. This is elaborated in Table 3.3, which links each of the recommendations to some specific feature of the 'Volcano' concept representation resource. The design of this concept representation resource reflects most of the recommendations.

> **Activity 3.4**
> *Look back at the paper-based design of the concept representation of 'heat' which you articulated in Activity 3.3. Carefully consider the Design for Presentation Recommendations provided in this section, and redesign your design to incorporate these prescriptions. Then, create a new table such as Table 3.3, and fill it in with information related to your own design to indicate how it incorporated the Recommendations.*

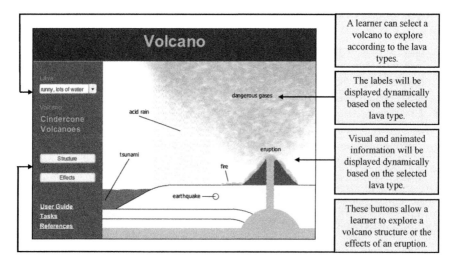

Fig. 3.13 'Volcano' concept representation resource (developed by the author's student)

3.6 A Study of Design of Concept Representation Resources

Table 3.3 Design features from the "Volcano" concept representation resource (crr)

Recommendations		Design features from the "Volcano" concept representation resource (crr)
Design for presentation	• Present information visually	• Information in the crr is presented mostly visually (e.g., cross-section of the volcano, and changes in eruptions). Text is used for buttons, labels, and instruction
	• Design for interaction	• The crr allows a learner to manipulate parameters through a pull-down menu (to select type of lava for exploration). Outcomes of manipulations are presented visually and numerically (e.g., cross section of the volcano, effects and animation of the eruption)
	• Design a holistic scenario	• Elements such as the cross-section of the volcano and the effects are arranged in a way that integrate into a single scenario
	• Design for a single screen	• Content of the crr is presented in a single screen
	• Design for small space	• The crr is designed for effective presentation in a 640 × 480 pixel screen area
	• Use audio and video only if it is the only option	• No audio or video content is present in the crr. Although audio could add some realism (e.g., explosion in eruption of the volcano), its presence is not necessary. Animation is used to add illustrative realism to the visual output
	• Use color in moderation	• Color use is limited in the design. Colors include gray, blue, maroon, black, green and yellow
	• Avoid unnecessary decorative elements	• No decorative elements are used in the crr. All elements are related to essential content
	• Design with a single font	• Only Arial font is used in the crr
	• Use frames to logically divide the screen area	• The screen is divided into functional areas. Left side of the screen contains control elements (pull-down menu, hot spots and buttons). Right side of the screen displays essential content

3.6.4 Call for Further Empirical Studies

The development of a concept representation requires: (a) the ability to identify a suitable concept from a discipline for development into a representation, (b) deep knowledge of the concept that is to be represented, (c) an understanding of pedagogically appropriate ways of representing the concept, (d) creativity in representing through interactive multimedia art, and (e) an understanding of an effective design for delivery via a specific technology. The study of the presentation design features of a concept representation resource resulted in an understanding of a number of useful recommendations as follows: present information visually, design for interaction, design a holistic scenario, design for a single screen, design for small space, use audio and video only if they are the only options, using color in moderation, avoid unnecessary decorative elements, design with a single font, and use frames to logically divide the screen area. While these recommendations for design for presentation should prove useful to designers of concept representations and other forms of digital resources, other aspects of design must be explored further. Future study might further explore links between pedagogical quality and specific design features. For example, correlation(s) between specific interaction used in the design and pedagogical quality might lead to further recommendation. In addition, more might be done in relation to understanding specific multimedia screen arrangements and effects on the cognitive effort required for conducting visual searches.

The study reported here used perceived pedagogical quality as a key measure to understand the effective features of a multimedia design. Further study might attempt to replicate this procedure. Rather than using a measure of perceived pedagogical quality as given by expert reviewers, measured achievement of learning outcomes is an option. However, this would require a huge amount of effort to collect such data. A large number of students would be required to use a significant number of digital resources for learning and then be tested to obtain such measures. Furthermore, this might require that attention be given to an additional variable of an activity; that is, the specific ways in which a digital resource for learning was used in a learning context when data were collected.

Lately, there has been an increase in concept representations and other digital resources available via mobile technologies such as iPods. Consideration needs to be given to design when a concept representation resource is to be delivered via devices whose screen size and interactions are different as compared to computers. Furthermore, these recommendations for design for presentation do not provide ideas regarding instructional uses of a concept representations and, therefore, although useful to designers, are of little use to teachers. Applying these recommendations alone will result in a concept representation design that is not necessarily optimized for instructional use. Further inquiry is required in order to develop more comprehensive recommendations that incorporate specific features of design for small screen and learning uses. The author has conducted such inquiry, and it is reported in the later chapter that discusses mobile technology and digital resources for learning.

Activity 3.5
Why do seasons change? What is your concept of season change? Begin by asking yourself what you understand about changes of seasons. Bring together all the parameters that affect season change. Approach some resources such as books and Internet sites. However, be careful, there are a lot of misconceptions about causes to season changes in books and Internet resources. Some of your misconceptions might also prevent you from articulating a cognitive resource, which will help you to design a conceptual

representation resource. Articulate your design as a single slide (you can use any graphic design or presentation software, unless you are skilled to use some kind of authoring or programming tool) to show your ideas for design. Refer to the design process introduced in this chapter, as well as to the design recommendations provided. Make sure you are able to discuss how these are integrated in your design.

References

Berger, M. (2004a). Heaps, complexes and concepts. *For the Learning of Mathematics, 24*(2), 2–6.
Berger, M. (2004b). Heaps, complexes and concepts. *For the Learning of Mathematics, 24*(3), 11–17.
Blunden, A. (2011). *Concepts in Vygotsky's cultural psychology*. Retrieved from http://home.mira.net/~andy/works/concepts-laboratory.htm
Bruner, J. S. (1960). *The process of education*. Cambridge, MA: Harvard University Press.
Bruner, J. S., Goodnow, J. J., & Austin, G. A. (1967). *A study of thinking*. New York, NY: Science Editions.
Canelos, J, Taylor, W., & Altschuld, J. (1982). Networking vs. rote learning strategies in concept acquisition. *Educational Communication and Technology—A Journal of Theory, Research, and Development, 30*(3), 141–149.
Carrier, C., Davidson, G., & Williams, M. (1985). The selection of instructional options in a computer-based coordinate concept lesson. *Educational Communication and Technology—A Journal of Theory, Research, and Development, 33* (3), 199–212.
Chai, C. S., & Quek, C. L. (2003). Using computers as cognitive tools. In S. C. Tan (Ed.), *Teaching and learning with technology: An Asia-Pacific perspective* (pp. 182–198). Singapore: Prentice Hall.
Chi, M. T. H. (2008). Three types of conceptual change: Belief revision, mental model transformation, and categorical shift. In S. Vosniadou (Ed.), *International handbook of research on conceptual change* (pp. 61–82). New York, NY: Routledge.
Chu, H. C., Hwang, G. J., & Tsai, C. C. (2010). A knowledge engineering approach to developing mindtools for context-aware ubiquitous learning. *Computers & Education, 54*(1), 289–297.
Churchill, D. (2005). Teachers' private theories and their design of technology-based learning. *British Journal of Educational Technology, 37*(4), 559–576.
Churchill, D. (2008). Mental models. In L. Tomei (Ed.), *Encyclopedia of information technology curriculum integration* (pp. 575–582). Hershey, PA: Idea Group Publishing.
Churchill, D. (2013). Concept model design and learning uses *Interactive Learning Environments, 21*(1), 54–67.
Churchill, D. (2014). Presentation design for "concept model" learning objects. *British Journal of Education Technology, 45*(1), 136–148.
Churchill, D., & Hedberg, J. (2008a). Learning objects, learning tasks and handhelds. In L. Lockyer, S. Bennett, S. Agostinho, & B. Harper (Eds.), *Handbook of research on learning design and learning objects: Issues, applications and technologies* (pp. 451–469). Hershey, PA: Information Science Reference.
Churchill, D., & Hedberg, J. (2008b). Learning object design considerations for small-screen handheld devices. *Computers & Education, 50*(3), 881–893.

Cisco Systems. (2001). *Reusable learning object strategy: Designing information and learning objects through concept, fact, procedure, process, and principle template.* San Jose, CA: Cisco Systems Inc.

Cohen, J. (1988). *Statistical power analysis for the behavioral sciences* (2nd ed.). Hillsdale, NJ: Erlbaum.

Collins, A. (1996). Design issues for learning environments. In S. Vosniadou, E. De Corte, & R. Glasser (Eds.), *International perspectives on the design of technology-supported learning environments.* Mahwah, NJ: Lawrence Erlbaum Associates, Publishers.

Davydov, V. V. (1999). What is real learning activity? In M. Hedegaard & J. Lompscher (Eds.), *Learning activity and development* (pp. 123–128). Aarhus, Denmark: Aarhus University Press.

Dawson, M. R. (2004). *Minds and machines: connectionism and psychological modeling.* Oxford, UK: Blackwell Publishing.

De Jong, T., & Van Joolingen, W.R. (1998). Scientific discovery learning with computer simulations of conceptual domains. *Review of Educational Research, 68*(2), 179–201.

De Jong, T., Ainsworth, S., Dobson, M., Van der Hulst, A., Levonen, J., Reimann, P., et al. (1998). Acquiring knowledge in science and mathematics: The use of multiple representations in technology-based learning environments. In A. Van Someren (Ed.), *Learning with multiple representations* (pp. 9–40). Oxford, UK: Elsevier Science Ltd.

Dewey, J. (1902). *The child and the curriculum.* Chicago, IL: University of Chicago Press.

Dewey, J. (1910). *How we think.* New York, NY: Prometheus Books.

Dewey, J. (1997). *How we think.* New York, NY: Dover Publications.

diSessa, A. A. (2008). A bird's-eye view of the "pieces" vs. "coherence" controversy (from the "pieces" side of the fence). In S. Vosniadou (Ed.),*International handbook of research on conceptual change* (pp. 35–60). New York: Routledge.

Engeström, Y. (1987). *Learning by expanding.* Helsinki: Orienta-konsultit.

Foo, S. Y., Ho, J., & Hedberg, J. (2005). Teachers' understanding of technology affordances and their impact on the design of engaging learning experiences. *Educational Media International, 42*(4), 297–316.

Fraser, A. (1999). *Web visualization for teachers.* Retrieved from http://fraser.cc/WebVis/

Gagne, R., & Driscoll, M. (1988). *Essentials of learning for instruction* (2nd ed.). Englewood Cliffs, NJ: Prentice Hall.

Gagné, R. M. (1966). *The conditions of learning.* New York, NY: Holt, Rinehart, & Winston.

Gagné, R. M. (1968). Learning hierarchies. *Educational Psychologist, 6*, 1–9.

Gagne, R. M. (1971). *Learning hierarchies.* Englewood Cliffs, NJ: Prentice Hall.

Gibbons, A. (2008). Model-centered instruction, the design and the designer. In D. Ifenthaler, P. Piarnay-Dummer, & J. M. Spector (Eds.), *Understanding models for learning and instruction* (pp. 161–173). New York, NY: Springer.

Hartnack, J. (1968). *Kant's theory of knowledge.* London: MacMillan.

Hicken, S., Sullivan, H., & Klein, J. (1992). Learner control modes and incentive variations in computer-delivered instruction. *Educational Technology: Research and Development, 40*(4), 15–26.

Hjørland, B. (2009). Concept theory. *Journal of the American Society for Information Science and Technology, 60*(8), 1519–1536.

Ivarsson, J., Schoultz, J., & Säljö, R. (2002). Map reading versus mind reading. In M. Limon & L. Mason (Eds.), *Reconsidering concept change: Issues in theory and practice* (pp. 77–99). Dordrecht: Kluwer Academic Publishers.

Johnson, T., & Lesh, R. (2003). A models and modeling perspective on technology-based representational media. In R. Lesh & H. Doerr (Eds.), *Beyond constructivism: A models and modeling perspectives on mathematics problem solving, learning and teaching* (pp. 3–34). Mahwah, NJ: Lawrence Erlbaum.

Jonassen, D. H. (1978). *What are cognitive tools?* Retrieved from http://www.cs.umu.se/kurser/TDBC12/HT99/Jonassen.html

References

Jonassen, D. H. (1986, November). *Attribute identification versus example comparison strategies in an interactive videodisc concept lesson*. Association for the Development of Computer-based Instructional Systems, Washington, DC.

Jonassen, D.H. (1996). *Computers in the classroom: Mindtools for critical thinking*. Englewood Cliffs, NJ: Merrill.

Jonassen, D. H. (2006). *Modeling with technology: Mindtools for concept change*. Upper Saddle River, NJ: Pearson Education Inc.

Jonassen, D. H., & Carr, C. (2000). Mindtools: Affording multiple knowledge representations in learning. In S. P. Lajoie (Ed.), *Computers as cognitive tools* (pp. 165–196). Mahwah, NJ: Lawrence Erlbaum.

Jonassen, D. H., & Reeves, T. C. (1996). Learning with technology: Using computers as cognitive tools. In D. H. Jonassen (Ed.), *Handbook of research for educational communication and technology* (pp. 693–719). New York, NY: Simon & Schuster Macmillan.

Kant, I. (1922). *Critique of pure reason*. London, UK: The Macmillan Company, Ltd. Retrieved from http://files.libertyfund.org/files/1442/0330_Bk.pdf

Kozulin, A. (1990). *Vygotsky's psychology: A biography of ideas*. Cambridge, MA: Harvard University Press.

Lajoie, S. P., & Derry, S. J. (2000). *Computers as cognitive tools*. Hillsdale, NJ: Lawrence Erlbaum.

Lawrence, S., & Margolis, E. (1999). *Concepts and cognitive science*. Retrieved from https://www.cs.nyu.edu/courses/fall07/G22.3033-006/CCS.pdf

Lesh, R., & Doerr, H. (2003). Foundations of a models and modelling perspective on mathematics teaching, learning and problem solving. In R. Lesh & H. Doerr (Eds.), *Beyond constructivism: A models and modeling perspectives on mathematics problem solving, learning and teaching* (pp. 3–34). Mahwah, NJ: Lawrence Erlbaum.

Li, J., Mei, C., Xu, W., & Qian, Y. (2015). Concept learning via granular computing: a cognitive viewpoint. *Information Sciences, 298*, 447–467.

Mayer, R. E. (1989). Models for understanding. *Review of Educational Research, 59*(1), 43–64.

Mayer, R. E. (2001). *Multimedia learning*. New York, NY: Cambridge University Press.

Mayer, R. E. (2002). Understanding concept change: A commentary. In M. Limon & L. Mason (Eds.), *Reconsidering concept change: Issues in theory and practice* (pp. 101–111). Dordrecht: Kluwer Academic Publishers.

Mayer, R. E. (2003). The promise of multimedia learning: Using the same instructional design methods across different media. *Learning and Instruction, 13*, 125–139.

Mayer, R. E., Dow, G., & Mayer, S. (2003). Multimedia learning in an interactive self-explaining environment: What works in the design of agent-based microworlds? *Journal of Educational Psychology, 95*(4), 806–813.

Merrill, M. D. (1983). Component display theory. In C. M. Reigeluth (Ed.), *Instructional design theories and models: An overview of their current status* (pp. 279–333). Hillsdale, NJ: Lawrence Erlbaum Associates.

Merrill, M. D. (1987). The new component design theory: Instructional design for courseware authoring. *Instructional Science, 16*, 19–34.

Merrill, M. D., Reigeluth, C. M., & Faust, G. W. (1979). The instructional quality profile: Curriculum evaluation and design. In H. F. O'Neal (Ed.), *Procedures for instructional systems development*. New York, NY: Academic Press.

Merrill, M. D., Richards, R. E., Schmidt, R., & Wood, N. D. (1977). *The instructional strategy diagnostic profile training manual*. Provo, UT: Brigham Young University, David O. McKay Institute.

Merrill, M. D., Tennyson, R. D., & Posey, L. O. (1992). *Teaching concepts: An instructional design guide*. Englewood Cliffs, NJ: Educational Technology Publications.

Montague, W. E. (1983). Instructional quality inventory. *Performance and Instruction, 22*(5), 11–14.

Newby, T. J., Ertmer, P. A., & Stepich, D. A. (1995). Instructional analogies and the learning of concepts. *Educational Technology Research and Development, 43*(1), 5–18.

Norman, D. A. (1983). Some observation on mental models. In D. Gentner & A. L. Stevens (Eds.), *Mental models* (pp. 7–14). Hillsdale, NJ: Erlbaum.

Pae, R. D. (1985). Beyond amplification: Using the computer to reorganize mental functioning. *Educational Psychologists, 20,* 167–182.

Piaget, J. (1972a). *The psychology of intelligence.* Totowa, NJ: Littlefield.

Piaget, J. (1972b). *The psychology of the child.* New York, NY: Basic Books.

Piaget, J. (1990). *The child's conception of the world.* New York, NY: Littlefield Adams.

Salomon, G., Perkins, D. N., & Globerson, T. (1991). Partners in cognition: Extending human intelligence with intelligent technologies. *Educational Researcher, 20*(3), 2–9.

Scott, H. P. (1997). *Developing science concepts in secondary classrooms: An analysis of pedagogical interactions from a Vygotskian perspective.* Retrieved from https://core.ac.uk/download/pdf/43730.pdf

Seel, N. M. (2003). Model-centered learning and instruction. *Technology, Instruction, Cognition and Learning, 1*(1), 59–85.

Sierpinska, A. (1993). The development of concepts according to Vygotsky. *Focus on Learning Problems in Mathematics, 15*(2), 87–107.

Singer, R. S., Nielsen, R. N., & Schweingruber, A. H. (2012). *Discipline-based education research: Understanding and improving learning in undergraduate science and engineering.* Washington DC: The National Academies Press.

Smith, J. P., diSessa, A. A., & Roschelle, J. (1993). Misconceptions reconceived: A constructivist analysis of knowledge in transition. *Journal of the Learning Sciences, 3*(2), 115–163.

Stock, W. G. (2010). Concepts and semantic relations in information science. *Journal of the American Society for Information Science and Technology, 61*(10), 1951–1969.

Tennyson, R. D. (1978). Pictorial support and specific instructions as design variables for children's concept and rule learning. *Educational Communication and Technology—A Journal of Theory, Research, and Development, 26*(4), 291–299.

Tennyson, R. D., & Buttrey, T. (1980). Advisement and management strategies as design variables in computer-assisted instruction. *Educational Communication and Technology—A Journal of Theory, Research, and Development, 28*(3), 169–176.

Tessmer, M., & Driscoll, M. P. (1986). Effects of diagrammatic display of coordinate concept definitions on concept classification performance. *Educational Communication and Technology—A Journal of Theory, Research, and Development, 24*(4), 195–205.

Traill, R. R. (2008). *Thinking by molecule, synapse, or both?—From Piaget's schema, to the selecting/editing of ncRNA.* Retrieved from http://www.ondwelle.com/OSM02.pdf

Turner, J. (1975). *Cognitive development.* London: Methuen.

Tyler, W. R. (1949). *Basic principles of curriculum and instruction.* Chicago, IL: Chicago University Press.

van Someren, A., Boshuizen, P. A., de Jong, T., & Reimann, P. (1998). Introduction. In A. van Someren (Ed.), *Learning with multiple representations* (pp. 1–5). Oxford, UK: Elsevier Science.

Vosniadou, S. (1994). Capturing and modeling the process of concept change. *Learning and Instruction, 4*(1), 45–69.

Vygotsky, S. L. (1962). *Thoughts and language.* Cambridge, MA: The MIT Press.

Vygotsky, S. L. (1978). *Mind in society.* Cambridge, MA: Harvard University Press.

Wellings, P. (2003). *School learning versus life learning: the interaction of spontaneous & scientific concepts in the development of higher mental processes.* Retrieved from http://ldt.stanford.edu/~paulaw/STANFORD/370x_paula_wellings_final_paper.pdf

Presentation Resources

4

Learning Outcomes:

- Describe what is a presentation resource;
- List different forms of presentation resources;
- Distinguish between presentation resources as a supplement to teaching and those for self-learning;
- Distinguish between external representation and a learner's knowledge; and
- Demonstrate understanding of visuals and interactivity as key affordances of representational technologies for design of presentation resources.

4.1 What Is a Presentation Resource?

A presentation resource is a digital media for education designed to explicitly present certain declarative knowledge (facts and information) with the intention for learners to remember, understand and reproduce that content as it was originally presented. Underlining assumption is that learning occurs by transfer of information, that is, by explicit teaching and presentation of content designed, arranged and presented for learners to internalize. Such an approach is associated with traditional teaching and learning practices, or so-called, instructivist pedagogy where teaching is based on a teacher (or technology and other resources) being a source of providing students with information (curriculum content segmented and arranged) in a ready-made format for passive learning (see Reeves 1998). Reeves writes:

These goals and objectives are drawn from a domain of knowledge, e.g., algebra, or extracted from observations of the behaviors of experts within a given domain, e.g., surgeons. Once goals and objectives are delineated, they are sequenced into learning hierarchies, generally representing a progression from lower to higher order learning. Then, direct instruction is designed to address each of the objectives in the hierarchy, often employing instructional strategies derived from behavioral psychology. Relatively little emphasis is put on the learner per se who is usually viewed as a passive recipient of instruction. CBE based on instructivist pedagogy generally treats learners as empty vessels to be filled with learning. Direct instruction demands that content be sharply defined and that instructional strategies focus as directly on prespecified content as possible.

Although there are educational contexts and content knowledge when direct presentation works effectively (e.g., presentation of facts and certain declarative information), this will be less than effective for achieving deep conceptual knowledge and new literacies and skills. Other forms of digital resources for learning, combined with learning activities, would be much more effective as a contemporary relevant strategy for the development of intellectually strong and contemporary relevant graduates.

Readers might be confused about differences between presentation and information display resources as both of these resources essentially deliver declarative information. We need to understand that this difference between information displays and presentation resources has to do with teacher-centered/instructivist pedagogy versus learning-centered pedagogy, or direct teaching vs. activity-based learning. Information displays are designed to display certain information in an organized way so that they can be used to mediate a learning activity. The primary purpose is not to consume and remember or understand the displayed information alone, rather the idea is to use that information to inform one's actions within a learning activity. Presentation resources, on the other hand, present information, which has been organized, simplified, and presented in segments and in ways in which learners' cognitive processing, that is, remembering, of that information is maximized. Information displays, unlike presentation resources, are not so much concerned with who the learners are specifically, their learning pace, age etc., rather, at the center of its design is how to effectively organize as much of the information as possible on a screen, and in a way that it is easier for someone to navigate, explore, and use it in learning activities. Furthermore, information displays are the only type of digital resource for learning that might not be originally designed for educational purposes. This means that a teacher and students can harvest such material from the Internet and other sources for use in their teaching and learning. Essentially, many web pages, journal articles, infographics, YouTube videos, etc., might be used as information resources in learning activities. However, in the context of this book, we are asking an important question "how to better design information resources given contemporary interactive and visual affordances of representational technology?" so that these can find effective utility in learning activities. Table 4.1 presents some essential differences between a presentation and an information display resources.

In this book, presentation resources are defined as digital media primarily and intentionally designed for either of the following two purposes:

Table 4.1 Comparison between presentation and information display digital resources for learning

Presentation resource	Information display
• A learner remembers information that is presented	• A learner uses information to accomplish a task specified by a learning activity
• Information is being presented for transfer	• Information is being displayed to inform a learning activity
• Content is presented temporally in a number of sequential screens	• Information is presented spatially, mostly in a single screen
• Navigation includes movement forward and backward to next chunk of content, selecting blocks of content from a central menu, or scrolling along a timeline	• Navigation is arranged to allow access to information chunks from within a single display
• Targets achievement of a specific learning outcome	• No learning outcome is targeted. This is determined by a learning activity where that information is to be used
• Intentionally designed for the purpose of teaching	• Not essentially designed for the purpose of teaching or learning, but it can be used in that context

(a) *An instructional presentation resource*—supplements and assists a teacher/lecturer/trainer/instructor to transfer certain knowledge to learners (such as is the case with PowerPoint, Prezi, Google Slides, Zoho Presentation, Haiku Desk or Keynote presentations), or

(b) *A self-learning presentation resource*—independently assist learners in self-consuming content of a screen and learning specific content being presented and reinforced—such as is the case with Computer-based/Managed Tutorials/Instructions (CBT/CMI), learning objects, recorded lectures, e-books, instructional videos, and screen capture recordings.

4.2 An Instructional Presentation Resource

An instructional presentation resource is a resource designed to support teacher presentations (e.g., a PowerPoint or Keynote slides used in a lecture). Traditional teacher-directed or instructivist practices are dominated with the presentation of content in an attempt to transfer knowledge from a source (teacher or a digital resource), through medium (technology) and messages (language and other modalities), to a passive recipient (a learner considered to be 'an empty vessel' to be 'filled' with that content knowledge). Most of what has been going on in such situations includes a teacher presenting certain content knowledge through direct teaching, often supported by audio-visual resources (digital and non-digital), and periodically checking if learners are learning by posing questions, or requiring them to complete worksheets (reinforcement), and subsequently preparing them to pass tests and exams. Knowledge content is explicitly presented/declared in a form, which is simplified and organized in a way that makes it easier for learners to remember it. Often, during such instructional situation, learners are taking notes, rephrasing and describing things in ways that they can be later studied, or use it to further independently consult other individuals in their networks, and learning material such worksheets, textbooks and web sites. A digital resource for learning used in such situations is a presentation resource that supplements a teacher. Contemporary technology enables students to record teachers' explanations, or their own observations, e.g., via recording features of a mobile device and note taking Apps. Skilled teachers will use a variety of strategies to help learners to remain focused during lectures, such as, well designed audio-visuals, various forms of attention grabbers, and asking or inviting questions. Technology can help to collect learners' answers and present summaries. However, no matter what means of presentation and supporting techniques are used, what can be achieved through such approaches is primarily declarative knowledge and surface learning, rather than deep conceptual knowledge. Even though information about a concept is provided to a learner in a presentation resource that does not constitute learning and the development of conceptual knowledge. Rather, that is a presentation of information and facts about a concept. Learning concepts requires conceptual knowledge construction and changes through active intellectual engagement. In other sections of this book, we look into more details about conceptual knowledge and explore suitable forms of digital resources for learning of this kind of curriculum content.

> **Activity 4.1**
> *Search Slideshare.net, identify presentations which demonstrate good instructional, presentational and visual design. Select one of these best examples, and describe your choice.*

Let us look more specifically at some of the key aspects of design of presentation resources for supplementing a teacher. This book does not intend to discuss the design of presentations in great details, as we are more concerned with the transformation of traditional teaching practice and adoption of learning centered approaches. In this context, we give more attention to digital resources for learning such as concept representations. Skills in the design of presentations that supplement teaching should be an integral competency of contemporary teachers and, thus, this should be a discussion at a more fundamental level of a teacher education program. However, here are some main points related to the effective design of presentations:

- *Presentation screen design—*
  - *Design of a presentation's opening and closing screens*—Opening screen (also called a title screen) should be designed to capture attention and get

learners focused and prepared for the main content to be presented. This screen might be designed to include a powerful visual representation that associates an audience of learners with the main ideas to follow in the presentation. This might set the overall look and feel (treatment), and include metaphorical representation of interface (which would be followed throughout the presentation in other screens as a tool that reminds learners about the main topic under the study). Furthermore, a supplementary screen might list the main points to be addressed in the presentation, and refer to prior knowledge required for learning the current topic. The closing screen might summarize the main points of the topic, and the final screen might include contact information of the presenter and credits to any copyrighted resources and reading material.
 – *Design a master slide with consistency (also called a template slide)*—A master slide is like a container that consistently frames every new slide to be filled in with content. Designing such a template slide can greatly facilitate the development of overall presentation and provide consistency for every subsequent screen to be designed.
 – *The master slide* should include areas for session headings, main content presentation areas for elements such as text, images, tables and a footer, determined background and color scheme to be used, text format (headings, subheadings, main content, meta-text, highlights, clues, signals and pointers), and navigation areas.

- *Content structuring and presentation*—A teacher as a designer must determine all content to be included in the presentation. Further decisions regard how that content will be presented, represented and structured. Most often, images and text are used to supplement each other and provide a supporting tool for the presenter to emphasize the main points, provide summaries, illustrates ideas, and provide examples and analogies. Later in this book, we will examine some theoretical ideas regarding the use of visuals, textual and verbal signals in communicating instructional content. Also, determining if additional content can be useful and included in the notes attached to slides. This area might contain pointers to additional resources, key questions to pay attention to, and any other additional content as determined by the teacher.
- *Navigation*—To determine navigation strategy, forward and backward buttons, main menu button, hyperlinks, and develop main menu structure if required.
- *Technical issues*—These issues address technical specifications, such as, duration of the presentation, number of colors to be used in the design, size of the presentation area, types of fonts available to the system, resolution of graphics, frame rate and size of animation, video codex, and audio format.

Presentation development software such as PowerPoint and Keynote provide templates, which can be used to easily populate with one's own content. Also, numerous templates are available for download from the Internet. However, the author of this book recommends that templates are not the best solution, and attempts should be made to be original and innovative in developing our own designs for particular contexts and content.

Emerging possibilities for presentations, such as Prezi, bring about a new concept for design. All content is structured in a single display, and navigation occurs by zooming on specific areas of display, and 'flying' to other areas based on backward or forward navigation. In addition, there are emerging forms of interactivity with technology that permit presenters to navigate between screens of content by using hands instead of a mouse or pointers (e.g., by using Myo device attached to an arm). These limit existing, while creating new design possibilities. Furthermore, emerging cloud-based tools for the design of presentations (e.g., Google Presentation and Zoho Presentation) bring the design to an online environment, enabling co-design and social discourse during the development.

4.3 Presentation Resource for Self-learning

In addition to presentation resources designed to supplement direct teaching/lecturing, technology affords the design of presentation resources for self-learning through the presentation of declarative knowledge content, that is, learning without a teacher, anytime and anywhere. Such resources contain all necessary information, explanations, and elaborations, and integrate representational modalities to enhance the effectiveness of presentation. Interactivity is most often used to facilitate navigation through the content, although the content representation itself can be significantly enhanced by use of interactive features. Even though such resources can contain elements of, for example, a concept representation resource (which can support concept learning), the original intention of a designer is to facilitate direct teaching and achieve learning by having students understand, remember and recall declarative knowledge content presented in a learner controlled pace. In certain cases, elements of practice resources are built in the design, in order to reinforce remembering and understanding of the content being presented.

Broadly speaking, this form of presentation resource can be (a) temporal media such as videos, (b) sequential media such as e-books, and (c) programmed media such as courseware or computer based or managed instruction. Although all of these are different media types, in the context of this book, they are united under the same category of digital resources for learning based on their intended purpose to communicate declarative knowledge content. Once again, digital resources for learning are not classified according to media types, but according to the forms of curriculum knowledge content they represent. Presentation resources are designed to represent declarative knowledge.

4.3.1 Video Presentation

There are various possibilities for the design of instructional videos. These include, at least, the following:

- *Video recorded lectures*—This can be achieved by using special lecture recoding platforms such as Panopto and Echo360, recording via online conferencing and real-time teaching environments such as Blackboard Collaborate or Adobe Connect, or by using screen recoding tools, such as TechSmith Camtasia.
- *Digital picture stories*—These are video compositions composed essentially of static images/photographs transiting from one to another, and accompanying narrations, text and background music.
- *Video records*—These are instructions recorded with a video camera, and special equipment such as microscopes, telescopes and remote cameras. Post-production using special software such as iMovie, allow the integration of recoded videos with graphics, animation, titles, audio and special effects. Special tools can be used to edit audio separately from the video (e.g., Audacity), and then merge it together with the video in a final product.
- *Animations*—This can include cartoons, animated sequences and diagrams, illustrated and animated processes, step-motion animation, and 3-dimensional animation.

4.3.2 E-Book Presentation

E-books are digital media that uses the same parading as traditional books for content presentation and navigation, with the exception and advantage that it can be delivered to a broad audience via the Internet, and deployed via a spectrum of devices such as a computer, mobile devices and wearables. Furthermore, the design of e-books can include all forms of digital media content, and include advanced interactive features and assist learners to, for example, highlight, annotate and save text for later uses, search content for keywords, bookmark pages, or listen to an electronic voice reading the text. However, designing an e-book should not simply be scanning pages from a traditional printed text and making these available as an online document, at least, not in the context of education. Contemporary technology allows easy conversion of analogue to digital, however, the design of e-books must leverage on representational affordances of contemporary technologies for learning. Contemporary tools, such as Apple iBook Author allow teachers to easily create e-books, integrating even some advanced interactive features with ease, such as interactive images, and deploy these via a variety of devices including iPods and iPads. Applications such as iBook Author, free teachers from the burden of technical complexity, and empower them to think about the design of content, rather than to struggle with complex technical issues.

4.3.3 Computer-Based Instructional Presentation

The third form of presentation resources for self-learning are programmed or authored media, such as, courseware or computer-based or managed instruction (CBI/CMI). Development of CBI courseware is based on traditional instructional design models such as the 'Systematic Design of Instruction' by Dick and Carey (1978, 1985, 1990, 1996), and builds on the theoretical constructs such as Gagné's 'Nine Events of Instruction' (Gagné et al. 1992). CBI courseware can be very complex, including elements of programmed instruction, intelligent tutorials and all forms of representations, expensive and sophisticated to produce. Essentially, the main idea on CBI courseware is that a computer is a teaching machine, enabling learners to learn at their own pace through pathways managed by the underlining structure. Table 4.2 shows main elements of a CBI courseware, and provides information regarding key features of each of these.

Although CBI courseware development processes can vary, depending on the context and purpose of development (e.g., commercial development, development of an external client, in-house development, or a simple development by an individual teacher), Fig. 4.1 shows an example of how it might occur from an initial meeting of the development team to the final summative evaluation.

> **Activity 4.2**
> *Instructional design is a critical step in the overall design of presentation resources for self-learning. Examine instructional design models listed at* http://www.instructionaldesign.org/models/ *and search the Internet for other resources. Which of the models listed appears most appropriate for the development of resources to support learning-centred as opposed to teacher-directed practice? Try to design an information display showing such a model.*

4.3.4 Learning Object

The author of this book previously argued the idea of a 'learning object' as an appropriate representation of digital resources for learning. However, his arguments and provision of an alternative definition of what a learning object might be, made no significant impact. Extensive, but most often less the useful discussions in the literature, and widely-spread disagreement of what a learning object might be, and how these can be classified, led the author to abound the use of this term, and adoption of the more generally understood term 'Digital Resources for Leaning' and, in a way, submerging learning objects under these as one of the possible forms of educational content in this current book.

Initially, the concept of the learning object emerged from the traditional, direct instruction courseware design ideas and professionals that attempted to articulate

4.3 Presentation Resource for Self-learning

Table 4.2 Main elements and key features of a CBI courseware

Main elements	Key features
Opening screens	• Gaining attention by using an interesting opening • Login and collecting information about a learner: user name, id, class and password (unless this is automatically determined by a learning management system used to deliver the CBI) • Automatically record date and time of access • Inform a learner about a lesson and objectives • Inform a learner how to use the courseware • Provide main navigation structure • Read record of previous use by the same learner—It is possible to begin from the point where a user left the courseware on the last visit
Main content and navigation	• Content navigation through paging structure: go from previous to current to next page, go to recently visited page, go to first or last page, search pages for a keyword • Keep information about pages visited and time spent at each page/section • Keep information about sections completed • Inform a learner about current page/pages visited/sections completed, pages left before completion of a section • Pages might contain multimedia elements and interactive components to enhance representation of curriculum content • Provide a map of a section with indication of visited areas
Programmed instruction	• Keep track of completed sections • Prevent users from entering one section without completing the other section • Allow access to quiz when all sections are completed, restrict to a single access to a quiz • Sections might follow with some drill and practice questions and remediation • Questions might preside a sections—used to identify 'advanced standing' or readiness for access to a section (pre-testing)
Quiz/Test	• Variety of questions: MCQ, true-false, fill-in-the-blank, match-and-marking, short answer, auditory, moving objects (e.g., puzzle) • Variety of interactions for questions: key-press, hot-spot, clickable-object, text-entry, target-area, pull-down, drag-slider • Randomize questions and their content to prevent copying or allowing multiple practices of a same question with different configuration • Present only certain number question from the bank of questions • Use of representations within questions • Enhanced interactivity in presentation of questions (e.g., use measuring tools, manipulation of parameters) • Allow access to external tools, sites, information • Provide feedback: if wrong: why is it wrong, hints about what to do to correct it, what to do next; if correct: acknowledge correctness, reinstate the correct answer, provide additional information, inform about what to do next

(continued)

Table 4.2 (continued)

Main elements	Key features
	• Allow each question to appear once, or allow multiple accesses to same questions until "mastery" is achieved • Track information about questions attended, results, time spent on a question, number of tries before getting the correct answer • Inform a learner about questions attended, time spent, time remaining to complete, and number of attempts and tries left
Record and presentation of results	• Present a learner with quantitative feedback: scores, grade, questions attempted and number of questions answered correctly or incorrectly, date of access, time spent within a lesson or a quiz • Present a learner with a certificate, voucher, or/and credit points • Present a learner with qualitative feedback: comment about performance, what to do next to improve performance or remediation • Record results in an external document or in a database (on the local machine, over the network/internet in a database or within the data-base of a learning management system)

more effective and economical strategies for the design, management and reuse of training/educational materials over computer-based networks. One of the dominant initial ideas was that curriculum content can be broken down into small, reusable instructional components that address a specific learning objective, and that could be tagged with metadata descriptors and deposited in digital libraries for primarily machine-driven and automated reuse (see Cisco Systems 2001; IMS Global Learning Consortium 2002). Up-to-date, there have been numerous other attempts to further define or redefine a learning object, and currently, there is a spectrum of, sometimes diverging views of what it might be. Here are some of these definitions presenting a variety of views of what a learning object may be:

- Any entity, digital or non-digital which can be used, re-used or referenced during technology-supported learning (IEEE 2001);
- Any digital resource used to support learning (Wiley 2000);
- Any digital resource used to mediate learning (Wiley and Edwards 2002);
- Small, stand-alone unit of instruction (Haamel and Jones, in ECC 2003);
- An instructional component that includes an instruction that teaches a specific learning objective and an assessment that measures achievement (NetG, in Wiley 2000);
- A collection of 7 ± 2 information objects, each containing content, practice and assessment components (Cisco Systems 2001);
- A reusable digital resource built in a lesson or a group of lessons (McGreal 2004);
- A combination of a knowledge object and a strategic object (Merrill 2000);
- A content object with a pedagogical component (Clifford 2002);
- An interactive practice exercise (Dunning 2002, in McGreal 2004);
- A virtual simulation resource for learning (Tubelo et al. 2016);

4.3 Presentation Resource for Self-learning

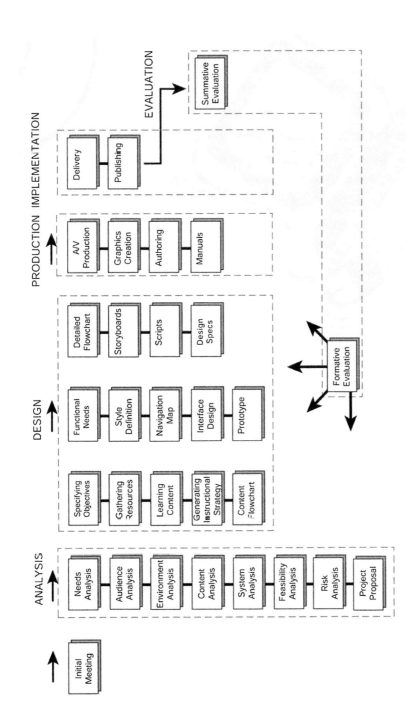

Fig. 4.1 An example of the CBI development process

- A personalized learning resource (Imran et al. 2016);
- An interactive digital resource illustrating one or a few interrelated concepts (Cochrane 2005); and
- An interactive visual representation (Churchill 2005).

These definitions appear to be articulated based on the three main learning theories: behaviorism, cognitivism and constructivism. For the behaviorist perspective (e.g., Haamel and Jones, in E-learning Competency Center 2003) all that is needed for learning is to appropriately present stimulus (material) and initiate responses. Responses are tracked by machine and remediation automatically provided until mastery is achieved. For cognitivism (e.g., Merrill 2000), learning objects must be directed at learners building mental representations and algorithms for their use. Learning is effective when material presented is isomorphic with an internal representation to be developed by a learner through '*incremental elaboration*' aided by instruction (see Merrill 2000). From a constructivist perspective (e.g., Churchill 2005), a learning object is a resource used to mediate a learning activity leading to learning outcomes, and learners' knowledge is constructed, transformed and applied through active engagement.

There is growing recognition that these ideas are incomplete and of limited use in context of any modernization of education. The academic community calls for reconsideration of what a learning object may be (e.g., Jonassen and Churchill 2004; Lukasiak et al. 2005; McGreal 2004). Friesen (2003) suggests that a learning object "need to be libelled, described, investigated and understood in ways that make the simplicity, compatibility and advantages claimed for them readily apparent to teachers, trainers and other practitioners". However, until now, this has not happened, and claimed advantages of a learning object such as *scalability*, *generatively* or *adaptability* (Gibbons 2000) are not well understood and appealing to educators. This might be because an average educator is more interested in improvements in teaching and learning through effective technology integration, rather than being replaced by a 'teaching machine' and resources capable of assembling lessons tailored for individual instruction. Merrill (2000) warns that with the current approaches "we are letting the idea of some mechanical principles drive what we are trying to do in psychology".

Current categorizations of learning objects do not appear to contribute to the solution of the problem. Wiley (2000) previously attempted to articulate a classification of learning objects. However, this classification has not been found in the literature to be of any use since it emerged. Wiley appears to classify learning objects according to parameters such as types and quantity of objects or elements contained and whether these can be extracted and reused in other learning objects (e.g., a single image, digital video, a web page, a machine-generated instructional module that monitors learner performance on practices and tests). However, even earlier classifications of educational resources, such as the one used by Alessi and Trollip (1995), might be more useful and relevant to teaching and learning. Alessi and Trollip suggest that computer-based educational resources can be classified into: (a) instructional modules or tutorials, (b) drill and practice, (c) simulations, and

(d) games. However, Alessi and Trollip's categories served the purpose for the classification of educational resources designed to instruct in a typically explicit instructivist way, or engage a learner in the practice of certain routine procedures, recall and recognition. Another classification of educational material that can be found is by MERLOT (Multimedia Educational Resource for Learning and Online Teaching) where learning objects are classified as: Animation, Assessment Tool, Assignment, Case Study, Collection, Development Tool, Drill and Practice, e-Portfolio, Learning Object Repository, Online Course, Open Journal—Article, Open Textbook, Presentation, Quiz/Test, Reference Material, Simulation, Social Networking Tool, Tutorial and Workshop and Training Material (see MERLOT, n. d.). This is a highly ambiguous categorization with overlapping categories, lacks any coherent theoretical underpinning and explicit links to curriculum content knowledge formats and, as such, is far from being effectively useful for designers and educators.

An alternative definition of a learning object and classification are needed to support diverse views and the needs of people involved in design (e.g., a designer who examines a subject matter, conceptualizes a potentially useful resource, and creates a blue print of it for production) and the reuse of learning objects (e.g., a teacher who plans to develop an activity for learning and locate learning objects to be used in that context). However, the up-to-date debate of what a learning object appears to be indeterminable. So, given that the issue of learning objects cannot easily be resolved, changes in thinking must follow. This would be possible when a definition is supported with a classification that includes a variety of categories, and where different categories are alighted with different perspectives and needs. In this book, the author proposes such a solution. However, at first, we must disregard all these naïve ideas of what a learning object is, and think in more general terms about digital resources specifically designed to support learning—digital resources for learning, and expand these in a way that will support the modernization of education. The 'digital resource for learning' term is adopted as the more appropriate representation of educational resources designed and delivered via technology-based environments.

However, in this book, we propose retaining the term 'learning object' as a specific form of presentation resource; that is, a digital resource for learning that explicitly presents specific curriculum content knowledge in a form most effective for direct instruction. Also, it is suggested that the most effective approach in this context is the learning object strategy proposed by Cisco (see Cisco Systems 2001). For Cisco, curriculum content can be broken down into small, reusable instructional/informational components, or information objects, that each address a single specific learning objective, and that could be tagged with metadata descriptors and deposited in digital libraries for primarily machine-driven and automated reuse. Therefore, the term 'reusable' is used in this strategy with both the learning object and the information object. According to this approach, a reusable learning object is a collection of 7 ± 2 pieces of reusable information objects. Each reusable information object contains information/presentation about a fact, concept, process, principles or procedure (Cisco provides guidelines for the design of each of these content forms); a practice component designed to improve retention and determine any remediation; and assessment components used to test if the specific learning outcome has been achieved and determine the component of any further learning. This 7 ± 2 number emerges from Miller's (1956) theory that proposes limits to human capacity for processing information, arguing that at one-time, human working memory might operate with 5–9 pieces of information. The components of a reusable information object are depicted in Fig. 4.2.

Although this approach acknowledges concepts, essentially, any concept learning is spontaneous rather than intentional, and the main purpose is to present information about the concept, rather than to engage learners in any deep conceptual changes through a learning activity. Building instructional modules or learning objects based on this strategy involves a system that packages these information objects automatically for learners to study independently. All that an instructor has to determine is a set of learning objectives to package in a learning object or a course initially (or in a set of learning objects), and then the system will retrieve related information objects, practice and assessment components, and package these in learning objects (or an instructional module). Alternatively, a pre-testing mechanism might determine where learners are at in terms of achievement of the curriculum specific learning outcomes, and the automatic packaging of learning objects will follow. Figure 4.3 illustrates the structure of a reusable learning object.

Although essentially being a data-based driven and mechanistic approach, the Cisco reusable learning object strategy might be a promising and effective approach for the management of traditional direct instruction with the purpose of declarative

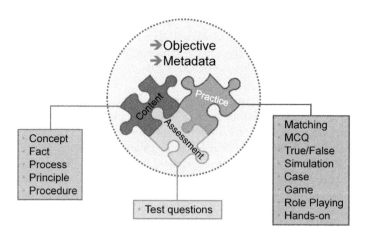

Fig. 4.2 Reusable information object according to Cisco System (2001)

4.3 Presentation Resource for Self-learning

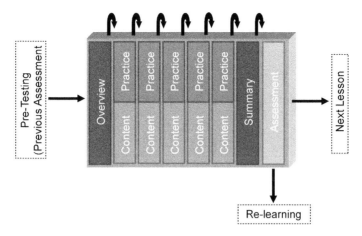

Fig. 4.3 Structure of a reusable learning object (Cisco Systems 2001)

knowledge content delivery. Although this is now more than a 15 years old strategy, those who subscribe to contemporary learning analytics claims, might find this highly relevant. Nevertheless, developing system architecture and content for this strategy will come at high expense and huge effort, but all that can be achieved are traditional learning outcomes addressing declarative knowledge. As we have noted so far in this book, the primary purpose of contemporary education in schools and universities should be the development of conceptual knowledge that is essential for disciplinary specific theoretical thinking, as well as new literacies emerging as important due to contemporary technological, social, cultural and economic developments. Perhaps, the Cisco strategy might at best fit in with learning in corporate environments.

> **Activity 4.3**
> *Look carefully at* Table 4.2. *Examine the typical elements included in the Computer-based Instruction (CBI) type of presentation resources. Now, consider the topic of "Introduction to Digital Resources for Learning (DLR)". Look at the presentation you developed in Activity 1.2 and think how this can be redesigned into a CBI type of presentation resource. Create a flowchart to show the content of a CMI to cover this topic. Expand on the following flow chart (add boxes as you wish). Also, use lines to connect the different boxes. Eventually, each of the boxes on your chart can become a single screen of the final CBI package. Flowcharting is an important stage in development; it assists the development team to articulate ideas and evaluate various instructional design issues.*
>
> *Also, think how you could reorganize your CBI into a reusable learning object type of resource.*

4.4 Theoretical Perspectives of Uses of Visuals and Interactive Representations in Instruction

When designing presentation resources, various modalities (or modes) can be integrated in a display in a way that supports communication and learning of declarative knowledge content. For De Jong et al. (1998), the term 'modality' indicates a particular form of expression such as text, animations, diagrams, graphs, algebraic notions, formula, tables and videos. Although visuals and main points summarized in textual format often dominate presentation resources, other modalities, such as sounds, animation, transitions and special effects are used to emphasize important points, provide signals and capture attention. Nevertheless, visuals are the most important mode of representations (or representational modality). By visuals, we mean the whole set of possibilities such as diagrams, charts, logos, signs, illustrations, cartoons, photographs, and even tables. When visuals are used with other modalities, e.g., text, these need to supplement each other and work in a way that enhance transfer and knowledge content learning. When multiple representational modalities are combined in a single knowledge content presentational piece, we refer to that resource as multimodal text in general, or a representation, more specifically in the context of teaching and learning.

This book proposes that visuals (visual affordances) are the most powerful mode of representation for all forms of digital learning resources. They can communicate maximum information in a smallest screen space. The second most important affordance of contemporary technologies for the design and presentation of information is interactivity (interactivity affordance). Interactivity makes possible for a large amount of information to be integrated, structured, presented and linked in a screen display of a resource, while making it possible to represent and illustrate conceptual properties, relationships and parameters. New or existing information can emerge based on configurations obtained through learners' interactions with screen elements. Also, other external parameters and data emerging spontaneously from an environment, in addition to screen interaction elements, can be used to manipulate information, for example, global positioning location obtained through GPS connectivity, or time of day.

Most critical for instructional presentation resources is how to effectively design and present information in a way that assists learners to follow, remember and understand the lecture. Visuals assist students to recognize patterns (e.g., comparisons, contrasts and regularities), and use these as mnemonics and schemas for understanding and remembering knowledge content. Visuals are prominently used in the design of presentation resources that supplement a lecture, while interactivity is limited and used mostly for navigation between screens. However, even with tools such as PowerPoint, some effective interactivity can be built into the screens. Nevertheless, the application of interactivity significantly increases in the design of presentation resources for self-learning.

4.4 Theoretical Perspectives of Uses of Visuals ...

Specific techniques to effectively create visuals to communicate data and information are best described in the collection of works by Tufte (1990, 1997, 2001): "Visual Explanations", "Envisioning Information" and "The Visual Display of Quantitative Information". Tufte suggests a range of visuals (e.g., graphs, illustrations, icons, pictures) to represent anything from everyday concepts to complex scientific information and data. For Tufte, visuals should be built on a single principle: present complexity through visual clarity. Tufte acknowledged that the possibilities for visualization of data and information are expanded with new technologies that allow representations in three-dimensional and animated formats. However, Tufte does not examine the use of visuals for teaching and learning, and he remains focused on effectiveness of communication of data, information and ideas in fields such as publishing, journalism, statistics or marketing. Nevertheless, a list of recommendations that he suggests, are valuable and should be considered in the design of visual material for education as well. Recommendations and principles are featured in Table 4.3.

Contemporary technology offers a spectrum of possibilities for the design and delivery of visuals. Previous research on text informs that learners are likely to learn more when text is supported with visual information, rather than with text alone (see Alesandrini 1984; Clark and Mayer 2016; Dale 1946; Dean and Enomoth 1983; Levie and Lentz 1982; Levin and Berry 1980; Mayer 1989; Paivio 1986; Shallert 1980). Purposefully included in this list of older publications are to indicate that the capabilities of visuals to support learning have been documented much before today's powerful multimedia-enabled computers, and a variety of mobile devices. Even as early as 1946, Edgar Dale (see Dale 1946) expanded on Confucius's saying "I hear and I forget—I see and I remember—I do and I understand" and developed what became widely known as the 'Cone of Experience'. Cone of Experience is a visual representation that summarizes Dale's classification of types of learning from the most concrete to most abstract experiences. For Dale, learning, usually, is a combination of concrete and abstract experiences, and he suggests that visualization becomes more important for understanding as learning experience becomes more abstract. See Fig. 4.4 for a modification of the original Edgar Dale's Cone of Experience.

Reflecting on Dale's proposal, teaching and learning should lead students to be active and gain experiences, engage in doing things, and use and/or develop media rich resources in these processes. This diagram suggests that for learning, it is essential to engage knowledge use, not just in passive consumption of knowledge content at the upper part of the triangle in the center (please see Chap. 1 and revisit the 3D curriculum model).

Paivio (1986) suggests another important idea that learning is empowered by visuals, because their content is processed simultaneously in image and verbal systems of memory. Based upon this idea, Mayer (1989) conducted a study to explore the impact of a visual display of some system (e.g., electric circuit or radar) upon learners' conceptual recall, verbatim retention and transfer of what they learned to solve new problems. A visual display for Mayer "... *highlights the major objects and actions in a system as well as the causal relations among them*" (p. 43).

Table 4.3 Edward Tufte's recommendations and principle for visual design—adapted and modified based on Venkatesh (2001)

Recommendation	Description	Example
Show cause and effect	When we try to comprehend something, we are looking for information to understand the underlying mechanisms. Reasoning is about examining causality. A visual should not only provide descriptive narration, but also explain the cause and effect	Tufte uses an example of John Snow's medical detective work examining the cause of Cholera epidemic in London in 1854 (see http://www.ph.ucla.edu/epi/snow.html). Comparing two sets of data about the number of deaths and their corresponding locations. Snow recast the one-dimensional temporal data sets into a two-dimensional spatial comparison that helped him pinpoint the contaminated pump well
Make comparisons	To be persuasive, which is the ultimate goal of communication, together with what is the cause, and what is the effect, the third important question that needs to be answered is, compared to what?	Citing the same example of the Cholera epidemic, Tufte describes how Snow's map with great clarity, presents several clues for comparison of the living and the dead, and clues about various locations etc.
Make displays multidimensional	Tufte argues for a feature of a design of information that utilizes multidimensionality in order to maximize the amount of information presentable	To demonstrate this principle, Tufte shows a 19th century map of Napoleon's 1812 march into Russia (see Chap. 2). The map shows multiple dimensions on a two-dimensional paper (e.g., the size of the army, direction the army is moving, temperature, and date). On a single sheet of paper with no text, Minards captures Napoleon's disastrous adventure to take Russia
Integrate words, numbers and images	Tufte stresses on the importance of telling a "coherent story". This means avoiding references for figures and examples, which are physically removed from the flow of the text. Information for comparison should be put side-by-side, that is, within the eye span, not stacked in time on subsequent pages	Again, Minard's map is the best example of how this is achieved

(continued)

4.4 Theoretical Perspectives of Uses of Visuals ...

Table 4.3 (continued)

Recommendation	Description	Example
Effectiveness of visual design depends upon the quality, relevance and integrity of the content	Good design is clear thinking made visible	Tufte features a book by Galileo published in 1613, which reports the discovery of sunspots and the rings of Saturn for the first time. The report of the discovery of sunspots has a simple drawing of the sun on each page to show daily observations. From these observations, he learned that the sun was rotating as the spots moved across the page and changed the apparent shape at the edges due to foreshortening
Sleight of hand	For Tufte, magic is expressed in five dimensions: 3-dimensional space, time, and what is revealed and concealed. Tufte calls magic the art of "disinformation design"	Tufte identifies several devices that magicians employ to misinform their viewers. They are: disguise, deny, conceal, obscure, manipulate, suppress context, prevent reflective analysis and distract. Hence effective information design involves doing exactly the opposite of what magicians do

*Please note that the percentages specified on the left of "We Tend to Remember" are only for illustration purposes and no corresponding evidence exists to confirm this to such specific percentage levels)

Fig. 4.4 Edgar Dale's Cone of Experience (modified by the author and others, such as Richard Felder who developed so called 'Cone of Learning')

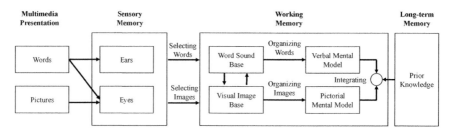

Fig. 4.5 Processing of visuals and verbal/words model (Mayer 2003)

For Mayer, a visual display, which he calls a '*conceptual model*', facilitates the development of learners' '*mental model*' of a system being learnt. By comparing two groups of learners, one that learnt with a conceptual model and another who learnt with conventional text information, Mayer understood that the visual model led to improved conceptual recall while at the same time, it resulted in reduced verbatim retention. As an explanation for this manifest, Mayer suggests that "... *the model helps students reorganize the material to fit with their conceptual model and when students actively reorganize the material they tend to lose the original presentation format*" (p. 59). Mayer acknowledged that there might be a problem if learners were expected to sit for a traditional test that expects the recall of information presented by books and teachers. However, the key understanding from Mayer's study is that learning with visual models improves the ability of learners to transfer what they learnt to solve new problems. Mayer further suggests that a possible reason for this transfer might be that students have constructed mind models that they could mentally manipulate when solving a new problem. Furthermore, Mayer (2003) expanded on these ideas and developed a model of how visual and verbal/textual information are processed during learning with multimedia material (see Fig. 4.5).

According to this model, words and pictures are processed through different sensory channels/memory. Certain elements of that information are then selected for processing thought working memory, resulting in an integrated mental model of the content being presented. This mental model then is contrasted and integrated with prior knowledge and, if a set of required conditions are met, stored in long-term memory. Based on such ideas, Mayer and his followers conducted a set of studies and developed the so-called, 'Theory of Multimedia Learning', providing a set of empirically developed guiding principles for the design of resources for learning for delivery via computer screens. These principles are:

- *Multimedia principle*—a resource for learning should integrate visual and verbal information, not verbal alone.
- *Split-attention principle*—words and pictures should be physically and temporally integrated in a screen.
- *Redundancy principle*—the same information should not be presented in more than one format within a screen.

- *Modality principle*—words should be spoken rather than written (in conversational rather than formal style, using a standard-accented human voice).
- *Segmenting principle*—multimedia messages should be presented in student-paced segments.
- *Pre-training principle*—names and characteristics of main concepts should be familiar to students.
- *Coherence*—extraneous material should be excluded.
- *Signalling*—cues should be used to highlight the organization of the essential material.

However, there might be limitations with this interpretation of the processing of pictures and words, especially when we consider contemporary representational technologies, interactive and integrated displays and multimodal text. For example, it is not clear how visuals and other modalities are cognitively separated from a single representation for processing into different sensory channels. Furthermore, learning is a complex phenomenon which most often includes an activity, rather than a mechanical process of inputting information and building mental representations from words and pictures and based on prior knowledge. In his later work, Mayer attempted to deal with this complexity by arguing that learning is a sense making and knowledge construction, however, this reaming to be at the surface rather than at any significantly deep theoretical level. Nevertheless, certain ideas and subsequent studies conducted by Mayer and colleagues subscribing to his theory of multimedia learning, provide useful ideas for the design of instructional material such as presentation resources.

Important
Knowledge is never a representation of the real world but a collection of conceptual structures adopted from an experience.

Van Someren (1998) proposes a similar idea in his edited book 'Learning with Multiple Representations' when suggesting that technology allows the integration of multiple representational formats into a single learning resource. This book explores a range of studies on different aspects of representations in learning. In one chapter of the book, van Someren et al. (1998) suggest, consistently with Mayer (2003) and Paivio (1986) that '*human cognitive architecture*' consists of different centres responsible for different modes of representations. For example, there are different centers for images and text processing. For these authors, what they call multiple representations, supports learning by allowing learners to cognitively link different representational modalities (e.g., visuals and auditory). Learners who learn in this way would be able to mentally change modes of internal representations, and this would facilitate independent problem solving and other reasoning tasks. A different chapter by Boshuizen and Hermina (1998) suggests that this is possible because different representational modalities are more efficient for dealing with different parts of a problem solving or reasoning task. In another chapter, De Jong et al. (1998) suggest that multiple representational modalities support different learning preferences and allow learners to select a suitable representation to be integrated in their personal knowledge construction process. However, De Jong et al. (1998) warns that the use of representations should be carefully planned in consideration of: (a) type of test to be used to test learners, (b) type of domain knowledge (more appropriate for "how it works" domains), (c) type of learners (more appropriate for novice learners), and (d) the type of support needed for learners to encode representations. Although the book provides useful discussion about the affordances of technology to bring together various media elements into multiple representational resources for learning, it fails short of addressing the importance of interactivity for enabling learners to manipulate these resources through their personal knowledge construction process and a learning activity. Interactivity was very briefly mentioned by Boshuizen and Hermina in their definition of a representation as "… *a format for recording, storing and presenting information together with a set of operators for modifying the information*" (p. 138). However, defining an aspect of a representation in terms of technical functionality might not be very helpful. This should be defined in terms of learners' interactions with screen elements and the manipulation of properties of displayed modalities. However, more serious concerns with this book is a concept of learning environment as an integrated multimodal representation. Any representation should only be considered as a tool for the mediation of learning activates, but neither activity nor any tool (including digital resource for learning) alone can constitute an environment. Technology can be a part or an extension, but not a replacement to an environment in which we find ourselves to exist. In addition, van Someren's book is similar to Mayer (1989) in discussing representation as a tool that improves an old approach to teaching and learning, thus, bringing to question how representations lead to improvements in learners' traditional test results. With new technology, the activity itself has to change (Salomon et al. 1991). With changes in activity, evaluation should focus on processes and artefacts created by learners through an activity where they construct and use knowledge (and develop new literacies). Thus, all this brings us to the problematic nature of a concept of a representation.

For us in this book, representation is a media design with the purpose to mediate the processes of knowledge construction and use. It is a visual (and interactive) tool that mediates our thinking and decisions. It represents disciplinary knowledge content required to complete an intellectual task (theoretical thinking) and, as such, it is not information to be remembered for later reproduction. Rather, some functional properties of a representation and its affordances become internalized through its intellectual use, and later becomes a form of a physiological tool and a resource in our cognition. Ideas, concepts, information and data displayed are represented, not in their raw formats, as they might exist in the world, but in more effective, organized and simplified ways though the integration of various representational modalities such as pictures, drawings, test, audio, video, animation special effects, and colors. When multiple modalities are used to represent a piece of content, often a term 'a representation' is suitable to refer to such a design. The problem with a representation is when this concept is used for an internal form of knowledge existing in one's mind. To make a presentation resource more educationally effective, its content should include representations of key knowledge content. However, learning, again, is not just copying these representations into learners' minds, but a reconstruction of an experience.

> **Important**
> A multiple representation, a pedagogical model or a digital resource for learning must be considered as a tool with a purpose to mediate a learning activity rather than as a vehicle used to display material to be copied to a learner's mind. In this case, the focus of our analysis in the design of learning experiences shifts to an activity and away from mapping of external into internal or vice versa.

Fraser (1999) distinguishes between a mental model, which 'exists' in the mind of a learner and a 'pedagogical model' (a representation) designed to facilitate a learner's construction of that mental model. He suggests that interactivity and visualization enable the creation of powerful pedagogical models, something that no previous technology was able to effectively combine for the purpose of learning. An important issue in Fraser's view is the division between a mental model as something in the mind and a pedagogical model as something in the world, and the two are not identical things. This division is, in fact, important, and literature confuses the matter by using the term representation to interchangeably refer to things of the mind and things of the world. This portrays a picture that there may be representations in the world, which can be copied or transported to, rather than deconstructed in the world through a learning experience. Von Glasersfeld (1997) suggests that representations exist only in the world but not in the mind. He writes that "... *the term representation is used for mental images that are supposed to reflect, or correspond to things that lie beyond our experiential interface*" and that this "... *use of representation is misguided, because it entails the belief that certain ideas we abstract from our experience correspond to a reality that lies beyond experience.*" For von Glasersfeld, knowledge is never a representation of the real world, but a collection of conceptual structures adopted from an experience. It is the learner who deconstructs segments parts of his or her experience into "*raw elementary particles*" and combines these into conceptual structures. This experience must be more than just learners' contact with instructional materials and it should include an "active struggle" with such materials (e.g., use of digital resources for learning) in order to subtract useful understanding, which informs thinking and decisions within a learning activity. A multiple representation, a pedagogical model or a digital resource for learning must be considered as a tool with the purpose to mediate a learning activity rather than as a strategy used to display material to be copied to a learner's mind. In this case, the focus of our analysis in the design of learning experiences shifts to an activity and away from mapping of external into internal or vice versa. A cognitive residue resulting from a tool-use experience can be considered as an 'interiorized' psychological tool. Interiorization of an external tool is not mapping or copying of an external representation into an internal cognitive residue. Interiorization possibly occurs through the deconstruction of an external tool and tool-using experience, and reconstruction of its elements into an intellectually useable residue. This process is likely to be mediated with other auxiliary means, which replace original elements of an external tool, prior knowledge and one's own cognitive capacity at a particular stage of conceptual development.

As noted in this book, in addition to visuals, a distinct feature of contemporary technologies and their affordances for representation is interactivity. White, as early as in 1984, writes that interactive visual capabilities of computer technology provide opportunities for representations to be developed as powerful tools for learning. Some years later, Fraser (1999) advises that the level to which a learner gains the same pedagogical benefit from a printout of a digital resource as from the digital resource viewed via a screen, is the extent to which nothing of pedagogical value was done by using technology. What difference does technology make? For Fraser, interactive visual capabilities of contemporary technology provide unique opportunities for the communication of mental models to learners through pedagogical models (representations). Fraser writes that:

> In the past, we relied on words, diagrams, equations, and gesticulations to build those models piece by piece in the minds of the students. We now have a new tool – not one that replaces the older ones, but one that greatly extends them: interactive computer visualization. Today, a teacher can build a pedagogical model, and both student and teacher can interact with it to explore the behaviour of the system in a way inconceivable in earlier times. The amazing thing is that such interactive models can be readily delivered through the Web not only into the classroom, where the teacher can use them to help communicate concepts, but also into the computer laboratory, the dormitory room, and the home, where the student can interact with them to explore ideas.

However, rather than thinking of interactivity as an affordance of technology that affords the design of a representation, as rightly suggested by White (1984) and Fraser (1999), the literature often discusses interactivity in terms of content navigation through structured instructional sequences with feedback and directions. It often appears in the literature that interactivity is traditionally discussed in the context of a learner's acquisition of subject matter from digital resources carefully designed to present appropriately paced content and corresponding cycles of question-interaction-feedback-remediation sequences. Digital resources are often considered to be the direct causes of learning in the same fashion that teachers are traditionally considered. Thus, these kinds of educational material are often perceived as a replacement for teachers and classroom teaching. Unlike learning from a teacher, such resources allow learners to revise and go through material as many times as they need. Interactions can be tracked and recorded into a database, which allows a teacher to obtain certain quantitative indicators regarding a learner's involvements with the resource (e.g., sections attended, duration of time spent in each section, and results from quizzes). Therefore, interactivity is expected to support learners to learn subject matter embedded in digital resources. For example, Jonassen (1988) writes that the quality of the interaction is generally a function of the nature of the learner's response and computer feedback, and that "if the response is consistent with the learner's information processing needs, then it is meaningful" (p. 101). This is also supported by Spector (1995) in Sims (1997) who suggests that although creating effective interface is important "… *the critical factor (of learning effectiveness) is more likely the learner's mental engagement or involvement with the subject material*". Sims (1997) writes that interactivity in educational material must support learning. Sims developed a classification of different levels of interactivity and proposed three dimensions by which interactivity may be perceived: engagement, control and interactive concept. The engagement dimension refers to interactivity for navigation or for instructional purpose. The control dimension refers to the level to which the resource or a learner makes navigational and/or learning decisions. The third dimension, interactive concept, indicates the type of interaction expected under the varying conditions defined by the content presented.

For us in this book, interactivity affords the design of digital resources that can be used as mediating tools in learning activities. It is a feature of a tool, not a cause of learning. Technology-based interactivity is what separates contemporary digital resources for learning from all previous forms of educational material such as print-based material, analogue video, audio, non-digital toys, and even manipulable material (e.g., pop-up books and Algebra Blocks). Although the digitization of traditional resources is made possible by contemporary technologies (e.g., scanning) and improved access, the simple conversion of these resources should not be understood as a creation of historically new kinds of educationally useful resources (e.g., by scanning a textbook and creating an electronic e-book). The fundamental question for any new tool in human praxis is how the tool is a product of historical development of previous generations of tools and socio-cultural developments of humans (Vygotsky 1978; Engeström 1987). As a new kind of tool in teaching and learning, digital resources for learning must build on our previous and emerging understandings of media, psychology and pedagogy, and extend upon affordances brought about by new and emerging technologies. Interactivity adds the critical dimension to the design of the forms of educational resources—the digital resources for learning.

In the context of more contemporary pedagogical approaches, learning is understood to result from conscious psychological processes, where these occur within an engagement in an activity (e.g., Davydov 1999; Engeström 1987; Jonassen and Rohrer-Murphy 1999; Hedegaard and Lompscher 1999). In these, a digital resource for learning is a tool that mediates an activity. However, no resource or a person is a direct cause of learning because knowledge does not directly transfer from a teacher, social context or a resource to a passive learner. In this thinking, it might not be appropriate to discuss interactivity as a cause of learning, but rather, only as an effective strategy for representing and organizing data, information, conceptual content and ideas into a digital resource for learning. The concept of "feedback" traditionally associated with interactivity also needs to be reconsidered in the context of more contemporary approaches. The major feedback that learners receive comes from their engagement in a learning activity (not from a digital resource for learning or other tools alone). A further issue with interactivity is that it is often discussed as a strategy that makes for easy navigation. Real-life situations require individuals to struggle with complexity and no educational activity should over-simplify that situation. Interactivity should be explored as a strategy that preserves this complexity.

In this book, we want to reiterate that visuals used in the design of presentation resources (and other forms of digital resources for learning) should strictly be the ones supporting representation of knowledge content. A significant problem arises when design includes irrelevant content, such as fun characters and decorations. Some teachers and designers hold the view that learning should be fun and, therefore, their design includes irrelevant fun-like characters and content-irrelevant multimedia with the intention to extrinsically motivate learners and make the learning process more entertaining. This is problematic in numerous ways, such as described below:

- Learning, most often, is not a fun activity, and a minority of individuals like to learn, unless it is purpose directed and related to personal goals. The strategy of making learning fun might work for some young learners (e.g., in lower primary school and kindergartens), as well as learners with special needs (e.g., autism), however, the very moment when disciplinary concepts become critical in a curriculum, it becomes much less important to worry about extrinsic motivation. Learning should be led by an interesting activity, but trying to make it fun, will not take us very far in teaching, at least not across all levels of schooling and university studies. Intrinsic motivation is critical for engagement, and engagement is strongly related to the achievement of learning outcomes. The designers of digital resources should think about aspects of activities where digital resources for learning will be used. This is what this module refers to as "design for learning uses". Engagement and intrinsic motivation occurs with these activities, where digital resources are tools that mediate these. Also, this is valid for the design of presentation resources which intends to either support teaching or be used as self-learning material.
- Unnecessary content (e.g., cartoon-like characters meant to be making learning fun) overloads cognitive capacity, that is, it creates unnecessary cognitive load, which is committed to analyzing irrelevant rather than relevant information. The cognitive load should not be focused on having fun rather than addressing the requirements of an activity where learning occurs.
- Motivation for learning is not caused by resources; rather it is a learning activity that facilitates students' motivation and engagement. When students are engaged in learning activities that they are interested in and that are related to their intrinsic motives, they are more likely to learn even from not so well-designed content. Engagement in learning is something that traditional teaching and presentation resources significantly fail to achieve.

- Creating content-related fun elements, animations and special sounds, while not contributing much to learning, unnecessarily complicates and makes considerably more expensive the process of design and the development of digital learning resources.

> **Important**
> Intrinsic motivation is critical for engagement, and engagement is strongly related to the achievement of learning outcomes.

In summary, visuals are powerful representational means for the communication of declarative knowledge content. In the case of instructional presentation resources, visuals significantly enhance teachers' ability to communicate declarative knowledge content in simplified ways; maximize the amount of content presented within specific time frame and a display; and empower learners with a framework for understanding the content. Interactive affordances add further possibilities to the design of representations to be utilized with in-presentation resources. When designing instructional presentation resources, visuals should always lead the design and text, and other modalities that should be used to supplement these and summarize and emphasize key aspects of information being delivered. This kind of resource aims to enhance and support teachers in delivering their lectures and, as such, alone, the resources should not be used as self-learning material. Alternative forms of presentation resources for self-learning of declarative knowledge content can be effectively designed by utilizing contemporary representational technologies. However, even though both of these kinds of presentation resources are designed with the intention to support traditional approaches to teaching and learning, they can find uses in the context of more contemporary, learning-centered, activity-based approaches. Presentation resources, if used in a learning activity, become information displays, delivering certain information to learners to use when completing their activities. In later parts of this book, we examine the concept of learning activity in greater details.

> **Activity 4.4**
> *Previously in Chap. 2, you designed an information display resource, which presented organized information about the atmosphere. Now, let's assume you want to teach a class about the atmosphere, and you need a presentation resource to help you in the process.*
>
> *Use Prezi.com to design an instructional presentation on the topic of 'Atmosphere' to support your teaching. Alternatively, you can design an instructional presentation resource to support a teacher to teach the topic of the 'Shape of a rain drop'.*

References

Alesandrini, R. L. (1984). Pictures and adult learning. *Instructional Science, 13*, 63–77.
Alessi, S. M., & Trollip, S. R. (1995). *Computer-based instruction: methods and development.* Englewood Cliffs, NJ: Prentice Hall Inc.
Boshuizen, P. A., & Hermina, J. M. (1998). Problem solving with multiple representations by multiple and single agents: An analysis of the issues involved. In A. Van Someren (Ed.), *Learning with multiple representations* (pp. 137–151). Kidlington, Oxford: Elsevier Science Ltd.
Churchill, D. (2005). Learning object: An interactive representation and a mediating tool in a learning activity. *Educational Media International, 42*(4), 333–349.
Cisco Systems. (2001). *Reusable learning object strategy: Designing information and learning objects through concept, fact, procedure, process, and principle template.* San Jose, CA: Cisco Systems Inc.
Clark, R. C., & Mayer, R. E. (2016). *E-learning and the science of instruction: Proven guidelines for consumers and designers of multimedia learning* (4th ed.). New Jersey, NJ: Wiley.
Clifford, R. (2002, August). *Adding a pedagogical dimension to SCORM* [Digital Audio Recording]. Oral presentation at the Online Instruction for 21st Century: Connecting Instructional Design to International Standards for Content Reusability, Brigham Young University, Rexburg, Idaho. Retrieved from http://zola.byu.edu/id2scorm/
Cochrane, T. (2005). Interactive QuickTime: Developing and evaluating multimedia learning objects to enhance both face-to-face and distance e-learning environments. *Interdisciplinary Journal of Knowledge and Learning Objects, 1*(1), 33–54.
Dale, E. (1946). *Audio-visual methods in teaching.* New York, NY: The Dryden Press.
Davydov, V. V. (1999). The content and unsolved problems of activity theory. In Y. Engerström, R. Miettinen, & R. Punamäki (Eds.), *Perspectives on activity theory* (pp. 39–52). Cambridge: Cambridge University Press.
De Jong, T. D., Ainsworth, S., Dobson, M., Hulst, A., Levonen, J., Reimann, P., et al. (1998). Acquiring knowledge in science and mathematics: The use of multiple representations in technology based learning environments. In A. Van Someren (Ed.), *Learning with multiple representations* (pp. 9–40). Kidlington, Oxford: Elsevier Science Ltd.
Dean, R. S., & Enomoth, P. A. (1983). Pictorial organization in prose learning. *Contemporary Educational Psychology, 8,* 20–27.
Dick, W., & Carey, L. M. (1978, 1985, 1990, 1996). *The systematic design of instruction.* Glenview, IL: Harper Collins Publishers.
E-learning Competency Center. (2003). *Explanation on learning objects.* Retrieved from http://www.ecc.org.sg/loc/ecplain.htm
Engeström, Y. (1987). *Learning by expanding.* Helsinki: Orienta-konsultit.
Fraser, A. (1999). Web visualization for teachers. *Chronicle of Higher Education, 48*, August 8, B8. Retrieved from http://fraser.cc/
Friesen, N. (2003). *Three objections to learning objects.* Retrieved from http://www.learningspaces.org/n/papers/objections.html
Gagné, R. M., Briggs, L. J., & Wager, W. W. (1992). *Principles of instructional design* (4th ed.). Fort Worth, TX: Harcourt Brace Jovanovich College Publishers.
Gibbons, A. (2000). *Model-centered instruction: Beyond simulation.* Retrieved from http://www.gwu.edu/~lto/gibbons.html
Hedegaard, M., & Lompscher, J. (Eds.). (1999). *Learning activity and development.* Aarhus, Denmark: Aarhus University Press.
IEEE. (2001). *WG12: Learning object metadata.* Retrieved from http://ltsc.ieee.org/wg12/
Imran, H., Belghis-Zadeh, M., Chang, T. W., & Graf, S. (2016). PLORS: A personalized learning object recommender system. *Vietnam Journal of Computer Science, 3*(1), 3–13.
IMS Global Learning Consortium. (2002). *Learning resource meta-data specification.* Retrieved from http://www.imsglobal.org/metadata/

References

Jonassen, D. (Ed.). (1988). *Instructional designs for microcomputer courseware*. Hillsdale, NJ: Lawrence Erlbaum.

Jonassen, D., & Churchill, D (2004). Is there learning orientation in learning objects? *International Journal of E-learning*, 32–42.

Jonassen, H. D., & Rohrer-Murphy, L. (1999). Activity theory as a framework for designing constructivist learning environment. *Educational Technology Research and Development, 47*(1), 61–99.

Levie, W. H., & Lentz, R. (1982). Effects of text illustrations: A review of research. *Educational Communication and Technology, 30*, 195–232.

Levin, J. R., & Berry, J. K. (1980). Children's learning of all the news that's fit to picture. *Educational Communication and Technology, 28*, 177–185.

Lukasiak, J., Agostinho, S., Bennet, S., Harper, B., Lockyer, L., & Powley, B. (2005). Learning objects and learning designs: An integrated system for reusable, adaptive and sharable learning content. *Research in Learning Technology, 13*(2), 151–169.

Mayer, R. E. (1989). Models for understanding. *Review of Educational Research, 59*(1), 43–64.

Mayer, R. E. (2003). The promise of multimedia learning: Using the same instructional design methods across different media. *Learning & Instruction, 13*, 125–139.

McGreal, R. (2004). Learning objects: A practical definition. *International Journal of Instructional Technology and Distance Learning, 1*(9), 21–32.

MERLOT. (n.d.). *Learning material types*. Retrieved from http://info.merlot.org/merlothelp/merlot_collection.htm#Learning_Material_Types

Merrill, M. D. (2000). Knowledge objects and mental models. In D. A. Wiley (Ed.), *The instructional use of learning objects*. Retrieved from http://reusability.org/read/chapters/merrill.doc

Miller, G. (1956). The magical number seven, plus or minus two: Some limits on our capacity for processing information. *The Psychological Review, 63*, 81–97.

Paivio, A. (1986). *Mental representation: A dual coding approach*. New York, NY: Oxford University Press.

Reeves, T. (1998). *Evaluating what really matters in computer-based education*. Retrieved from http://eduworks.com/Documents/Workshops/EdMedia1998/docs/reeves.html

Salomon, G., Perkins, D. N., & Globerson, T. (1991). Partners in cognition: Extending human intelligence with intelligent technologies. *Educational Researcher*, 2–9.

Shallert, D. L. (1980). The role of illustrations in reading comprehension. In R. Spiro, B. Bruce, & W. Brewer (Eds.), *Theoretical issues in reading comprehension* (pp. 503–524). Hillsdale, NJ: Earlbaum.

Sims, R. (1997). *Interactivity: A forgotten art?* Retrieved from http://intro.base.org/docs/interact/

Spector, M. J. (1995). Integrating and humanizing the process of automating instructional design. In R. D. Tennyson & A. E. Barron (Eds.), *Automating instructional design: Computer-based development and delivery tools*. Berlin: Springer.

Tubelo, R. A., Branco, V. L. C., Dahmer, A., Samuel, S. M. W., & Collares, F. M. (2016). The influence of a learning object with virtual simulation for dentistry: A randomized controlled trial. *International Journal of Medical Informatics, 85*(1), 68–75.

Tufte, E. (1997). *Visual explanations*. Cheshire, CT: Graphics Press LLC.

Tufte, E. (2001). *The visual display of quantitative information*. Cheshire, CT: Graphics Press LLC.

Tufte, E. (1990). *Envisioning information*. Cheshire, CT: Graphics Press LLC.

Van Someren, A. (Ed.). (1998). *Learning with multiple representations*. Kidlington, Oxford: Elsevier Science Ltd.

Van Someren, A., Boshuizen, P. A., de Jong, T., & Reimann, P. (1998). Introduction. In A. Van Someren (Ed.), *Learning with multiple representations* (pp. 1–5). Kidlington, Oxford, UK: Elsevier Science Ltd.

Venkatesh, R. (2001). *Visual design for instructional content*. Retrieved from http://www.elearningpost.com/articles/archives/visual_design_for_instructional_content_part_i

Von Glassersfeld, E. (1997). *Piaget's legacy: Cognition as adaptive activity*. Retrieved from http://www.umass.edu/srri/vonGlasersfeld/onlinePapers/html/245.html

Vygotsky, S. L. (1978). *Mind in society*. Cambridge, MA: Harward University Press.

White, B. Y. (1984). Designing computer games to help students understand Newton's laws of motion. *Cognition and Instruction, 1,* 69–108.

Wiley, D., & Edwards, E. (2002). *Online self-organizing social systems: The decentralized future of online learning*. Retrieved from http://wiley.ed.usu.edu/docs/ososs.pdf

Wiley, D. A. (2000). Connecting learning objects to instructional design theory: A definition, a metaphor, and a taxonomy. In D. A. Wiley (Ed.), *The instructional use of learning objects*. Retrieved from http://reusability.org/read/chapters/wiley.doc

Practice Resources

Learning Outcomes:

- Describe what is a practice resource;
- Design more effective drill & practice resources; and
- Design a digital resource for procedural knowledge development.

5.1 What Is a Practice Resource?

In addition to declarative and conceptual knowledge, curriculum content for most subjects includes procedural knowledge, such as, knowledge of problem solving procedures, algorithms, configuration of lab equipment, and other conceptual and practical tasks requiring skills. Procedural knowledge is best described as curriculum knowledge content of "tasks specific rules, skills, actions, and sequences of actions employed to reach goals" (see Cauley 1986).

Practice resources primarily aim at assisting the development of this form of knowledge for learners. Such resources do not simply present declarative information about a procedure we expect learners to remember. Rather, if effectively designed, these resources allow learners to learn with and through interaction and engagement with the content of the display. Contemporary representational technology tools, with their visual and interactive affordances, allow for the design, development and delivery of resources that can effectively be used in this context. For this to be achieved, we need to move beyond simple forms of practice items most widely used—drill & practice forms, such as, short-answer and multiple choice questions with simple wrong or right responses, when ineffective or no feedback is provided at all—and adopt a design approach where representations and interactivity are used to provide a tool for the development of procedural knowledge.

> **Important**
> Contemporary representational technology tools, with their visual and interactive affordances, allow for design, development and delivery of resources that can effectively be used in the context of development of procedural knowledge.

However, most often practice resources are designed and used as a means for drill & practice, and quizzes that check students' recollection of certain factual and declarative knowledge that they are expected to remember for reproduction at exams. Practice resources are most often embedded within presentation resources, and used as a means of reinforcing chunks of information that learners learn.

In the approach proposed in this book, practice resources are separated from other forms of digital resources for learning, with the purpose to allow optimal reusability within a variety of resources other than presentations. Furthermore, this separation allows designers to focus more on the development of resources to target procedural knowledge content specified by a curriculum, rather than to continue focusing on the design of resources for transfer of facts and declarative information, and subsequent checking if that knowledge has been remembered.

In this chapter, we will examine some of the possibilities for more effective design of practice resources. At the same time, we will look at some fundamental instructional principles for designing interactive drill & practice, so that such resources can be made more educationally effective. We will discuss practice items in two forms: drill & practice (including quizzes), and procedure practice, and acknowledge the possibility for games to be considered under this category of digital resources for learning.

> **Activity 5.1**
> *How would you design a practice item for the learning of a procedure of measuring patient's blood pressure? Sketch your idea, or try prototyping something with a tool of your choice.*

5.2 Drill & Practice Resources

The drill & practice form of practice resources has been most widely used in education in presentation resources, such as, in instructional multimedia packages and computer based instruction, or within on-line learning management systems.

Numerous technology tools such as Hot Potatoes, tools within an e-learning system, such as, Moodle or Blackboard, and even Web 2.0 platforms such as those empowered by Google Forms, allow for the easy creation and delivery of drill & practice questions. Teachers around the world have been using these tools to leverage upon their affordances, and develop drill & practice questions for implementation in their teaching. This looks promising to teachers, as it gives them a sense of creating interactive resources for their own use with ease. Teachers appear empowered to quickly create a set of drill & practice questions by copying text from somewhere else (e.g., a Word document), and pasting into their resources for configuration. Resources can be easily implemented and teachers can collect responses from students automatically, thus, removing the required time and effort to manually check through students' work. Often, these are used as a tool for assessment.

However, there are limitations and further room for considerable improvements in such practice. Although teachers are easily embracing these tools, often it appears, based on the author's review of numerous drill & practice questions that sound instructional design principles are absent most often. Furthermore, it appears that rarely, visual and interactive affordances of contemporary representational technology were utilized within question or corresponding feedback.

We will use a simple example to illustrate this limitation, and propose some design principles. Let's say a drill & practice question is created to ask a learner the question presented in Fig. 5.1.

Teachers, using one of the technology tools mentioned previously, can easily create such a question. However, what happens most often is that, once student selects a response A, B, C or D by pressing a corresponding key on a keyboard (or clicking on the selected answer by a mouse, or a finger via a mobile device), they are told if they are correct or incorrect. Often, feedback is limited to simple text, such as, 'Right!', 'Well done!', 'You are correct', 'Wrong', 'Incorrect', etc. In some

---

Classification of Triangles

What is the proper name for a triangle that has 2 side of equal length?

A. Isosceles Triangle
B. Scalene Triangle
C. Equilateral Triangle
D. Right Angled Triangle

Fig. 5.1 An example of a simple practice resource

instances, students receive, for example, a green tick (✓) acknowledging correctness, or an alternative red sign (✖), acknowledging incorrectness. These are usually automatically provided by the system supporting the development of such a resource. Furthermore, the system might also provide auditory feedback in the forms of a pleasing sound when a correct response is selected, or a disturbing sound if an incorrect response is selected. Rarely, students are given the opportunity to try again and correct their mistakes; neither authoring tools in available platforms support this to be integrated in design of a practice resource.

So, what should be done in terms of design to make this more effective as a practice resource? The first option is to do with the presentation of the question. Visual representation can be used to more effectively present this question in a way that will support learning. For example, this can promote learning of mathematical representations, as well as the linking of mathematics to language by corresponding the visual to textual information. So, the question might appear, as presented in Fig. 5.2.

There are some additional elements included in this screen. These include additional instructions on how to answer the questions, as well as some formatting of the text to highlight important and related information. Furthermore, and probably most importantly, attention should be given to the role of feedback in such resources. Telling learners that they are 'wrong' or 'correct' does not carry any significant educational value. Feedback must be constructive, and serve as a tool for learning. These are some guiding principles in respect to feedback:

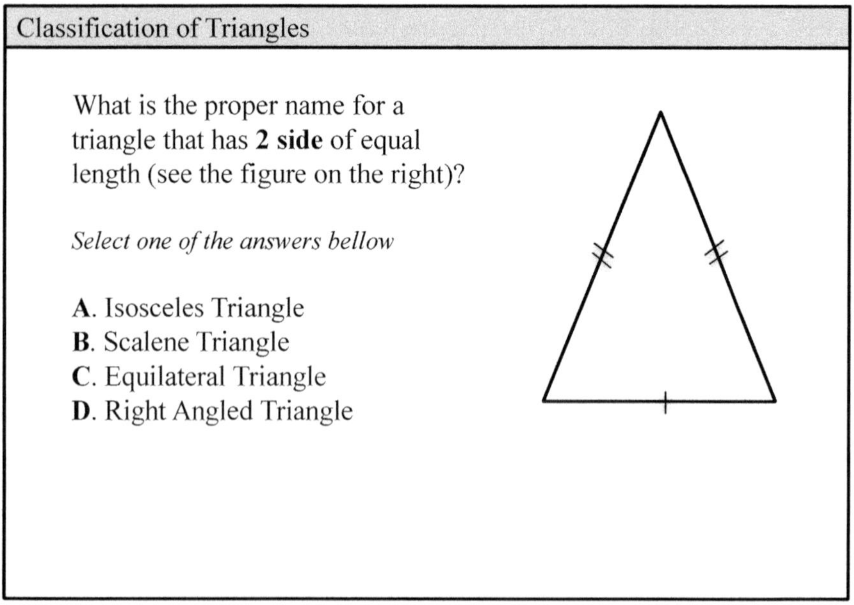

Classification of Triangles

What is the proper name for a triangle that has **2 side** of equal length (see the figure on the right)?

Select one of the answers bellow

A. Isosceles Triangle
B. Scalene Triangle
C. Equilateral Triangle
D. Right Angled Triangle

Fig. 5.2 More effective display of a practice resources (visual representation is used to enhance presentation and support learning)

5.2 Drill & Practice Resources

- When a learner answers a question *correctly*, this should be used as an opportunity to provide further information, and extend his or her knowledge beyond the sole content of the question. So, the feedback might be: *"Correct! A scalene triangle can also be a right-angled triangle"*. Instructions on what to do next will then be provided, e.g., '*Click go to the next question*'.
- When a learner answers the question *incorrectly*, this should be used as an opportunity to point to his or her mistake(s), provide some information that can help the learner to improve (remediation), and provide another opportunity to answer the question. So, for example, if a learner selected "*C. Equilateral triangle*" as an answer, the feedback might be: "*Incorrect! Equilateral triangles have 3 sides of equal length. You are looking for a triangle that has only two sides of equal length. Please try again*". The feedback might even contain a graphical representation of an equilateral triangle. In this way, a learner can focus on the mistake made, and will attempt to correct this mistake by considering new information provided.
- When a learner is *partially correct*, that is, in the example if he or she selects "*D. Right-angled triangle*" as an answer, this should be acknowledged and further information provided with an opportunity to provide an answer in the next attempt.

> **Important**
> A practice resource must include appropriate feedback provided to learners based on their responses. Providing feedback is a critical aspect of the design of practice resources. Learners should be given an opportunity to reflect on their responses.

In addition to limitations associated with the feedback, not providing learners an opportunity to correct their mistakes is another serious limitation of many of the drill & practice questions reviewed by the author. Learners should be given an opportunity to correct their incorrect answer by thinking more about the question asked and responses they provided. It would not make much sense to provide more than one additional attempt, as a learner might easily guess the correct answer by eliminating previous unsuccessful attempts. If a learner was not successful in the second attempt, then, remediation can be provided (some other resources may be used to learn relevant content).

5.3 Procedure and Practice Resources

However, until this stage, it can be reasonably assumed that this kind of drill & practice does not fully address procedural knowledge. It appears that these are more about practicing recall of declarative knowledge. What can be done to build

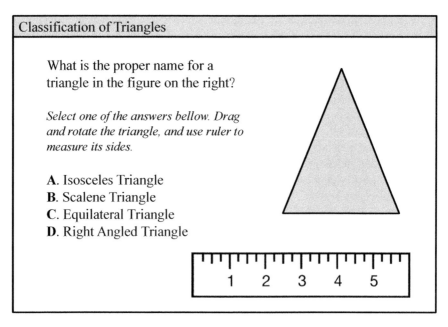

Fig. 5.3 An example that integrates aspects of procedural knowledge

procedure in the process of answering questions? This is illustrated in the redesigned example featured in Fig. 5.3.

Rather than telling a learner that the triangle under question has two sides of equal length, he or she could be instructed to use a ruler and measure the lengths of the sides, and based on these, determine the answer. Such questions can become even more sophisticated by providing an option to select a tool for this task, for example, a protractor instead of a ruler, just a protractor, or both of these tools.

There are a number of ways how this question can be designed and answered by a learner. One option presented so far, is multiple choice where a learner can press a key on a keyboard, or click on a selected answer. An alternative can be that a learner checks a box next to the selected answer, or drag and drop a selected answer in an answer box. However, these interaction possibilities do not, in essence, change the effectiveness of this resource for learning and, moreover, these might overload cognitive processing. Also, an option is to have a text input box for a learner to type in his or her answer. We must note that in the case of open-ended answers, a learner might be penalized and told he/she is wrong because of a spelling mistake, rather that of knowledge of content (e.g., if they misspell isosceles). Also, in these cases, a learner might produce an anticipated partially correct answer (e.g., isosceles angled triangle), or incorrect answer (e.g., equilateral), or a totally unanticipated answer (e.g., Bermuda triangle). For each specific question, a designer must determine the most appropriate form of interaction that can be used to answer a question, so that the most appropriate feedback can be applied to support learning.

5.3 Procedure and Practice Resources

> **Important**
> A designer must determine the most appropriate form of an interaction that can be used to answer a question, so that the most appropriate feedback can be applied to support learning.

A single design of a resource can be articulated in a form that affords multiple practices, and even prevents the copying of answers between learners. Figure 5.4 illustrates such a design.

Affordances of contemporary representational technologies allow that an image of a triangle is randomized, that is, selected from several images available to the resource, or drawn dynamically by a program. It can be presented as different forms of a triangle with different sizes of sides and angles. At the same time, the scale on the ruler can be randomized, so that each time a learner activates the question, a different combination is presented, requiring different answers. Internal logic of the resource will calculate the required answer and will compare that value to the value given by a learner. Again, feedback will play a critical role in enabling a learner to learn from this experience, and extend his or her knowledge even when the correct answer is provided.

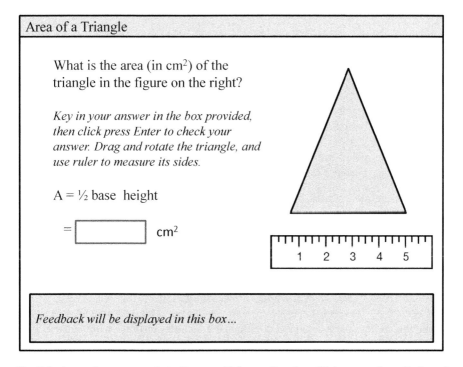

Fig. 5.4 A practice resource that allows multiple practices by utilizing a random display of parameters

A key problem is that designing such items is beyond the competencies of average teachers and instructional designers, as well as beyond the features that standard learning management tools provide and, therefore, require more extensive involvement of a technical specialist to implement such ideas. Nevertheless, instructional designers, as well as teachers, have always been professional who bridge between curriculum requirements and actual implementation, and they need to be fully aware of these possibilities when designing and deciding on forms of resource to use in their practice. Help should be sought from technical specialists who can implement their ideas by developing these resources in a form ready for implementation (e.g., multimedia developers or programmers).

Activity 5.2
Consider this question:

When exposed to lower air pressure, the boiling point of water:
A: Increases
B: Decreases
C: Does not change

Examine this question carefully, and attend to the following:

- *How would you design a practice item to engage learners to use certain procedures, such as using measuring instruments (e.g., temperature gauge) to answer this question?*
- *What feedback you should provide for an incorrect response? What about feedback for a correct answer?*
- *How to reframe this question to make it more real-life and authentic (e.g., "It takes much longer to boil eggs in the hills than in the plains, because?")?*
- *How can this question be randomized in other to prevent learners from copying answers from each other?*

For learning, practice items can be designed to fully address the requirement of a procedural knowledge in numerous cases, or at least to bring learners' understanding and skills close to those that they would require in working with real tools. Ultimately, in many cases, learners would be required to move to use and work with real tools to complete their learning of procedures.

Figure 5.5 shows an example of such resources. This example was designed while the author was working at a technical education institute with teachers from the Mechanical Maintenance department. These teachers held the belief that technology resources are good for the learning of declarative knowledge, but these cannot really help them to teach the procedures required in the maintenance of

5.3 Procedure and Practice Resources

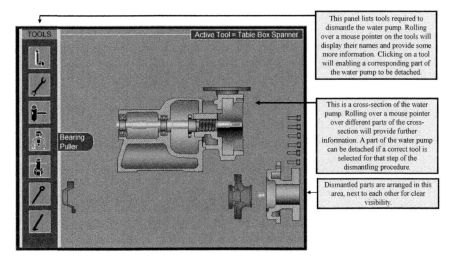

Fig. 5.5 'Water Pump Maintenance' Practice resource

various equipment. Presented with this challenge, the author was determined to prove the contrary, and through this process, the practice resource presented in Fig. 5.5 was developed.

This practice resource shows a cross section of a water pump. The task for a learner is to dismantle the pump, and assemble it back in a particular order of steps. Parts of the pump must be removed in a specific order, or put back together in the reverse order. Each part of the pump can only be removed if a specific tool is selected for use. So, a learner is conditioned to select a specific tool (e.g., bearing puller), in order to remove a specific part (e.g., bearings). Various interactive elements drive learners to approach the procedure in the correct order by using correct tools. For example, from the beginning, a learner is not able to move any part of the pump by dragging it away from the cross section. A pop-up message instructs a learner that he or she should select the appropriate tools to approach the first step of the procedure. Then, once a learner has selected a spanner he or she will be able to remove the first part (casing cover). Rolling a mouse pointer over the cross section of the pump will display pop-ups with names and short descriptions of the different parts. The same will apply when a learner moves the mouse pointer over different tools on the left of the display.

Finally, the learners visit a workshop, and work on a real pump using real tools. However, by this time, they will have a well-established understanding of what is involved in dismantling and assembling a water pump, and able to visualize mentally how the pump looks inside, how parts are distributed and what tools are required. This dramatically reduces the amount of time required to learn to perform the final real-life procedure, while making learning possible at anytime and anywhere beyond the workshop (not to mention possibilities of minimizing accidents, damage to real equipment and limitations in terms of the number of real pumps available for students to practice).

When this practice resource was used in a classroom with learners, it was observed that they were exceptionally enthusiastic and engaged. Some learners even set up a competition between themselves to compete who will dismantle and assemble the water pump faster. This gave a special dimension of a 'game' to this particular practice digital learning resource.

Nevertheless, this particular practice resource is obviously different from the previously discussed case of drill & practice format. Because such a resource contains a certain degree of realism, that is, they reassemble, or simulate real world, in this book, we argue that such resources are a special form of *practice simulation* (e.g., Rutherford-Hemming and Lioce 2016; Sunnqvist et al. 2016). Other forms of practice resource might include those that incorporate aspects of *digital games* (e.g., Beserra et al. 2016; Hainey et al. 2016; Reinders 2012). When we think of a game in teaching and learning, there are a number of possibilities. This means that the idea of games cannot be limited only to a specific form of digital resources for learning. Most relevant to this chapter is that there are digital resources for learning incorporating representations and interactivity to drive a learner to practice certain procedures in game-like fashion. In this sense, a game is a form of a representation resource. The design of such resources most often places a learner in a situation to pursue a certain goal, such as high scores, moving to the next level of complexity, or competing against the machine or others. Essentially, what learners are doing is not about learning new conceptual knowledge (although some conceptualizations might occur incidentally), rather, they repetitively practice certain procedures until some level of mastery is achieved. Games can be considered as a special form of learning activity as well. In this case, the game is not a digital resource, but a strategic approach to achieving learning outcomes. Furthermore, a game might be a complex, digital and social environment, where multiple networked players engage in interactivity, collaboration, competition, and achieving specific goals. In the case of a digital game as a special form of presentation resource, it is a digital resource designed to mediate a learning activity—not an activity in itself—rather than just a resource used in a learning process.

> **Activity 5.3**
> *Design a practice resource to help a learner to practice a procedure of using a protector to measure angle sizes.*

References

Beserra, V., Nussbaum, M., & Grass, A. (2016). Using a fine-grained multiple-choice response format in educational drill-and-practice video games. *Interactive Learning Environments*, 1–16.

Cauley, K. M. (1986). *Studying knowledge acquisition: Distinctions among procedural, conceptual and logical knowledge.* Retrieved from ERIC database. (ED278682).

References

Hainey, T., Connolly, T. M., Boyle, E. A., Wilson, A., & Razak, A. (2016). A systematic literature review of games-based learning empirical evidence in primary education. *Computers & Education, 102*, 202–223.

Reinders, H. (2012). *Digital games in language learning and teaching.* New York, NY: Palgrave and Macmillan.

Rutherford-Hemming, T., & Lioce, L. (2016). Utilization of the standards of best practice simulation: A descriptive study. *Journal of Nursing Education and Practice, 6*(3), 1.

Sunnqvist, C., Karlsson, K., Lindell, L., & Fors, U. (2016). Virtual patient simulation in psychiatric care–A pilot study of digital support for collaborate learning. *Nurse Education in Practice, 17,* 30–35.

Data Display Resources

6

Learning Outcomes:

- Describe what is a data display resource;
- Discuss differences between information and data displays, and data displays and conceptual resources;
- Identify data display resources; and
- Design data display resources.

6.1 What Is a Data Display Resource?

Data display resources are interfaces designed for the accessing of data that can be useful for learners in their learning activities. Such resources are best designed to allow learners to use simulated tools to collect some data, and engage in the processes of data organization and analysis in search for patterns, understandings and generalizations that can be applied in their decision making with a learning activity.

In addition to information (facts and declarative knowledge) and concepts (conceptual knowledge) through the process of working on learning activities, learners can collect and work with data. An effectively designed leaning activity might require learners to engage in the procedure of collecting, organizing, analysing and decision-making based on data. Results of this procedure can further lead to generalizations and abstractions, and subsequent knowledge uses, while the process of working with data can support the development of new literacies. Therefore, these kinds of digital resources for learning target development of procedural knowledge of disciplinary in a specific way in dealing with data in the context of activities such as research and problem solving.

It is important to understand the differences between data and information in the context of this book. Data are unprocessed, disorganized and fragmented measurements, facts, observations and statements collected from an environment, people, or generated by natural or artificial systems. On the other side, information is processed and organized data presented in a form that can be communicated and used directly. An important part of a learning activity should be to engage learners to conduct research, work with data and create information, most desirably, by using digital representational technology to process and organize data in useful formats. In our approach in this book, information useful for learning activities is presented via information display resources, while data are presented via data display resources. A data display resource allows a learner to collect, organize, analyse and use data in decision-making within a learning activity. When data are organized, and presented in a representation (e.g., pie chart, table or a country data on a map), then, that is information rather that a data display resource. However, the most important difference between information and a data display is that in a data display resource, learners are engaged in collecting and working with raw data. Sometimes, specific tools are required to accomplish data collection, while analytical tools are most often deployed within a learning activity.

> **Important**
> The design of resources for mobile technology application needs to pay attention to issues including, at least, the design for presentation via small screens and the design for mobile learning uses.

Direct instruction, that is, teaching-centred practice, leads teachers to take 'shortcuts', giving ready-made answers and information to learners, and expecting them to remember facts, declarative knowledge and drilled-down procedures. Although, to a certain extent, this might prepare learners for examinations, this does not give full attention to their intellectual development and deep knowledge within disciplines (e.g., concept knowledge). It is important that shortcuts are not taken in contemporary education, and that learners are provided with educational experiences which bring to them an opportunity to use tools, struggle with complexities, think and innovate within and across disciplines. At the same time, students should be given opportunities to develop new literacies (e.g., digital literacy) required by contemporary living, learning, working, and socializing. Engaging students to collect and work with data, conduct analysis, generalize, abstract and use their knowledge to solve problems, will promote these essentials of modern day teaching and learning. Furthermore, working with data, especially in digital formats, will promote the development of aspects of new literacies. We live in the time of 'Big Data' and developing literacies are essential to working with data and make sense of them, is an important task for education today.

6.1 What Is a Data Display Resource?

Activity 6.1
Look at the data displayed at the "Weather Underground" at the https://www.wunderground.com/. Explore this map and its features, such as searching for a specific location, or identifying your own location. Attend to the following questions:

- *Are there any patterns between geographical locations and weather patterns?*
- *What might be the causes to the higher temperatures that this map might reveal?*
- *What would be the most desirable place to leave in the world in terms of the consistently high quality of weather?*
- *Compare the weather across at least five major cities in China. What can you observe?*
- *What other data would be useful to have on this map?*
- *Are there any design features you think could be effectively integrated in this map to make it more effective (e.g., winds, air pollution, web cams and blog data from various locations)?*

Rather than providing ready-made answers, we should engage students in experiences where they arrive at these answers themselves. However, this process is not arbitrary, rather, it is carefully planned and managed by a teacher whose role in the process is that of a learning designer and a facilitator or learning. That process deploys data, information, knowledge, tools and philosophies of a specific discipline. How disciplines arrive at knowledge differs and is based on their underlining philosophical understanding of what are constituted truths, and how such truths are generated. However, without going any further into this philosophical debate, let us return to our main focus in this book and discuss data display resources.

Important
A learning activity should engage learners to conduct research, work with data and create information, most desirably, by using digital representational technology to process and organize data in useful formats. Learners should be provided with an opportunity to use tools, data, information and knowledge, struggle with complexities, and think and innovate within and across disciplines.

Data display resources are interactive and visual digital resources for learning that allow a learner to collect, access and work with data they need in order to complete their learning activities. More effective data display resources do not simply display data that we want learners to work with. These might not be just interfaces for data access and interrogation, as commonly found in tools for accessing and interrogating data (such as in the "Real-time Air Quality Index Visual Map In Task A). Rather, these might include the following features that specifically have the intension to extend learning:

- Realistic contexts where data are collected (e.g., data collected from a number of simulated patients in a hospital who display certain symptoms);
- Tools used to collect and present data (e.g., measuring instruments such as hearth rate, body temperature and blood pressure);
- Data record, display and organization features (e.g., records with tables and graphs where data from multiple patients are displayed);
- Some information (declarative knowledge) about key tools and properties might be included, or learners pointing to other resources (e.g., information display resources); and
- Some analytical features might be included (e.g., how will blood pressure change under specific condition), although this is more characteristic for conceptual resources.

Data should be presented in an authentic way as they emerge from a realistic context. Learners might learn not just about the relationship and properties of that data, but also where data originates, how they are collected and analysed, and how decisions are made based on that data. Data might take many forms, such as numerical measurements, observational data and interview statements, and can be presented authentically with the use of various modalities supported by contemporary representational technologies, such as text, numbers, colours, shapes, audio, video, animation, etc.

Data might be internally stored within a digital resource. This is usually the case when there is a limited and static dataset. Also, data can be generated within the resource based on a learners' interaction (e.g., throwing a dice and recoding instances of resulting number, or randomly displayed data of water discharge of a river). Alternatively, data can be accessed from external databases via a network. This is the case when we want learners to access data from larger and dynamic databases, whether managed by ourselves or by others, or commercial and non-commercial sources on the Internet. Also, this might be the case when we want learners to collect real-time data from instruments at remote locations accessible via the Internet (e.g., environmental monitoring instruments, remotely-operated telescope/microscope, or web cams). Contemporary technologies allow, so-called, 'mashing' which enables data from multiple sources to be mixed and presented in a single resource (e.g., mashing weather data from AccuWether and similar sources with Google Maps from Google, to deliver a bland of data including geographical locations and weather parameters such as temperature, humidity, wind direction and strength, and rainfall). Technologies, such as Google, provide an Application Programming Interface (API) that allows their data to be accessed and reused.

Readers might arrive at the conclusion that such a kind of digital resource for learning is useful only in cases where we deal with hard data (e.g., numerical data that can be manipulated mathematically or statistically), such as in mathematics and science subjects. However, data exist across different disciplines such as in humanities and even languages, and it might be largely available in various soft forms such as interview data, opinions, records, sounds, blog posts, images and videos. Context and tools for the collection and access to different forms of data will differ. These tools are authentic to specific disciplines.

How data are presented within a data display resource is an important factor. Even quantitative data might not be always displayed as numbers alone. For example, the size of a geometric object such as a circular and rectangular bar can correspond to a numeric value; values can be represented through pitch of a sound, or positive and negative values can be represented through blue and red colours. However, usually, these forms of representations are used to supplement raw data or some parameters that are defined based on that data. In the case of a data display resource, focus is on providing learners with authentic data, so that they can organize, manipulate and analyse and use emerging generalizations and abstractions when working on their learning activities. With differences with conceptual resources, data display resources are less concerned with the relationships existing between different aspects of data. It is a learning activity that drives learners to extract these if needed.

> **Activity 6.2**
> *The UK Department of Transport provides a map with a data count at different count points across the country:*
> http://www.dft.gov.uk/traffic-counts/cp.php.
> *Examine the interface to the data, as well as the data provided. Think about and describe what kind of activity you could set up for learners to work with this data and use it to develop certain knowledge.*

6.2 Examples of Data Display Resource Designed Specifically for Learning Purposes

The examples presented in Tasks A and B have been developed for general use by anyone interested in accessing the data presented. In this part of the chapter, some examples specifically designed for learning will be presented.

The example in Fig. 6.1 shows a data display resource which presents a scenario (in a form of an image of a lake), allowing a learner to collect water parameters at different locations. After choosing a location on the lake, a learner selects various

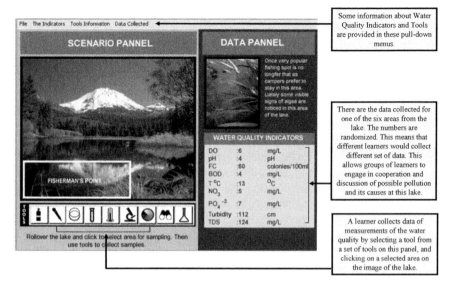

Fig. 6.1 'Water pollution' data display resource

tools to collect measurements such at temperature, fecal coliform, total dissolved solids, level of phosphorous, acidity level, and turbidity. Learners collect these measurements at different locations on the lake. Once data are captured, they are recorded in the resources and displayed in a summary table that allows a learner to compare data from across different locations on the lake. Descriptive information provided within this environment briefs learners about various tools and data included in the data display resource.

An activity might require learners to solve a problem based on specific data extracted from the scenario. As a more immediate step, learners would engage in extracting data from the resources and reorganizing externally for analysis. The data are randomized within possible data-ranges, allowing different learners to work on different combinations of data leading to a variety of conclusions. For example, if a level of dissolved oxygen is low, and level of phosphorous high, this might indicate an algae problem. The following figure shows a screen from the "Water Quality" data display digital resource for learning.

Another example shown in Fig. 6.2 is from a business course with a focus on Cost Accounting. This digital resource for learning shows a floor plan of a virtual company. Learners can navigate different departments of this virtual factory, including general department, administration department, marketing department, supplies department, assembly department, and finishing department, and access data such as, the department's sections and operations, staff and their salaries, various expenditures such as electricity, material requisitions and costs, machines used in processes and their costs, usage of electricity and required operators, and

6.2 Examples of Data Display Resource Designed Specifically ...

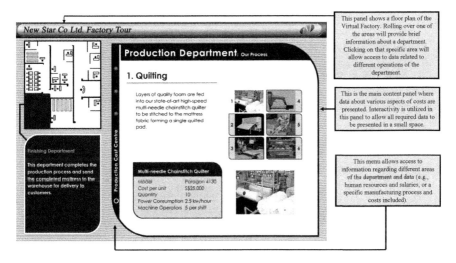

Fig. 6.2 'Virtual factory' data display resource

production output. Learners can use these data to complete a variety of tasks such as to develop a cost information flow diagram, depicting the providers and users of cost information within the organization, and a cost analysis table, and based on these, propose approaches to more effective cost accounting.

We will make note about one more example of a data display resource. This particular resource was developed to allow learners to work with data, which they collected in real-time based on the opinions of their classmates. The resource was developed for postgraduate learners of an education related program. The learners were largely practicing schoolteachers. The main idea was for these learners to examine their collective thinking about the roles of technology in teaching and learning, and through this, to be engaged in identifying conceptual limitations that affect effective technology integration. The students were presented with data that originates from their own community and were collected in real-time. They were presented with the resources shown in Fig. 6.3.

This resource presents two sets of questions relevant to technology in education, based on two perspectives, as follows:

- From a perspective of technology (e.g., Internet, collaborative tools and multimedia content), to indicate the extent to which they see specific affordance as useful for their practice, by dragging the slider from 0 [not useful] to 5-[highly useful]; and
- From a perspective of their own practice (e.g., lecture, demonstration and practice), indicate the extent to which technology can help them in their work, by dragging a slider from 0 [technology is not useful], to 5 [technology can completely replace a teacher in this activity].

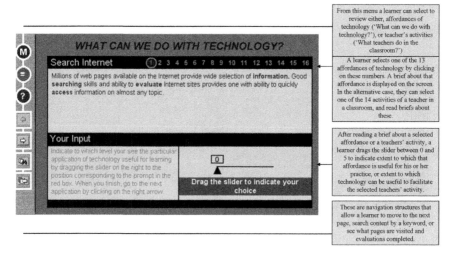

Fig. 6.3 'What can we do with technology?' digital resource for learning

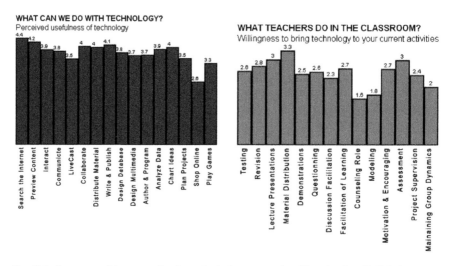

Fig. 6.4 Summary of data emerging from the 'what can we do with technology?' digital resource for learning

All the data collected from students (across different classes) are summarized in the two graphs as shown below. This can be already considered to be information generated based on the raw data collected (Fig. 6.4).

The central idea of this experience is to initiate students' critical reflection and discourse about what they observe from the data, and how their own thinking contributes to this collective understanding. Learners can be engaged in further activities, such as, to discuss in a forum and present their view about issues that affect technology integration has in schools, and apply certain statistics to identify statistically significant relationships. An activity might also require students to develop a proposal for their schools about the directions for adoption of technology, or develop an intervention to help teachers to transform aspects of their thinking.

In this specific example, we can see how a data display resource might be based on non-existent data, that is, data that emerges in the context of a learners' activity and use of a digital resource for learning. From the perspective of procedural knowledge, students, in this particular instance, learn about the procedure of collecting data to inform education leadership decisions.

With these examples, we see three different ways of how data can be presented to learners. In the first example, hard data (random numerical values for various water quality indicators) are presented. Data are extracted by learners through specific tools used in the process. Data sources are generated based on underlining mathematical logic. Alternatively, data can be extracted from data sources on the Internet. In the second example, there are a bland of soft and hard data presented through the interface. The data are embedded in the resource and displayed based on the learners' exploration. Learners place attention and use various pieces of data as directed by a learning activity. In this case, learners do not use any specific tools, as data are not measurable, rather they are specified.

Activity 6.3
It is not always easy to distinguishing between different forms of digital resources for learning. Carefully examine the "Digital Multimeter" digital resource for learning illustrated in Fig. 6.5. Attend to the following questions:

- *What would be the main purpose of this resource?*
- *What kind of data are available in this resource?*
- *How are the data collected?*
- *How does the resource support data organization and analysis?*
- *Given it all, do you think this digital resource for learning will identify more as a conceptual representation or a data display?*
- *Do you have any recommendations for the improved design of this digital resource for learning?*

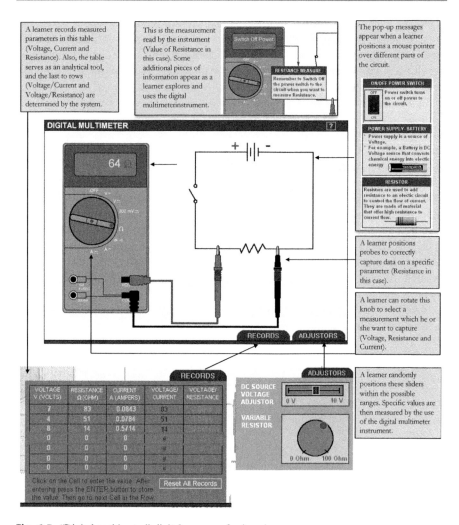

Fig. 6.5 "Digital multimeter" digital resource for learning

6.3 Designing Data Display Resources

The design of a data display digital resources for learning might occur in the way as explained below. This description is provided as a guide, however, as noted in the design of other forms of digital resources for learning, the process can vary in complexity depending on whether you are designing it, for example, for your own teaching, for your colleagues, for other teachers in your institution, or for an external client and as a part of a larger project development team. In some cases, storyboarding, flowcharting, evaluation and various project documents might be

6.3 Designing Data Display Resources

needed and signed off before actual production. In other cases, the process can be completed in a more casual manner. Nevertheless, in here, some key conceptual issues related to the design of data displays are presented.

- *Start by identifying a topic/concept*—Usually, this is determined based on some concept from a curriculum that could be developed through a learning activity involving working with data (conceptual knowledge), and/or where learning of a procedure involved in working with data is required to be learnt (procedural knowledge). A topic can be identified by a designer or requested by a client. The purpose of a data display digital resource could be to support the development of conceptual knowledge, or even to support the development of procedural knowledge involved in data capture, collection, management and analysis. Let us use the data display digital resource for learning featured in Fig. 6.1 as an example to illustrate this process. The topic/concept selected for the design and development in this example is "Water Quality" and associated parameters (represented by data) that determines it.
- *Determine data-set to be used in the resource*—This might include:

  - Data from a real source (e.g., collected by distant measuring instruments and probes or provided by data providers in real-time);
  - Real data collected by learners and fed to the resource;
  - Data collected by sensors and instruments which are attached or are a part of a device used for delivery;
  - An artificial data set created by a designer based on certain regularities;
  - Data that emerges through the use of a digital resource, e.g., by multiple users providing input to data set based on their interaction and feedback; or
  - An algorithm for mathematically-driven generation of data based on interaction with the resource.

- In the case of "Water Quality" data display resources, an artificial data set is integrated into the resource and includes parameters/indicators and data generated by a mathematical algorithm randomly within possible ranges. These numeric data include the following:

  - Dissolved Oxygen (DO);
  - pH;
  - Fecal Coliform (FC);
  - Biochemical Oxygen Demand (BOD);
  - Temperature (C);
  - Total Phosphates (PO_4);
  - Nitrates (NO_3-);
  - Turbidity (T); and
  - Total Dissolved Solids (TDS).

- *Identify a scenario/context to be used to present data to learners*—In the case of the "Water Quality" example, the context is a scenario of a lake. Learners can collect data from various parts of this lake. A certain level of authenticity is always useful as it informs learners about a real context within which specific data emerges.
- *Identify tools needed for the data collection (if any tool is needed)*—Each of the data are collected by a specific instrument or extracted by specific test, and in the case of the "Water Quality" example, these include the following:

  - Accu Vac Check for Dissolved Oxygen (DO);
  - Hach Pcket Pal Ph Meter for pH;
  - Colisan EasyGel Test for Fecal Coliform (FC);
  - 5 h BOD Test for Biochemical Oxygen Demand (BOD);
  - Thermometer for Temperature (C);
  - Model NI Test for Nitrates (NO_3-);
  - Model PO Test for Total Phosphates (PO_4);
  - TurbiMeter for Turbidity (T); and
  - TDS Meter for Total Dissolved Solids (TDS).

- In the case of the "Water Quality" data display resource, learners simply select a tool (one of the icons below the lake scenario), and by clicking on a specific target area, they record a measurement/data. The data collected from a specific location of the lake are displayed immediately on the bottom right part of the screen, and stored in the emerging data record (see Fig. 6.1). Some designs of data displays might include simulated instruments and tests so that learners can be exposed to their operation and use.
- *Determine level of analysis if any, and presentation of data (textual, numeric, or/and graphical)*—A certain level of data analysis and representation can be included in the data display resource, although the main purpose is to provide data to learners to analyse within their learning activity. For example, data collected as numbers might be represented as graphical objects (e.g., as a bars of a bar chart, or as blue and red colours for positive and negative values). Some level of data analysis can be included (e.g., a pie chart showing proportions and percentages), however, almost always, conclusions/generalizations and abstractions are left open for learners to make, test and refine through their activity. In the case of the "Water Quality" data display resource, data collected are organized and presented in a summary table, making it easier for learners to engage in further analysis and generalization (see Fig. 6.6).
- *Determine any declarative information to include in the resource*—Some declarative information might be useful to include in the data display resource. Usually, this includes information about parameters, procedures and tools. In the context of the "Water Quality" data display resources, learners can access declarative information related to each of the parameter and tools. Figure 6.7 demonstrates how declarative information is included in the "Water Quality" data display resource.

6.3 Designing Data Display Resources

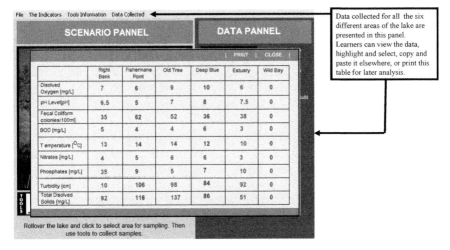

Fig. 6.6 Display of data collected within the "water quality" digital resource for learning

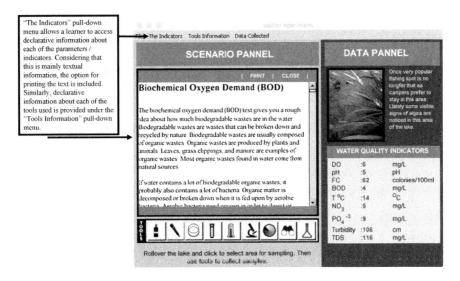

Fig. 6.7 Declarative information displayed within the "water quality" resource

- *Design and prototype data display resource*—once all the necessary components are collected, and ideas are clear, a prototype, either a functional one developed with a final development tool (e.g., Flash, HTM5 or App Inventor), or a mock-up of the screens developed with something easier, such as, PowerPoint, can be created and evaluated. Once feedback from the evaluation is collected, a final decision can be articulated in the design before the full production is carried out. Evaluation can focus on the subject matter content, data completeness, accuracy and presentation, interface design and presentation, language, appropriateness for learners, etc.

Activity 6.4
The Air Quality Index (AQI), also called Air Pollution Index (API), informs the public of the local level of air pollution, and the potential health risk it could impose. People use the AQI to help them make decisions, for example, on outdoor activities.

A network of air quality monitoring stations across countries has been set up to measure concentrations of pollutants in the air at fixed time intervals. The national air quality standards will usually be used as the reference for the AQI (e.g., by US Environmental Agency). Some countries, like South Africa, Canada and Hong Kong use a variation of this index. For example, Hong Kong introduced an Air Quality Health Indicator (AQHI) which considers various statistics explicated from actual intervention by health agencies in dealing with people affected by poor air quality (see "Overview of Hong Kong's Air Quality Health Index" at https://aqicn.org/faq/2015-06-03/overview-of-hong-kongs-air-quality-health-index/ *for more information about how this is calculated).*

Air pollutants commonly used in AQI include: Nitrogen dioxide (NO_2), Sulphur dioxide (SO_2), Ozone (O_3), Carbon monoxide (CO), suspended particulates smaller than 10 μm in aerodynamic diameter (PM10), and suspended particulates smaller than 2.5 μm in aerodynamic diameter (PM2.5). Some countries also monitor lead (Pb) and visibility (e.g., Australia), and incorporate these into the AQI calculation, while some other countries exclude SO_2 and CO, or O_3 (e.g., China). Calculation of the AQI is usually based on 1-hour, 8-hour, or 24-hour average monitoring data.

World Quality Index project provides data on the air pollutants across the Globe. Access this display at https://aqicn.org/map/world/ *and examine data at various locations.*

In this activity, you should design a data display resource that can be used by learners in activities that leads them to learn about AQI and various air pollution parameters. Consider what aspects of the https://aqicn.org/map/world/ *you can adopt, and how to provide a simplified design that is more relevant for learning. For example, how to integrate an experience of data collection, do you need to integrate any tools, and how to provide more authentic contexts for data collection?*

Here some references for you to study, so that you can understand more about the Air Quality Index:

- *Air Quality Index Wikipedia article (Pay attention to US approach to AQI)* https://en.wikipedia.org/wiki/Air_quality_index
- *A Beginner's Guide to Air Quality Instant-Cast and Now-Cast* https://aqicn.org/faq/2015-03-15/air-quality-nowcast-a-beginners-guide/

You can conduct your own search to find other resources that can help you to understand the AQI and how best to design your digital resource for learning.

Using Digital Resources for Learning in a Learning Activity

7

Learning Outcomes:

- Describe what is a Learning Design;
- Discuss a concept of a human activity in general, and a learning activity more specifically;
- Discuss a concept of tool mediation in a learning activity;
- Identify and select digital resources for learning that can serve as tools in a learning activity; and
- Develop and implement a learning design based on the RASE framework.

7.1 An Idea of a Learning Design

So far, we have discussed different forms of digital resources for learning including: information displays, presentation resources, practice resources, conceptual representations, and data display resources. How can these digital resources for learning be used in the most effective way in teaching? In this chapter, we will explore some theoretical issues and practical aspects of the design of educational activities for the utility of digital resources for learning.

> **Important**
> Teaching suitably for today and the future enables learners to construct knowledge for themselves, learn, not just information and procedures, but

> also develop deep conceptual knowledge that supports theoretical thinking and develop new literacies.

As readers might notice, in this book, the author argues that traditional education practices need to change in order for teaching to be appropriate, given the developments and the needs of the contemporary world. Teaching suitably for today and the future is what enables learners to construct knowledge for themselves; to learn, not just information and procedures, but also develop deep conceptual knowledge that supports theoretical thinking[1]; and in addition to disciplinary content, learn and develop competencies, mindsets and new literacies for living, working, socializing and learning in the modern world. Such teaching, we argue, is learning-centred, rather than traditionally teacher-centred, or even student-centred. A student-centred idea is a way to move teaching practices away from traditional approaches, however, we need to step ahead beyond this, towards the one that gives full recognition to aspects of relevant learning theories, understanding of how humans learn, and how human knowledge is used in application and innovation. A teacher's role in such teaching is to design learning experiences for learners, and this plan for the achievement of learning outcomes we call a *learning design* (Churchill et al. 2013). A learning design is a plan for the engagement of learners in a learning-centred activity where they use resources and work on projects, research, design and explore solutions to problems, and pursue innovations. The foundation of a learner's knowledge are those conceptual forms which learners develop for themselves through learning-centred activities and the use of resources, test through applications, used as a base to construct further knowledge and create innovation. These conceptual forms have personal and socio-cultural history, and are developing along the trajectory of knowledge humanity that has disciplines up to the current stage. In other words, these are resources developed within our culture to mediate our disciplinary and cross-disciplinary activities. These aid our intellectual activities, that is, enable us to engage in theoretical thinking in a way that, for example, a contemporary scientist, an engineer, a medical doctor, an economist or a mathematician does. Conceptual representations might be one of the most important digital resources for learning in this context. However, although certain digital learning resources originated based on a traditional idea of transmission of information from a resource to passive learners (e.g., presentation resources), these still have potential for use in effective learning designs and support the development of conceptual knowledge, in addition to being declarative and procedural.

---

[1]Theoretical thinking refers to "the development of deep structural strategies, the children's growing understanding of basic features and relationships laying not at the surface of the learning material, but demanding abstraction from the phenomenon and penetrating into the substance" (Hedegaard and Lompscher 1999, p. 13).

7.1 An Idea of a Learning Design

Before we continue a discussion about how to develop a learning design and use of digital resources for learning in that context, we will examine some key theoretical assumptions and ideas. These relate to a concept of a learning design to the following: (a) a human activity in general; (b) a learning activity as a specific form of a human activity; and (c) digital resources as mediating tools used in learning activities.

7.2 A Concept of a Human Activity

Teaching and learning are separate, but connected forms of human activities. Engeström (1987) articulated a general representational framework of any human activity (see Fig. 7.1). An activity can be as small as making a cup of tea, or as large as national education. According to this framework, a subject in an activity transforms an object into an outcome. For example, a builder transforms bricks, mortar, wood material, roof tiles, armature, etc., into a house. As a human acts on nature to transform it, and in order to deal with challenges and reach an outcome, he or she deploys various tools. An outcome, in our example of a builder, is the final house being sold and profit to be made from it, while tools are, for example, a blue print, reference documents, Construction Calculator App, a mortar mixer, measuring instruments, a wheelbarrow, a saw, a hammer, a power drill, a trowel, a brick jointer, a plumb and a chalk line.

> **Important**
> In an activity, learners learn from an experience by receiving feedback from the environment they are acting upon.

In an activity, a subject and an object are in a relationship where "… the subject is transforming the object, while the properties of the object penetrate into the subject and transform him or her" (Kutti 1997, p. 32). In other words, a subject learns from an experience by receiving feedback from the environment he is acting upon. This process is mediated by tools (or supporting artefacts and resources) whose properties

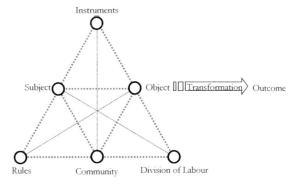

Fig. 7.1 A representational framework of an activity (modified from Engeström 1987)

and uses might also penetrate into a subject and transform him or her. For example, a number of studies have investigated how the integration of technology in teaching lead to the transformation of teachers and their pedagogical practices (e.g., Hardman 2005; Glover et al. 2015; Murphy and Manzanares 2008; Peruski and Mishra 2004). Often, a subject in an activity collaborates, and is not an "…unaided individual divorced from a social group and from supporting artifacts" (Nardi 1997, p. 67). When an activity involves collaboration amongst multiple individuals, there is always a division of labour. In addition, an activity is carried out according to certain rules, standards, requirements and framing parameters. Tools, community, division of labour and rules, are both enabling and constraining meaning that these all mediate goal-directed actions that can be executed within an activity.

For example, school education is one large and complex activity system with a community composed of teachers, principals and deputies, administrative staff, councillors, heads of departments, laboratory technicians, etc., all working together on transforming objects of their activity (learners) into an outcome (school graduate). All these members of the community execute different actions essential in completing this transformation (e.g., someone teaches mathematics, someone social science, while someone takes care of learner administration). Within this community, there is a division of labour (for example, principal and teachers do different things and have different powers) and there are rules (e.g., curriculum and assessment requirements). Often, *contradictions* arise in an activity between different nodes (e.g., subject and rules, or community and division of labour), and these contradictions cause changes in the activity itself (see Lim 2002; Murphy and Manzanares 2008). Contradictions might emerge with other activities that in some way relate or affect the current activity (e.g., a tool making activity). Thus, human activities, in general, are usually under continuous change.

7.3 A Learning Activity and a Learning Design

Learning activity is a specific kind of human activity (see Davydov 1999). It is unique in that it is characterized by voluntary learning—a subject of the activity is a learner, its motive is learning, and the object is the material to be learnt (or 'appropriated' in Davidov's term) through transformation into an outcome. For Hedegaard and Lompscher (1999), learning activity is "directed towards the acquisition of societal knowledge and skills through their individual re-production by means of special actions upon *learning objects*" (p. 12).

Relevant literature suggests that an outcome of a learner's activity should be the development of '*theoretical thinking*' (Chaiklin 1999; Davydov 1999; Hedegaard and Lompscher 1999). Theoretical thinking is important for learners because "development of creative abilities, initiatives, self-understanding, and, finally, the development of their personality depend on it" (Davydov 1999, p. 132). The development of theoretical thinking is achieved through activities "related to the conceptual foundations of the subject matter being taught, which in turn are related to the societal traditions within which this knowledge was originally developed" (Chaiklin 1999, p. 189). For Davydov (1999), to design an activity which supports the

7.3 A Learning Activity and a Learning Design

development of theoretical thinking "one needs to use such material that the children could perform the respective transformations and make object-related or mental experiments with the material" (p. 128). Furthermore, Davydov (1999) suggests that, often, learning does not occur because "textbooks and methodical recommendations for the instruction of particular school subjects do not meet the requirement of the very learning material and the intended way of how to introduce the subject into the teaching/learning process" (p. 130). Hence, as Chaiklin (1999) suggests, in order to realize the development of theoretical thinking "the key is to have a significantly good analysis of the subject matter, such that one can create a *framework of learning task* within which variations in pupil motives and motivation can find expression" (p. 188).

A motive for a subject (a learner) in a learning activity is to achieve learning outcomes specified by a curriculum, or perhaps, to achieve a high grade in exams (an outcome). However, in practice, how many learners are motivated to learn? This represents one of the key challenges for educators—how to motivate learners, and how to sustain that motivation and engagement throughout learning. What might be a solution to this problem? How to design activities that are engaging and sustain the motivation of learners?

In many human activities other than a learning activity, learning emerges as a special component of this experience (i.e., learning is incidental). For Engeström (1987), learning might occur in the context of at least three kinds of activities other than a learning activity: work, science and art. Learning outcomes per se are not a motive behind these activities—rather, a motive may be, for example, to answer an interesting inquiry (science), design computer graphics (art), or make money for living (work). Engeström (1987) illustrates this by using an example where a child is allowed to go outside and play once he completed his homework. In this case, a motive for an activity and learning is play, not learning.

As it is a challenge for teachers to create learning activities where learners are motivated to learn, a strategy we call here '*masking*' is proposed as a solution. It means that we can design activities that on the surface are not learning activities, but are designed with an intention to result in learning, such as projects, problem solving and inquiries. These activities are learning-centred from the point of intention of their designers (teachers). Such activities make it possible for learners to learn with tools they use while transforming objects (materials) into an outcome (artefact), as well, from the development of an outcome. Often, in such a learning design, learners as subjects of an activity create learning artefacts (outcome of an activity) in formats such as (see Jonassen and Rohrer-Murphy 1999):

- *Physical artefacts*—e.g., a robot or a cardboard model;
- *Soft artefacts*—e.g., a computer-based model or a multimedia presentation; and
- *Cognitive artefacts*—e.g., a solution to a problem, or an idea or a theory based on inquiry.

In these activities, educational resources (including digital resources for learning) are tools, rather than material to be transformed into an outcome (as would be the case in a learning activity), that is, the use of tools and transformation lead to incidental learning. A plan for executing such an activity we refer to as 'a learning design'. From a teachers' perspective, these activities remain to be teaching activities, that is, a teacher is a subject of activity, a learning design is his or her tool, and he or she transforms an object (learners' knowledge) into an outcome (achievement of a learning outcome). Therefore, teaching, in this context, is learning-centred. So, when we talk about a learning design, we think of a plan developed by a teacher to serve as a tool in his/her teaching activity on one side, and on the other, from a learners' perspective, a framework for an activity where learners are engaged and motivated to participate. A learning design can be implemented in various environments, inside or outside of a class, online, blended mode, MOOC (Massive open online course), and even as a self-learning module.

> **Important**
> 'Masking' is a strategy where we design activities that on surface are not learning activities, but are designed with an intention to result in learning, such as projects, problem solving and inquiries. These activities are learning-centred from the point of intention of their designers (teachers).

Here is one example that illustrates a learning design. School learners in their mathematics and history class (cross-disciplinary engagement) are engaged in an activity to create models of Egyptian pyramids in Giza near Cairo. Three groups of learners in a class create one of the three different pyramids at that site: Menkaure, Khafre and Khufu pyramids. The fourth group of learners prepare a model of a terrain at Giza where these three models of pyramids once constructed are to be positioned. The fifth group of learners are "Khufu Pharaoh's advisors" who must select and illustrate a set of objects that the pharaoh will take into a pyramid for the 'afterlife'. This group will also prepare a hieroglyphic message of Pharaoh's legacy upon his death. Each group will have to create a small display board with an explanation/illustration of their artefact. This board will be placed on the final model of the site at Giza. The groups will then present their experiences and the final artefact to other classes, and showcase it during the school's open house day.

Each of the groups works on its own part of this project. This activity structure creates a community whose groups and members have specific roles and tasks (division of labor). The groups' tasks are mediated by certain rules that exist. Some rules are integral to their tasks, e.g., a model of a pyramid should show a cross section allowing an inner view. Rules might be imposed by other activities, e.g., pyramids must be designed according to a scaled measurement imposed by the size of the final site where they will be displayed or, objects that Pharaoh might take with him are subject to the size and capacity of a pyramid.

A variety of resources is used in these activities. Most of the learning occurs through the use and application of these resources, as well as through social engagement, decisions and action taken with others. Some are digital learning resources from websites (e.g., http://www.pbs.org/wgbh/nova/pyramid/) where learners explore information about ancient Egyptian culture and history (an information display resource or a presentation resource, depending on its design); a satellite image of Giza from Google Earth (an information resource); interactive resources allowing the exploration of rules which exist in similar triangles (a concept representation resource); a calculator used to calculate scaled-down measurements; or a mathematics e-book used as reference in relation to the construction of polyhedral objects (a presentation resource). Some tools are technical, such as scissors and drawing instruments. Technology-based tools might also be used to create a virtual model to be used as references for the creation of physical models (e.g., Google SketchUp).

What is a motive for learners to participate in this project? They might be motivated to participate because of a particular purpose, e.g., to participate in an inter-schools competition and win, or to provide a useful model for a local travel agency to brief potential tourist travellers about pyramids in Egypt and, in this way, acquire a donation for the school's sport club from the agency, or simply because the activity gives them play time. However, aligning any outcome with the motive of each member of a group is always difficult to achieve. This is something that teachers need to monitor during such kinds of activities. For Kutti (1997), an object and a motive themselves undergo changes through an activity and they might only reveal themselves in the process of doing. A teacher might deploy a variety of supporting strategies to deal with this challenge.

For us in this book, we see theoretical thinking in a discipline to be strongly related and dependent upon conceptual knowledge. Accordingly, we place emphasis on the usefulness of conceptual representations resources, as representations of disciplinary conceptual tools, and a special form of interactive and visual digital resources for learning. Technology opens the opportunity for design, development and delivery of interactive visual material for the effective manipulation and exploration by learners engaged in an activity which results in the development of conceptual knowledge required for theoretical thinking. We concur with Chaiklin (1999) that deep subject matter analysis is essential for learning design and the design of tools that would permit this to happen. This kind of analysis demands good subject matter expertize and understanding of the ways in which kernels of a subject matter evolved historically, and how learners can reproduce through an activity this knowledge and experience. We hope that our classification of digital learning resources will contribute to be a resolution of this problem. However, importantly, we do not see digital resources as learning objects of a learning activity. Rather, we see these as tools prescribed by a learning design which the learner uses during their activity. In this context, we would like to emphasize some important ideas about tools and how these connect to learning.

Important
Deep subject matter analysis is essential for learning design and of digital resources for learning. Digital resources are not objects of a learning activity. Rather, these are tools prescribed by learning design which learners use during their activity.

7.4 Learning Resources and Tool Mediation

Humans have developed and used tools throughout history to extend their own intellectual and physical capabilities. These tools are 'crystallized' social experience and cultural knowledge developed through human history (Kaptelinin 1997; Kutti 1997). Human activities, in general, include the conscious use of tools, and are outcome directed. In their mediating role, tools create connections between humans and the world (Nardi 1997). For Jonassen (1978), some "species of animals have discovered tools, but have been unable to conceive needs to construct tools or incorporate tools into their culture" in a way that humans do, because humans are conscious and motivated organisms which construct their subjectivity while adjusting to, and acting upon, their objective world. Tools enable us to carry on with otherwise impossible activities, e.g., flying, cutting through metal or viewing and manipulating micro-biological organisms, Nano-materials and DNA. Tools also amplify our intellectual capacity and make it possible to carry on with activities that are beyond our cognitive abilities, that is, tools mediate and extend our thinking. Engerström (1991, in Kutti 1997) writes that "… humans can control their own behavior—not 'from the inside', on the basis of biological urges, but 'from the outside' using and creating artifacts" (p. 12). For Kaptelinin (1997), tool mediation leads to "…the formation of 'functional organ,' the combination of natural human abilities with the capacities of external components—tools—to perform a new function or to perform an existing one more efficiently" (p. 109). Therefore, the use of tools "… shapes the way people act and, through the process of internalization, greatly influence the nature of mental development" (Kaptelinin 1997, p. 109). Kutti (1997) divides tools into material/physical tools and tools for thinking, while for Kaptelinin, tools are "external (like hammer or scissors) and internal (like concepts and heuristics)" (p. 109). Tool use leads to "mastery" (Zinchenko 1986, in Nardi 1997) and "internalization" (Leont'ev 1978; Vygotsky 1978) of features of these tools into ones knowledge and cognition. For Vygotsky (1978), tools are not only the means for manipulating reality, but they are also mediators of human cognitive functioning. We can think of tools as physical, but also digital, and conceptual resources (or a combination of these).

Now, if we consider that learning occurs in an activity (incidentally or directly), then resources used in that activity are mediating tools. It applies to digital resources for learning as well. Overall, a subject is using tools to transform an object of an activity and, at the same time, properties of the tool penetrate into the subject's cognition and transform his or her psychological activity. So, a tool can be an internal conceptual resource we use in thinking and making decisions about action upon an object of an activity. In the absence of internal conceptual resources, such tools can be supplied from outside and, in the case of this book, as digital resources for learning. In this sense, a tool is directed at internal cognitive, and indirectly at a physical activity in the world.

7.4 Learning Resources and Tool Mediation

Learning is a phenomenon that qualitatively and quantitatively increases an individual's intellectual capability through the gradual interiorization of external experiences. There are two aspects to consider when discussing learning: (a) learning as an internal cognitive phenomenon, and (b) an activity as an object-oriented, outcome-directed, tool-mediated and external phenomenon. In simpler terms, cognition occurs in the head[2] and an activity occurs in the world, and the two are connected through consciousness (see Jonassen and Rohrer-Murphy 1999). In other words, thinking and doing together create context and experience for learning, therefore, a learning design must focus on what and how will learners' think, and what they will be doing in that context. Consciousness is metaphorically described as a plane where acts of thought take place (see Leont'ev 1978). Vygotsky (1962, 1978) made a distinction between natural psychological functions given to us by nature (e.g., memory, thinking, or imagination) and higher psychological functions, essentially socio-cultural in their origin (e.g. inner speech, formation of concepts, mathematical operations or theoretical thinking). For Vygotsky (1978), human cognitive activity is mediated by signs. A sign is an artificial, self-generated, second order stimulus that for Vygotsky, "transfers the psychological operation to higher and qualitatively new forms and permits humans, by the aid of extrinsic stimuli, to control their behavior from outside" (p. 40). The sign acts as a tool of a psychological activity and, for Vygotsky (1962, 1978), the use of tools and their subsequent interiorization, contribute to the development of higher psychological functions.[3] Interiorized signs mediate the higher psychological functions and, the use of external tools might lead to 'cognitive residue' or resources that can serve such purposes (that is, as a mediating sign). This interiorization is not cognitive mapping or copying of an external activity and tools; rather, it is achieved through the internal reconstruction of certain elements of external experiences into acts of thought. Higher psychological functions do not replace natural psychological functions, but are developed upon them, not as natural or biological, but as 'cultural extensions.' In Vygosky's terms, scientific evidence suggests that the human cognitive system has not changed biologically over the last few thousand years. So, how is it that today, we are smarter, able to develop machines and theories, create technologies and solve, for example, complex mathematical, medical, and engineering problems, in particular, rapidly since the beginning of the 20th century? The answer lies in the availability of conceptual tools that not just supplement our thinking and inner speech, but also our imagination and creativity.

> **Important**
> Use of tools and their subsequent interiorization, contribute to the development of higher psychological functions. Interiorized aspects of tools mediate

---

[2]There is also concepts of distributed cognition, which holds that thinking is distributed across the individuals and artifacts.

[3]Vygotsky (1978) emphasizes that psychological activity is not limited to use of tools and signs only—other issue, such as social interaction, play further roles.

> the higher psychological functions, and might lead to 'cognitive residue' or resources that can serve such mediating purposes in further learning and activities.

We have already established that where cognitive resources are limited, external tools might mediate an activity, and make it possible for us to overcome our limitations in respect to the achievement of outcomes. This would allow individuals to perform tasks that are beyond their current developmental level, while internalization of these tools might potentially lead to a new 'zone of proximal development' being reached (Vygotsky 1978). However, this interiorization will occur only if tools are principally designed and used to serve this purpose. Thus, much attention in the author's work in this book is given to the design and use of concept representation resources as the most suitable form of digital resources for such learning purposes.

Representational technologies open a spectrum of opportunities, or affordances for design, development and the implementation of digital learning resources which can serve as mediating tools. Furthermore, as Salomon et al. (1991) suggest, technology tools offer the opportunities for individuals in partnerships that increases the overall intellectual capacity of this joint system (*a functional organ*). Technology is not only an extension to the body, but it is also an extension to the mind, that is, it is a tool that can extend the limits of our intellectual capacity. Kutti (1997) suggests that technology provides other supporting functions in an activity. These supporting functions "…are directed not towards manipulating or transforming the object but making the activity run" (p. 35). Technology might be used, for example, to automate some operations, make tools and procedures visible and comprehensible, explicate rules and the division of labour, connect a community in a network, and enable communication and collective actions.

7.5 Learning Design Model and Uses of Digital Resources for Learning

These theoretical foundations present important ideas for a difference to be made in the ways how digital resources for learning are designed and used in learning. Here is a summary of some of the key points, and synthesis of these in a concrete model or a framework for a learning design. In addition to a learning design and design of learning activities, this will also help us to better understand the design of digital resources for learning in a way that they support integration in learning experiences:

- Activity-theoretical perspective places an Activity at the centre of analysis in the articulation of a learning design;

7.5 Learning Design Model and Uses of Digital Resources for Learning

- A teacher's role is to design an activity for learners to engage with when achieving an outcome.[4] The outcome of an activity from a teacher perspective is the achievement of a learning outcome(s). The outcome of an activity from a learner perspective is a physical, digital or a conceptual artefact to be produced for some meaningful purpose;
- The further role of a teacher is to identify and prescribe Resources (including digital resources for learning) which serve as mediating tools in an activity;
- The achievement of learning outcomes occurs incidentally in an activity, partly through resource mediation. Changes in the artefact (outcome of an activity) cause discourse, reflection and the reuse of resources, and these contribute to the achievement of learning outcomes as well;
- An activity might include group work (division of labour), collaboration (community), and framing parameters (rules). These are both, framing and supporting factors. In addition, other activities of learners (parallel activities) might have an impact on learning (e.g., learning activities in other subjects);
- The outcome of an activity, that is an artefact produced, should be evaluated by a learner, a teacher and/or community of participating learners (Evaluation). Feedback emerging from evaluation can provide a further mediating tool for learning. Furthermore, an important aspect of mediation can be achieved through the inclusion of supporting resources and strategies (Support). Support is required to ensure that learners are provided help, and where possible with strategies to independently, or in collaboration with other learners, effectively utilize resources and solve emerging difficulties, while Evaluation informs both learners and teachers about progress, and serves as a strategy for understanding what else needs to be done in order to ensure learning outcomes are achieved.

Based on these, four aspects of a learning design emerge as prominent: (a) an *Activity* that has an outcome; (b) *Resources*, or tools whose features when interiorized through a learning experience, in addition to the experience itself, change learners' knowledge; (c) *Support*, which might be essential for individual learners and communities during the implementation of a learning design; and (d) *Evaluation* of artefacts produced by learners in the activity, and timely provision of feedback and further ideas for its revision and improvement. Hence, our proposed model of a learning design contains four key elements: Resources, Activity, Support and Evaluation, and we call this learning design model the *RASE*. See Fig. 7.2 for visual representation and a summary of the RASE Learning Design model.

---

[4]This book does not argue that all teachers should produce digital resources for learning in their own. This job might be left to professional technology developers to accomplish. However, teachers might be the ones articulating what digital resources should be produced, and developing a blue prints or storyboards for implementation.

Fig. 7.2 The RASE learning design model

7.5.1 Resources

Resources include (a) content resources (e.g., digital resources for learning, textbooks, lecture presentations), (b) material (e.g., chemicals for an experiment, paint and canvas), and (c) instruments and software that learners use when working on their activity (e.g., laboratory tools, brushes, calculators, rulers, statistical analysis software, word processing software). In addition to digital resources for learning, there are various software tools that learners can use in an activity, e.g., a Mind Mapping tool such as MindMeister, image/video editing tool such as iMovie, professional software such as AutoCAD and Mathematica, and model building and experimentation software such as Interactive Physics and Stella. When integrating digital resources in learning design, it should be done in a way that leads learners to learn with, rather than just learn from these resources. Digital resources are mediating tools in an activity, they are not representations to be copied in someone's mind in original format. Rather, tool using experience leads to interiorization that is a reconstruction of the tool-using experience in one's cognition. Since the main purpose of this book is to examine digital resources for learning, we will shift our attention in the remainder of this chapter to other elements of the RASE.

7.5.2 Learning Activity

In general, when we talk about an activity, we are thinking of various kinds of inquiries, problems and projects for learners to work on. An activity provides a focus for learners to engage in an outcome-directed set of actions. Learning

7.5 Learning Design Model and Uses of Digital Resources for Learning

emerges as a part of the process of adaptability to the conditions of the activity, that is, learning is voluntary and directed as an applied strategy towards achieving a particular outcome. An activity provides learners with a context and an experience where learning occurs through tool mediation, collaboration exploration, reflection, testing and understanding emerging ideas, generalizing, abstracting and applying knowledge. Digital resources for learning, such as conceptual representation resources, are mediating tools that a learner uses while completing their activity.

For Jonassen (2000), learning is most effective when it occurs in the context of an activity that engages learners to solve ill-structured, authentic, complex and dynamic problems. These types of problems differ significantly from logical, well-structured problems with a single solution (including logical problems, algorithmic problems, story problems, and rule-using problems). These ill-structured types of problems include: decision making, case study, troubleshooting, diagnosis solution problems, strategic performance tasks, design tasks, and dilemmas, all of which require learners to engage in deep thinking, examination of multiple possibilities, deployment of multiple theoretical perspectives, uses of tools, creation of artefacts, and exploration of possible solutions. Churchill and Hedberg (2008) classify Jonassen's problem types into four categories including application of rules, incidents-based decision making, strategic solution and role taking (see Table 7.1).

Understanding how different types of digital resources for learning support different types of activities can provide useful heuristics for selecting digital resources from repositories and the Internet more generally. In addition, the framework might also be useful for the designers of digital resources in suggesting ones that might be useful to develop. Table 7.2 links different types of digital resources for learning to different types of problems.

Table 7.1 Types of problem activities and their focus (from Churchill and Hedberg 2008)

	Rule-based	Incident-based	Strategy-based	Role-based
Description of the category	Explicate, practice and apply standard procedures and rules in the solution. Learners meaningfully and reflectively apply procedures and processes	Exposure and participation in authentic and realistic events or incidents. The activity require learners to reflect and take decisions based on their responses to events	Explore the strategies employed to achieve goals. Often the strategy options are generated as part of the solution	Participate as a player and participant in a setting that models a real world issue. Learners negotiate, apply judgments experience subrogation and employ multiple perspectives
Type of problem under the category (based on Jonassen 2000)	Logical problems Algorithmic problems Story problems Rule-using problems	Decision making Case study	Troubleshooting Diagnosis solution problems Strategic performance tasks Design tasks	Dilemmas

Table 7.2 Different types of problems and digital resources for learning

Type of LO	Type of an activity			
	Rule-based	Incident-based	Strategy-based	Role-based
Presentation resource	Instruction how to execute certain algorithm (e.g., calculate area of a triangle)[a]	Presentation slides instructing issues to consider when making a decision in relation to an event or incident (e.g., what to do if a driver refuses to produce his or her license)	Description of the strategy and procedure to be used in solving a problem (e.g., how to troubleshoot a faulty computer)	Instruction how to act in a situation requiring an answer to a controversial question (e.g., what to do if a learner with special needs fails to submit an assignment)
Practice resource	A practice resource that allows a learner to repeatedly practice the application of a rule (e.g., calculate circumference of a circle with given diameter)	Practice requiring action based on an emerging event or incident (e.g., select a medication for a patient based on symptoms presented)	Practice that allows a learner to dismantle and assemble a certain system and explore its components (e.g., dismantling and assembling a water pump)	Practice that requires a learner to interact with a virtual character and negotiate a solution (e.g., negotiating court case settlement)
Conceptual representation resource	A representation that enables a learner to construct internal model of a rule to be used in the solution of an algorithmic problem (e.g., representation of how to divide two numbers)	A representation that allows a learner to explore if-than or cause-and-effect scenario (e.g., effect of the spread of birth flu on markets in Asia)	A representation of a concept which guides an expert in diagnosing a problem and proposing solution (e.g., concept of Ohm's Law)	A representation of value system held by an expert that supports his or her judgment (e.g., value system of a movie producer who produced a controversial film)
Information display resource	An illustrated story problem (e.g., James has to go to the airport to meet his father. How long it would take him to get there based on given parameters)	An interactive table of some useful information or a flow graph of decision-making process (e.g., trigonometric table)	Information with a list and description of items (e.g., items required for the interior design of an apartment)	An organized collection of articles (e.g., newspaper clips allowing a learner to explore them, for example, by navigating along a time)

(continued)

7.5 Learning Design Model and Uses of Digital Resources for Learning

Table 7.2 (continued)

Type of LO	Type of an activity			
	Rule-based	Incident-based	Strategy-based	Role-based
Data display resource	A simple real-life scenario that provides few variables that can be captured and used in the rule to solve a problem (e.g., click on a vehicle to capture how fast it is going)	A realistic scenario that provides data that are used to make a decision (e.g., collecting water quality indicators form the lake)	A representation that allows the collection of data from a realistic scenario that shapes the strategy applied in solving a problem (e.g., collecting performance data from a faulty engine)	A scenario that allows a learner to collect the views of different people affected by the situation (e.g., collecting views about the war in Iraq)

[a]These are suggested rather than absolute possibilities

Activity 7.1
The following table displays a list of examples of activities. Complete the rest of this table by describing possible digital resources for learning that can be used to mediate each of the activities listed. You can recommend multiple resources, however, for each of the activities, provide at least one description of an example. If possible, search the Internet and various repositories of digital resources and provide links to those that might be appropriate to mediate these activities.

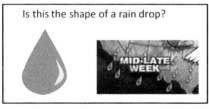

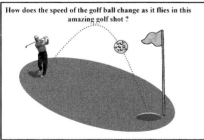

Fig. 7.3 Examples of problem questions

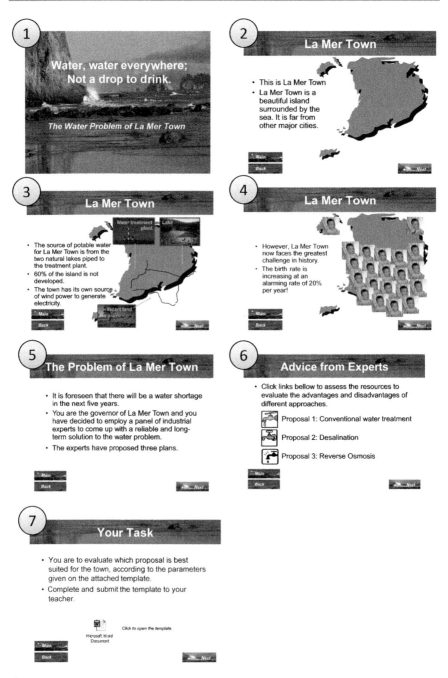

Fig. 7.4 An activity and resources introduced with the aid of a presentation (note slide 6 which provides links to digital resources for learning on three different topics)

7.5 Learning Design Model and Uses of Digital Resources for Learning 149

Example of an activity	*Proposed digital resources for learning*
A design project (e.g., design an experiment to test scientific hypothesis)	
Case study (e.g., a case of how a scientist identified a new physics regularity)	
A problem solving learning task (e.g., minimizing friction in the design of a ski)	
Develop a documentary movie on a specific issue of interest (e.g., GM food pros and cons)	
A poster to promote a controversial scientific issue (e.g., Nuclear energy)	
Planning a science day in your school	
Develop software to control the mechanical transfer of power	
Role-play (e.g., defending the right to conduct science experiments with small animals)	
Create an aerial map of an area surrounding and including the school	
Develop a digital story to promote an artistic creation	
Write a proposal for suitable water treatment technology to overcome a water shortage problem	
Plan a menu for foreign visitors	
Design a model to demonstrate how friction plays an important role in motion	
Create a visual representation (e.g. mind map) that illustrates the rise and fall of Napoleon Bonaparte	
Maintain a blog that describes the benefits of living in a particular country	
Develop a presentation about 21st-century artefacts that will no longer be useful in the Year 3000	
Collect and organize material to support an argument for or against Brexit	

An activity might be simply presented and triggered, as in the examples of problems/inquiries in Fig. 7.3. Further scaffolding/supporting a structure can then be provided to direct learners further (e.g., templates, rubrics and recommended resources).

Alternatively, an activity might be presented as an interesting scenario through the display of a problem or a project with the aid of multimedia to initiate interest, display clear instructions to follow and provide links to resources (see Fig. 7.4).

Activity 7.2
Select one of the examples of the activities presented in Activity 7.1. Now, look at the example of a presentation of an activity illustrated in Fig. 7.4. *For your selected example of an activity from Activity 7.1, describe a scenario*

> *you would recommend to introduce the activity to students and provide links to the resources and supporting templates for completion of the required work. You might use PowerPoint or other tools to develop slides to introduce the activity.*

7.5.3 Support

The purpose of support is to provide learners with essential scaffolding while enabling the development of learning skills and independence. For teachers, one aim is to reduce redundancy and workload. Support might anticipate a learners' difficulty, such as understanding an activity, using tools or working in groups. In addition, teachers must track and record ongoing difficulties and issues that need to be addressed during learning, and share these with learners. Three modes of support are possible: teacher-learner, learner-learner, and learner-resources. Support can take place in a classroom and in-online environments such as through forums, Wikis, Blogs and social networking spaces.

Support can be seen as anticipatory based on foreseen learners' needs or something unforeseen that emerges through learning. Depending on the course, support structures such as FAQs can be planned and implemented in light of anticipated needs. The objective of anticipatory support is to ensure learners have access to a body of resources when they need help, rather than being dependent on asking teachers for help. Here are some specific strategies:

- Build content and materials which form a FAQ Page;
- Create a "How Do I?" or "Help Me" Forum;
- Create a Glossary of course-related terms;
- Use checklists and rubrics for activities; and
- Use other social networking platforms and synchronous tools such as chat.

Overall, support should aim to lead learners to become more independent. Teachers should give frequent, early, positive feedback that supports learners' beliefs that they can do well. Furthermore, learners also need rules and parameters for their work. For example, before learners can ask a teacher for help, they must first ask their classmates through a forum and/or search the Internet for solutions to their problem(s). In this way, learners are expected to take responsibility for their learning and to support other learners in their groups.

7.5.4 Evaluation

An activity should require learners to work on tasks, and develop and produce artefacts that evidence their learning. Outcomes of an activity can be a conceptual artefact (e.g., an idea or a concept presented in a written report), a hard artefact (e.g., a model of an electric circuit), or a soft artefact (e.g., a multimedia report). Artefacts produced by learners should undergo peer and expert review and revision before final submission. This process may also involve learners' presentations and peer/expert feedback. The produced artefacts should be evaluated in a way that learners can reflect upon feedback and take further action towards a more coherent achievement of the learning outcomes.

Evaluation of learning during the semester is an essential part of effective learning-centered teaching practice. Evaluation needs to be formative in order to enable learners to constantly improve their learning. This evidence of learner learning enables the teacher to monitor progress and provide further formative guides to help improve learning achievements. Learners also need to record their progress in completing the tasks set, so they too can monitor their learning and the improvements they make. Rubrics can be provided to enable learners to conduct self-evaluation as well. Rubrics might, for example, play an important role in the learning process to orientate learners to the standards that need to be achieved in their work.

Activity 7.3
Select one of the digital resources for learning you developed previously through the chapters (e.g., atmosphere, protractor or season changes). Propose a learning activity for learners to make use of that digital resource in learning.

7.6 An Example of Digital Resource for Learning Used Within an Activity

A group of school learners were presented with a problem requiring them to identify the height of objects in their school environment, such as, school buildings, lampposts and trees. This challenge was part of a larger cross-curriculum activity that involved learners in designing a small-scale model of their school (which subsequently used it as a miniature set for their digital video projects). The learners worked in small teams and obtained measurements of different objects in their environment in order to construct a model to an appropriate scale. Although they were able to simply use a tape measure to measure parameters, this was not possible with vertical objects such as trees, lampposts and buildings. Divided into small groups, they were given a tape measure to measure the distance from a group member to the object (e.g., a tree) and an inclinometer to measure the angle of elevation from the horizontal plane at a group member's position to the top of an object (see Fig. 7.5). The groups were also provided with a mobile device equipped with a camera feature to collect evidence of their data collection, which they needed for the subsequent presentation of their solutions and approaches.

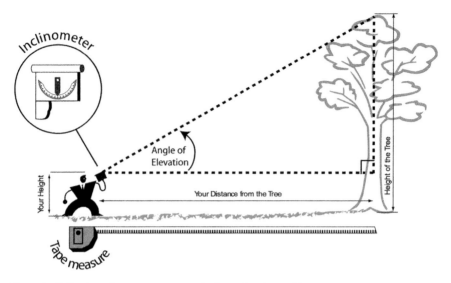

Fig. 7.5 Collection of measurements required to solve the problem

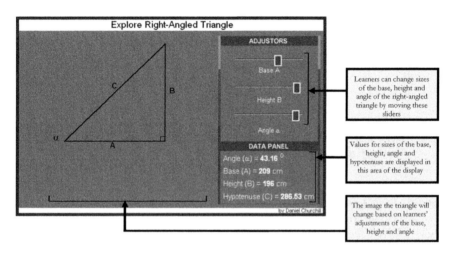

Fig. 7.6 "Exploring right-angled triangle" digital resource for learning

A digital resource for learning used in this project is presented in Fig. 7.6. This digital resource for learning is a conceptual representation called "Explore Right-angled Triangle". This resource could possibly be used in a variety learning activities enabling learners to develop mathematical concepts such as Pythagorean Theorem, similar triangles, trigonometric rules and the rules for calculating missing parameters.

7.6 An Example of Digital Resource for Learning Used Within an Activity

The learners manipulate the values for the base, height and an angle of a triangle, and then examine changes in the value of the hypotenuse by repositioning a set of corresponding sliders. This allows learners to keep the angle constant while changing the sides of the triangle and examining the ratio that exists between the sides. The changes are represented:

- Numerically as numbers relating to the sides and angles of the triangle; and
- Visually as a dynamic drawing of a triangle.

The learners were provided, amongst other resources, with this digital resource for learning. Prior to going into the field, the learners explored this resource via a computer screen. They were told that it would later be helpful during their fieldwork. Their initial exploration of the content was supported by a set of questions and graphical organizers (templates) which directed them to approach this exploration in a systematic way: e.g., to collect some values in a template table, to compare different rows and columns in search of patterns, and build some preliminary generalizations about the concepts represented by the resource. Once the learners moved outside of the classroom to collect the measurements of the objects, some mobile devices with the resources were made available for them to use as a reference tool while they interpreted the situation and explored possible solutions. The solution to the problem of finding heights of tall objects is based on the ratio of the base and height of a triangle that remains constant for any size of right-angled triangle with the same angle of elevation. Groups of learners were encouraged to discuss and share their problem-solving approaches. Once the groups arrived at their solutions, a representative of each group was required to present their solution to the rest of the class. The presentation contained a proposed solution to the problem of calculating the height of tall objects, an approach to the solution was based on the conceptual representation resource and digital photos they collected with the mobile device of the objects that they measured.

Several weeks later, the learners were asked to estimate the values of a ratio of the sides of a right-angled triangle with given sizes of an angle provided to them. They were also asked to recall their experience with the resource used and to explore whether this recall would help them in their estimation. Interesting patterns were observed as the learners begun to employ auxiliary means to help them in this estimation. Some learners sketched triangles on paper. Others used their pens, rulers and other objects as arms of a constructed angle. Some learners used their fingers as arms of an angle in attempting to reconstruct elements of the digital resource in the air in front of their eyes. These behaviours indicated that some form of interaction between mental structures (cognitive residues from the previous activity and interaction with the content of the resource) and physical objects (auxiliary means) were occurring. Aspects of an activity involving the resource were reconstructed as a cognitive resource in a similar way to the way children learn to work with numbers. Vygotsky (1962) observed that when learning to count or perform simple addition or subtraction, young children are likely to use their own fingers as auxiliary means. Children will later begin to hide their hands behind their backs and keep using their fingers to aid the process; the auxiliary means disappears from the visual field but remains physically present. Slowly, children will stop using their fingers, or other auxiliary means and the process will become more internal. Auxiliary means do not disappear, however, through the internalization of an external activity, they begin to operate purely in the mind, that is, they take the form of an internal tool for support of their theoretical thinking.

In the remaining part of this project, learners were constructing their miniature set based on a specified scale. Finally, they were to use their models to construct a short Play-Doh[5] animation. It was observed that some learners frequently accessed the digital resource during the process of construction. In some way, the resource became a useful calculator and a conceptual supplement to learners in this context.

> **Activity 7.4**
> *By this stage you should be ready to design a complete learning design plan. The following template will assist you in completing such a task and delivering your learning design for implementation* via *a digital or other environments. Complete the form for a selected learning unit of your choice. Pay attention to important concepts covered in this Chapter, and reflect on these in the 'Theoretical Perspectives' part of this form.*

Learning Design Planning
(Based on the RASE framework)

Topic of a Learning Unit:

[ ]

Learning Outcomes:
Specify learning outcomes (maximum 3)

1.
2.
3.

---

[5]Play-Doh, also called plasteline or plasteline clay, is a soft modeling material used by children to build models, structures and art work. See the official Play-Doh site for more information http://playdoh.hasbro.com/

7.6 An Example of Digital Resource for Learning Used Within an Activity

Plot the learning outcomes in the graph below:

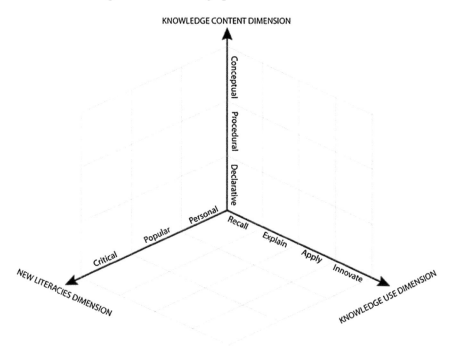

Activity:
Describe an activity for learners to achieve the learning outcome(s).
Describe what learners will deliver at the end of their activity.
Describe a scenario you will present to introduce the activity.

Resources:
List resources learners will use in the activity (include some digital resources for learning).

Support:
How learner learning be supported, develop any template to scaffold their work for the activity, list any additional resources to be used in case learners need further assistance, etc.

Evaluation:
How will you evaluate learners' artefacts developed in the activity? Develop a list of criteria for satisfactory completion of the activity (you can try using http://rubistar.4teachers.org/index.php to develop a rubric for this purpose).

Develop an e-learning environment to implement your learning design
You have several options to do this:

- Develop it inside of a learning management space or other system (e.g., Moodle, Course Sites, iTunesU, Canvas, Scholastic, EdModo, Facebook);
- Develop it as a web site (e.g., Google Sites);
- Develop it as a blog or wiki (e.g., Blogger, Wikispaces);
- Develop it as WebQuest;

- Develop it with a presentation tool such as PowerPoint; or
- Develop it as e-book with iBookAuthor.

My learning design is available for viewing at:

Theoretical Perspective:
The last part of your activity is to write a short paragraph to describe how important the theoretical concepts introduced in this chapter are in underlining your learning design, that is, how you think learning will occur.

References

Chaiklin, S. (1999). Developmental teaching in upper-secondary school. Introduction. In M. Hedegaard & J. Lompscher (Eds.), *Learning activity and development* (pp. 187–210). Aarhus, Denmark: Aarhus University Press.

Churchill, D., & Hedberg, J. (2008). Learning objects, learning tasks and handhelds. In L. Lockyer, S. Bennett, S. Agostinho, & B. Harper (Eds.), *Handbook of research on learning design and learning objects: Issues, applications and technologies*. Hershey, PA: Idea Group Publishing.

Churchill, D., King, M., & Fox, B. (2013). Learning design for science education in the 21st century. *Journal of the Institute for Educational Research, 45*(2), 404–421.

Davydov, V. V. (1999). The content and unsolved problems of activity theory. In Y. Engerström, R. Miettinen, & R. Punamäki (Eds.), *Perspectives on activity theory* (pp. 39–52). Cambridge, UK: Cambridge University Press.

Engeström, Y. (1987). *Learning by expanding*. Helsinki, Finland: Orienta-konsultit.

Engeström, Y. (1991). Activity theory and individual and social transformation. *Multidisciplinary Newsletter for Activity Theory,* (7/8), 6–17.

Glover, M., Czerniewicz, L., Walji, S., Deacon, A., & Small, J. (2015, October). *Approaches from the literature: Activity theory, new tools and changing educators' practices*. Poster presented at the HELTASA Conference 2015, North-West University, South Africa. Retrieved from http://roer4d.org/wp-content/uploads/2014/01/HELTASA-2015-poster-AO.pdf

Hardman, J. (2005). An exploratory case study of computer use in a primary school mathematics classroom: New technology, new pedagogy?: Research: Information and communication technologies. *Perspectives in Education: Research on ICTs and Education in South Africa, 4*(23), 1–13.

Hedegaard, M., & Lompscher, J. (Eds.). (1999). *Learning activity and development*. Aarhus, Denmark: Aarhus University Press.

Jonassen, D. (1978). *What are cognitive tools?* Retrieved from http://www.cs.umu.se/kurser/TDBC12/HT99/Jonassen.html

Jonassen, D. (2000). Towards design theory of problem solving. *Educational Technology Research and Development, 48*(4), 63–85.

Jonassen, H. D., & Rohrer-Murphy, L. (1999). Activity theory as a framework for designing constructivist learning environment. *Educational Technology Research and Development, 47*(1), 61–99.

Kaptelinin, V. (1997). Activity theory: Implications for human-computer interaction. In B. A. Nardi (Ed.), *Context and consciousness: Activity theory and human-computer interaction* (pp. 103–116). Cambridge, MA: The MIT Press.

Kutti, K. (1997). Activity theory as a potential framework for human-computer interaction research. In B. A. Nardi (Ed.), *Context and consciousness: Activity theory and human-computer interaction* (pp. 17–44). Cambridge, MA: The MIT Press.

Leont'ev, A. N. (1978). *Activity, consciousness and personality*. Englewood Cliffs, NJ: Prentice Hall.

Lim, C. P. (2002). A theoretical framework for the study of ICT in schools: A proposal. *British Journal of Educational Technology, 44*(3), 411–421.

Murphy, E., & Manzanares, M. A. R. (2008). Contradictions between the virtual and physical high school classroom: A third-generation activity theory perspective. *British Journal of Educational Technology, 39*(6), 1061–1072.

Nardi, B. A. (1997). Activity theory and human-computer interaction. In B. A. Nardi (Ed.), *Context and consciousness: Activity theory and human-computer interaction* (pp. 7–16). Cambridge, MA: The MIT Press.

Peruski, L., & Mishra, P. (2004). Webs of activity in online course design and teaching. *ALT-J. Research in Learning Technology, 12*(1), 37–49.

Salomon, G., Perkins, D.N., & Globerson, T. (1991). Partners in cognition: Extending human intelligence with intelligent technologies. *Educational Researcher, 20*, 2–9.

Vygotsky, S. L. (1962). *Thoughts and language*. Cambridge, MA: The MIT Press.

Vygotsky, S. L. (1978). *Mind in society*. Cambridge, MA: Harvard University Press.

Zinchenko, V. P. (1986). Ergonomics and informatics. *Problems in Philosophy, 7*, 53–64.

Repository of Digital Resources for Learning

> **Learning Outcomes:**
>
> - Discuss limitation(s) of traditional learning management systems and repository systems in terms of delivery and management of digital resources for learning;
> - Describe how Web 2.0 affordances can be utilized to advance traditional repository systems; and
> - Develop a set of recommendations for the development of a repository of digital resources of learning that provides integration with curriculum, supports the learning design process and leverages upon affordances of Web 2.0.

8.1 Repository of Digital Resources for Learning

In this chapter, we will explore the needs and rationale for a repository system of digital resources for learning. Initiatives such as those promoted under the Open Education Resources, as well as the most current learning management strategies fail to adequately address the issue of a repository, provide links of resources to curriculum, support learning design or integrate affordances of contemporary and popular Web 2.0 tools. As mentioned previously, to gain the maximum outcome of the strategy presented in this book, institutions should engage in a systematic curriculum analysis and the identification of digital resources for learning to be developed, sourced from elsewhere, and organized for reuse. In addition, relevant policies should be constructed in a way that promotes learning-centered pedagogy and, hence, the system should also be developed in a way that reflects these.

A traditional repository system focuses on providing a platform for resources to be deposited, managed and reused. Most of education institutions use some form of learning management system such as Moodle. Although such a system is open and able to integrate a repository, e.g., Alfresco, and various cloud-based systems, e.g., Google Docs and DropBox, these are still optional components not utilized by many teachers. Teachers would usually upload digital resources in their own course spaces, so that only their own students can access these. File management features in a system would allow that teacher to reuse the resources in his other courses, however, if any update to a resource is made, most often that resource needs to be replaced (unless it is kept externally, for example, in Google Docs). Other teachers and students would not have access and knowledge of the existence of these resources. Is some cases, a system utilizes administrator-managed metadata to facilitate searching and management of resources. Such a system might also facilitate issues related to existing institutional policies, integration with other platforms at an institution, as well as assist in dealing with copyright related aspects. The system is primarily focused on content resources management, (that is, it is content-centered), and does not pay full attention to the uniqueness of users (teachers and students) and the ways they reuse and manage content in their own ways (user-centered and learning-centered). Such a system originates from the IT industry, and largely, it is becoming more obvious that this industry alone fails to understand the unique aspects and needs of education today. A different repository system can change this and will provide institutions with a powerful environment and tool for resource development, sharing, reusing and social networking in ways that are user- and learning-centric. In this chapter, a proposal for such systems will be explicated with a central argument that it should leverage upon practices, paradigms and affordance of Web 2.0. The chapter will discuss a social repository system previously developed by the author that can be used as a model for the development of a suitable social repository of digital resources for learning.

Important
A repository of digital resources for learning must link the resources to the curriculum, support learning design, and incorporate social networking tools to maximize reusability, and further developments.

Activity 8.1
Select one of these two repositories of educational content: Merlot https://www.merlot.org/ or MIT Open Courseware at http://ocw.mit.edu/. Browse the selected repository for features, and search for some resources based on a topic of your choice. Pay attention to how the resources are cataloged and

how they are presented. Evaluate the repository in terms of the following questions:

- *How are resources/material categorized? Is this of a use to teachers and learners?*
- *What metadata about resources are in place (e.g., description, material type, and author)? How are these useful to teachers who are searching for resources to integrate in their learning designs?*
- *How the resources are linked to any curriculum requirement/learning outcomes?*
- *How does the repository system integrate with any learning management system?*
- *How does the repository system support the development of a learning design?*
- *What are strengths and weaknesses of this repository system?*

8.2 Web 2.0 Paradigm and the Social Web

Web 2.0 refers to a number of innovative Internet tools and corresponding practices of individuals and communities. Social bookmarking, networking, and other Web 2.0 technologies are increasingly popular today. These emerging popular tools have the ability to engage enormous numbers of ordinary people in socializing, working, and even learning. For Richardson (2006), we "are at the beginning of a radically different relationship with the Internet, one that has long-standing implications for educators and students" (p. 133). These include blogs, micro-blogs, wikis, social networking, social bookmarking, social content sharing, syndication feeds, and podcasting. The major aspects of the Web 2.0 are (Churchill 2007):

- *Read-Write Web*—Web 2.0 applications engage users not only to consume, but also to create and publish content.
- *Subscribing to Information*—In Web 2.0, users subscribe to information based on their preferences. Then, the information is delivered to specific locations as it becomes available. This is made possible through "syndication feeds" or RSS.
- *Social Spaces*—Web 2.0 applications are usually about engaging people in collective activities in a social space where they network and exchange bookmarks, resources, and ideas.
- *The Internet as a Platform*—Web 2.0 also signifies a gradual transformation of the Internet into a platform that contains tools traditionally understood as being native only to desktop computers (e.g., Google Docs).

- *Open Source*—There are now various applications offered for download and free use (e.g., Drupal, Twiki, ELGG, and Moodle). Rather than being designed in strictly secretive and protected formats, Web 2.0 applications are designed for "remixability."

Web 2.0 applications have gained huge popularity across the globe and have become one of the most socially engaging phenomena in human history. Information from major news sources suggests that millions of people around the world currently visit Web 2.0 sites on a daily basis. These "digital citizens" (Katz 1997) provide their contribution in a multitude of forms, such as multimedia content, blogs, comments, and tags. They develop new partnerships and discover knowledge from a pool of collective intelligence that exists in these environments. Sites such as the YouTube digital video repository, attracts millions of hits a day, while ordinary Internet users publish millions of video clips to this site and regularly comment upon, rank, tag and recommend these resources. Wikipedia houses millions of articles in over 100 languages (Wikipedia, n.d.), and it has become one of the world's most visited websites, with millions of hits and thousands of edits and new articles per day (Giles 2005). Blogs have contributed to the enormous growth of Internet sites over the last few years. Tens of thousands of blogs are created every day by ordinary Internet users (Reynolds 2006). Facebook, Skype, WhatsApp, Google Hangouts and Viber have transformed interaction and become primarily a channel for networking and communications that increasingly replaces email, SMS-ing and telephone talks.

Some of the popular Web 2.0 applications combine social bookmarking, networking and repositories into one platform, e.g., Delicious, SlideShare and YouTube. These systems introduce a powerful new way of working with Internet content and social networks. A typical social bookmarking/repository system allows online storage and management of resources (e.g., bookmarks, videos and presentation slides) that can be accessed anytime, anywhere, via any browser, and any web-enabled device. Such systems enable resources to be tagged by user-defined keywords or tags instead being meta-tagged by administrators. The social dimensions of these systems enable the sharing of bookmarks/resources with others, as well as ranking, subscribing, discussing resources and networking. Through exploring such social spaces, a user can locate relevant resources based not only on personal search and selection, but also on tags, user recommendations, and popularity. Rather than acting alone, a user mobilizes 'collective intelligence' of the community to locate useful resources. The process of locating resources is referred to as 'community plumbing'. Also, such technology allows users to subscribe to new resources provided by specific users and marked by specific tags, and to save and manage these in their own personal spaces for later use. In addition, such systems also effectively integrate across other Web 2.0 environments, such as, for example, blogs, wikies, and mash-ups. It is possible to embed resources and forward feeds to other places, such as in blogs, wikis and learning management systems. Another important Web 2.0 application is the social networking environment, such as Facebook, for example, which provides numerous ideas for what a social repository should integrate. These environments allow users to manage their profiles, share certain content, network, communicate and, in some cases, collaborate on tasks. Such environments might also integrate other Web 2.0 tolls such as blogs, wikis, file management and sharing. In addition, open source codes and various community-developed plugins enable extensions to standard functionalities found in a social networking environment such as Facebook. An example of a social networking environment more specifically designed for education is Edmodo. Teachers around the world are using Edmodo as an alternative to the standard learning management system.

The literature claims that Web 2.0 has the potential to transform education technology and applications (see Churchill 2007; Du and Wagner 2007; Hsu 2007; Parker and Chao 2007). In light of the popularity of Web 2.0, educators should not miss the opportunity to leverage these technologies and associated human practices for the benefits to teaching and learning. Thus, systems such as repositories, learning management and digital portfolios of students' work should be developed and used in line with the changing paradigm and technological developments.

Although these technologies have the potential to be effectively applied in teaching and learning, integrating innovation in education is often a slow process that is likely to encounter resistance. Emerging technologies have not been timely explored and adopted in education around the World due to a number of reasons such as institutional policy, teacher resistance, parents' expectation, lack of resources, lack of professional development, or simply because these challenge traditional mindsets and expectations.

Over the last few years at The University of Hong Kong, the author has been examining pioneering educational applications of Web 2.0 through projects that have explored the educational applications of blogs and wikis (Churchill 2009); examined pioneering Web 2.0 educational practices around the world; use of social networking to support teaching and learning (Jie and Churchill 2012); and explored possibilities for Web 2.0 environments to be used as extension and even an alternatives to the traditional learning management systems (Churchill 2009). More recently, the focus has been on the synergy between Web 2.0 and mobile technologies (e.g., Gu et al. 2014).

Activity 8.2
SlideShare is a very popular repository of presentations. There are hundreds of presentations on a spectrum of topics available in this repository. Some are designed for education purposes, thus, these can serve as presentation resources, while others are designed for various other informational purposes. SlideShare is available at http://www.slideshare.net/.

Review this repository, and in particular, pay attention to its social features. Search for a resource on a topic of your choice, then access that resource. Now, look at the page where the selected resource is displayed, and answer the following questions:

- On the right-hand side of the screen, there is a list of recommended presentations. What criteria are used to determine what presentations to recommend to you?
- If you click on the "Share" button under the displayed presentation, a number of options will appear. What do these options allow you to do?
- Below the displayed presentation, there are some owner/author's information. Below that, there is a "Follow" button. What does this allow you to do? Why might following an owner/author be important in the context of the reuse of digital resources for learning?
- Under this button, there are options to share this presentation on LinkedIn, Facebook or Twitter. What are the benefits of having such a feature in a repository system?
- Further down the page, there are information about people who like this presentation, user comments, as well as statistical information informing, for example, how many times the presentation has been viewed, shared or downloaded. Why are these pieces of information important, and what do they tell us about the resource even before we start previewing it?
- What can SlideShare teach as about any repository of digital resources for learning?

8.3 An Example of a System Based on Web 2.0 Ideas that Can Serve as a Model for a Repository of Digital Resources for Learning

Teachers in education institutions use resources on a daily basis for activities such as lesson preparation, student support, and the delivery of teaching. These include all forms of digital resources for learning and other media such as presentation slides, web sites, videos, images, articles, notes, worksheets, course outlines, assignments, examples of student work, etc. Also, students regularly use resources; they reference a large amount of materials and articles from journal databases or Internet sites when working on classroom activities and projects, writing assignments, or pursuing independent learning. Which resources are used by teachers and students? Which ones are found useful for their teaching and learning, and other meta-information about these resources is currently not collected in academic learning management systems or repository systems? In other words, there is no strategy for leveraging upon collective intelligence across an institution in the contexts of the use and reuse of resources in teaching and learning.

Through a teaching development grant funded by the Faculty Education at The University of Hong Kong, the author attempted to address this problem by developing a prototype of a social repository system based on Web 2.0 ideas. The

8.3 An Example of a System Based on Web 2.0 Ideas ...

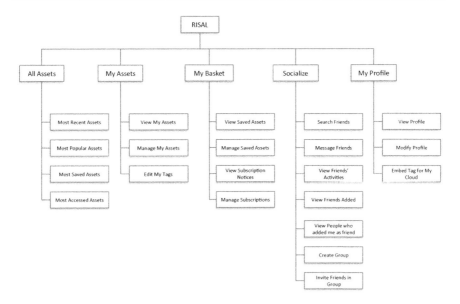

Fig. 8.1 Structure of the RISAL system

system is called RISAL—Repository of Interactive Social Assets for Learning (see Churchill et al. 2009). The system was built initially by enhancing and customizing PLIGG open source code. Figure 8.1 shows the structure of the RISAL system. The system interface with explanation of its functions is displayed in Fig. 8.2.

The RISAL supports students and teachers to manage, share and reuse bookmarks and resources (assets), create networks, and subscribe to information in the context of their activities such as learning design planning for teachers, or assignments and projects for students. The fundamental idea of the RISAL is that instead of keeping resources on one's own computer, or buried within a learning management system space, one can place them in cloud space for access anytime, anywhere and any device. Then, these resources can be shared with others, such as colleagues and students, or accessed for personal purposes. When assets are stored in one's own personal space, a teacher or a student will add a set of custom tags that describe the resource from his or her own stand point. This practice of tagging is an important strategy for the sharing and management of resources, as well as a tool that promotes social networking by students and teachers. Thus, the system and collection of bookmarks can serve as an important tool for teaching and learning, which promotes use of the technology, and supports the culture of sharing and collaboration. Figure 8.3 shows a single item of a resource displayed in the RISAL with a description of the functionalities.

The RISAL system allows teachers and students to explore resources, create favourite sub-collections on different topics, create social networks (e.g., with people whose resources they find useful or with whom they work as partners in teaching assignments or a group project), and to subscribe to new resources.

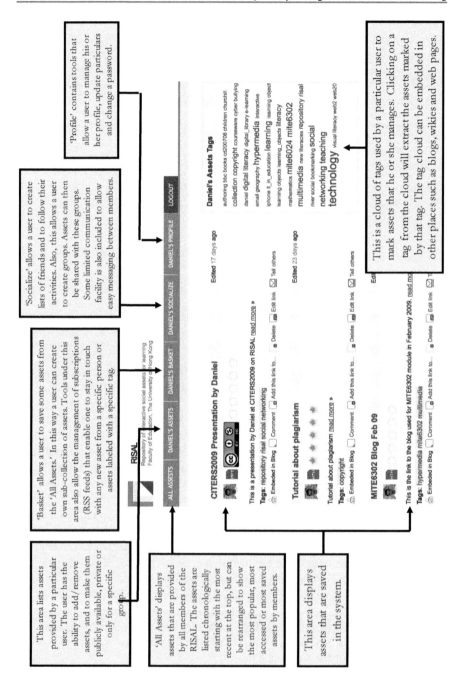

Fig. 8.2 Main interface of the RISAL and functionalities

8.3 An Example of a System Based on Web 2.0 Ideas ...

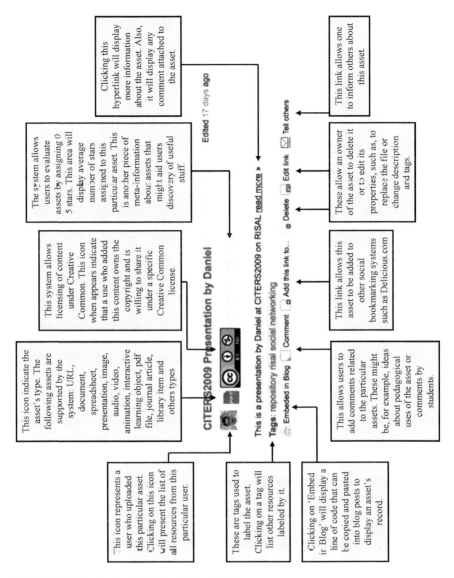

Fig. 8.3 'Anatomy' of a single item in the RISAL

Teachers or learners can use and re-use the RISAL resources when preparing lessons and assignments, writing articles, or developing research proposals. The teachers can also identify students' interests, patterns of networking, and use of resources. Further, the system can be prescribed for students to use during various learning and assessment activities (in classrooms and on-line). Teachers may use the resources in their learning designs, Moodle course, or course blog pages. The system enables teachers to network with other teachers with whom they share similar interests. This might serve to connect compatible teachers and result in increased collaborative activities, such as joint research projects, research student supervision and publishing, not just teaching. The system has the potential to support inter-disciplinary inquiry and multidisciplinary collaboration as resources and access to people from different disciplines are made possible. The variety of media and social activities supported by the system also provide tools for diverse learning experiences and support multiple forms of learning and assessment.

The collection of resources in the RISAL system reflects resources valued and used by the university community of students and teachers. The collection of bookmarks of sites from the Internet, for example, represent a subset of the Internet content that is specifically perceived as relevant by this institution's members. Similarly, a collection of links to the institution's library resources represent a subset of the items perceived useful by students and teachers in specific disciplines. Meta-information about assets such as tags, 'owner' information, and comments facilitate the additional classification of resources into more specific segments that better meet the learning and teaching needs of the students and teachers.

The system is also designed to promote good copyright practices. When users upload their own resources to their collections, they are asked to certify that they own the copyright(s) for these assets (not necessary for bookmarks, and links to library items). The system incorporates the practices of the Creative Commons and provides users with a sense of ownership for their resources, as well as providing the tools to select when and how they want to share the resources with others. Others, in this sense, are able to use and develop these resources further based on their own needs.

Since the RISAL was first introduced in December 2008, the author has received numerous expressions of interest and formed strategic partnerships for further development into a more comprehensive set of tools for university-wide support for teaching and learning. Recognizing the potential of the system (and other emerging Web 2.0 ideas), the author is currently pursuing funding to develop the RISAL's features into a more comprehensive platform. It is intended to focus on the following areas of further enhancements:

- *Extend social networking features*—Emphasis on social engagement is unique to Web 2.0 applications. The current RISAL system concentrates primarily in the development of bookmarking and repository features, and the social networking features of the system remain underdeveloped. Social networking features enable individuals to more effectively manage lists of "friends" (those with similar interests who wish to communicate about specific topics) and groups for sharing of resources and tracking of activities. For example, a teacher might create a special group (based on his/her class or a group of research students) and share specific resources with these students. In addition, the teacher might track the group members' activities (resources that they bookmark, or new items in their collections). A student might connect to 'friends' (other

8.3 An Example of a System Based on Web 2.0 Ideas ...

students) and create project groups to share resources, track activities, collaborate and form connections. The system should also contain suitable communication features to allow the flow of information, such as messaging and alerts about new resources or comments. Social networking features of the RISAL system will help provide valuable feedback through peer feedback and discussions within a social space as ideas (relative to the course learning outcomes) are developing. The importance of feedback to students for learning in progress has been emphasized as an important pedagogical intervention (Salter 2008). In this aspect, the system might be useful for other purposes. For example, a head of a department might create a group consisting of the department's teachers and share resources such as curriculum documents, and minutes of meetings. Similarly, a group of teachers might use the system to plan co-teaching activities or develop a curriculum. Research project collaborators might create a space for the exchange of files and collaboration. The system would allow for easy feedback to this kind of work in progress and shared resource development.

- *Develop mechanism for linking resources to learning outcomes*—This is an important feature that would support activities such as learning design preparation by teachers and independent learning or project work by students. For example, when preparing a lesson, a teacher might decide to explore resources that are linked to specific learning outcomes listed in the curriculum. The teacher will then decide which of these resources to use in his/her lesson. This approach has the potential to help teachers align the lesson resources and activities closely with the desired course learning outcomes and may result in huge time savings on lesson preparation and resource development. In addition, this creates possibilities for content to be continuously improved through redevelopment. At the same time, comments and tags attached to the resources might serve as a platform for sharing pedagogical ideas for the reuse of these resources to achieve specific learning outcomes. A self-directed student might identify certain learning needs through the system and relate these to specific learning outcomes. Then, they may explore resources that are linked to these learning outcomes. In this way, the system will support increased self-directedness and the lifelong learning of students by encouraging/allowing the students to also contribute to new knowledge creation.
- *Develop a set of players to display rather than download content such as videos and PowerPoint presentations*—The current RISAL system allows access to resources that are downloaded on a local computer for preview. This is not an effective strategy for the delivery of resources via the Web. In addition, this does not provide adequate protection of the intellectual property rights in some cases. The new feature will allow media to be streamed and displayed within web browsers or Mobile Apps (e.g., by utility of streaming technology, conversions and HTML5). This will also generate scripts, which allows resources to be embedded in other locations such as blogs, wikis, presentations, and web pages.
- *Develop digital portfolio features*—A portfolio used for educational purposes is a collection of student work and self-reflection in the learning of a

subject/course/program which demonstrates the student's effort and achievement. A digital portfolio is a blog-like space that can accept materials in electronic formats including text, graphics, audio and video, and allow them to be integrated. Such a portfolio enables learners to document their learning journey, report their projects and assignments, and maintain reflections that can assist in later revisions and further studies. A student reflecting on their own learning promotes an attitude of inquiry that allows them to integrate learning, discover meaning and relevance of the course material, acquire voice and authority, increase self-directedness, and connect with the world (see Kusnic and Finley 1993). The planned features would enable both teachers and students, to develop the digital portfolio space including: a course home page by a teacher; a group space (e.g., group project work presentation); or an individual portfolio space. In this way, the system will support portfolio- and project-based assessment strategies. In addition, the system will also support formative assessment as various stages of students' progressive work can be presented and evaluated in the digital portfolio. Also, the plan is to explore the development of mechanism that would support teachers to plan activities based on the RASE learning design model.
- *Go Mobile*—Mobile phones and tablets have become powerful Internet–enabled computer devices. In an increasing number of countries and regions, mobile phone penetration is well over 100%. Globally, there are more than a billion mobile Internet subscribers, and this is likely to increase. Most of our students and teachers are likely to possess an Internet-enabled mobile phone. We believe it will be very effective to enable certain features of the RISAL system for access via mobile phones. The features might allow, for example, access to files, storing of bookmarks, integration with a phone camera and audio recording features with the repository and digital portfolio, tracking of activities of friends, GPS records, and communication.
- *Develop features to allow bookmarking of the library items*—This feature will allow institutional library records of books and other material to be added in RISAL. In this way, members will create subsets of library resources perceived as useful in the contexts of their learning and disciplines. Since it will also be possible to tag and comment on these resources, RISAL has the potential to add an important social dimension to the currently limited social features of the traditional library catalogue. In addition, integration with some major digital libraries will be explored (e.g., Scopus, EBSCOhost and ProQuest).
- *Explore more effective integration with a learning management systems*— Integration of the RISAL with learning management systems might provide a tool for teachers to prepare on-line lessons by combining the affordances of the two systems. Previously in this chapter, we noted limitations of the current approaches and tools of a learning management system such as Moodle. The RISAL might provide an important extension to the overall learning technology infrastructure in line with contemporary developments.

8.4 What Is Useful from RISAL in Relation to a Repository of Digital Resources for Learning Presented in This Book?

In this book, we introduced the following kinds of digital resources for learning: information display resource, presentation resource, practice resource, conceptual representation resource and data display resources. These types of digital resources for learning are derived according to the different forms of curriculum content including declarative, procedural and conceptual knowledge. Previous approaches are either associated digital resources for learning with traditional teacher-centred instruction and needs (e.g., Alessi and Trollip 1995), or simply categorized resources based on media forms (e.g., digital video, audio, computer based package, and simulation). In the case of this book, different forms of curriculum content can be represented with different forms of digital resources for learning. The proposed approach to learning design will further ensure the instruction does not limit itself only on covering curriculum content, that is, the Knowledge Dimension, but also addresses the Knowledge Use Dimension of that curriculum. Central to this is that a learning-centred instruction approach and a learning design require active and engaging learning activates where digital resources are used as a mediating tool in this process, and where emerging knowledge is put to immediate use. In this approach, it is not only that students acquire knowledge, but also they use and experiment with that knowledge, refine it, reflect and develop theoretical thinking with a discipline. In this sense, the central activity of a teacher is the development of learning designs, while for students, it is working on problem solving and projects where knowledge is developed and used. A repository of digital resources for learning must effectively facilitate these.

Furthermore, any repository of digital resources of learning should be built upon contemporary and popular digital practices and technologies, that is, Web 2.0 or Social Web. Based on previous experience of working of developing the RISAL system, the author argues that the following should be considered in the development of a repository of digital resources for learning:

- The repository of digital resources for learning should be social networking technology, not just a repository of content and file sharing.
- The repository should enable *Folxonomy*, that is, user tagging of resources.
- The repository should support community plumbing in addition to searching by keywords.
- The repository should support subscriptions and syndications based on tags, type of a digital resource for learning, resource users and resource owners (and possibly by the kind of activity it supports).
- The repository should support integration with other internal environments (e.g., an institution's learning management systems), external environments (e.g., Google Docs), and possibly with other popular repositories of learning resources such as Merlot (see http://www.merlot.org).

- The repository should be available for access and use via mobile and emerging technologies.
- There should be a commenting feature available for each of the digital resources in the repository to allow users to discuss how to use these, suggest ideas for others and ask for suggestions.
- The repository should enable individual users to recommend resources.
- There should be a feature that allows the ranking of the resources and tracking of, for example, the number of reuses and number of unique users.
- The repository system should incorporate a set of tools to allow users to harvest and manage resources in their own personal spaces for later reuse in learning designs, portfolios, learning management systems, blogs, etc.

> **Important**
> Through exploration and use, and a repository of digital resources for learning, a teacher or a learner can locate relevant resources based not only on personal search and selection, but also based on links to learning outcomes and activities, tags, user recommendations, and popularity.

In addition, a useful feature for the repository of digital resources for learning would be a mechanism that links these to learning outcomes specified by the curriculum. A digital resource for learning can be associated with different learning outcomes simultaneously, depending on how teachers see it being useful. Once a teacher decides to use a specific digital resource for learning in his or her learning design, the system would require that related learning outcomes are indicated. Availability of such information would prove useful and give ideas to teachers in the planning of their learning designs. For this to be achieved, a database of the curriculum must be in place. This places a requirement on an institution to systematically approach curriculum design in a formal way so that learning outcomes are clearly listed and regularly updated. If such a database does not exist, as is unfortunately the case with many institutions, a teacher might be asked to briefly describe the intended use of that resource. Figure 8.4 is an illustration of a single digital resource for learning display in a possible repository.

In addition, a repository might integrate ideas and practices of popular commercial platforms such as eBay and Amazon. Idea practices by such platforms profile users and present recommendations. So, the repository might keep and analyze search histories, resources use and make comparisons with users with similar patterns, all for the purpose of making recommendations of resources that might meet that current user profile.

8.4 What Is Useful from RISAL in Relation ...

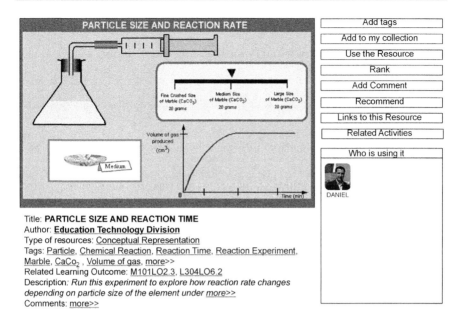

Fig. 8.4 An illustration of a single digital resource display in a repository

Another option is for a repository to contain a database of learning designs and a tool for constructing these. It would be useful for teachers to have an idea from their colleagues about the possible uses of a specific resource. This might be a powerful strategy to promote learning-centered practice across the community of teachers. However, this needs more detailed discussion and this book leaves this for some other occasion.

> **Activity 8.3**
>
> *Collect all the digital resources for learning you developed through this book so far. Tag each of these resources according to the schema illustrated in Fig. 8.4 (include fields: Title, Author, Type of resource, Tags, Relate Learning Outcomes, Description). Are there any other fields you would like to propose? You might need to develop some related learning outcomes for your resources. Think about different learning outcomes that your digital resources can be used for to be achieved with suitable activities. Furthermore, think and list features that need to be built in a repository system to support the development of learning designs.*

References

Alessi, S. M., & Trollip, S. R. (1995). *Computer-based instruction: Methods and development*. Englewood Cliffs, NJ: Prentice-Hall.
Churchill, D. (2007). Web 2.0 and possibilities for educational applications. *Educational Technology, 47*(2), 24–29.
Churchill, D. (2009). Educational applications of Web 2.0: Using blogs to support teaching and learning. *British Journal of Educational Technology, 40*(1), 179–183.
Churchill, D., Wong, W., Law, N., Salter, D., & Tai, B. (2009). Social bookmarking-repository-networking: Possibilities for support of teaching and learning in higher education. *Serials Review, 35*(3), 142–148.
Du, H. S., & Wagner, C. (2007). Learning with weblogs: Enhancing cognitive and social knowledge construction. *IEEE Transactions on Professional Communication, 50*(1), 1–16.
Giles, J. (2005). Internet encyclopedias go head to head. *Nature, 438,* 900–901.
Gu, J., Churchill, D., & Jie, L. (2014). Mobile web 2.0 in the workplace: A case study of employees informal learning. *British Journal of Education Technology, 45*(6), 1049–1059.
Hsu, J. (2007). Innovative technologies for education and learning: Education and knowledge-oriented applications of blogs, wikis, podcasts, and more. *International Journal of Information & Communication Technology Education, 3*(3), 70–89.
Jie, L., & Churchill, D. (2012). The effect of social interaction on learning engagement in a social networking environment. *Interactive Learning Environments, 22*(4), 401–417.
Katz, J. (1997). The Digital Citizen. *Wired, 5*(12). Retrieved from http://www.wired.com/wired/reprints/digicit.html
Kusnic, E., & Finley, M. L. (1993). Student self-evaluation: An introduction and rationale. In J. MacGregor (Ed.), *Student self-evaluation* (pp. 5–14). San Francisco, CA: Jossey Bass Inc., Publishers.
Parker, K. R., & Chao, J. T. (2007). Wiki as a teaching tool. *Interdisciplinary Journal of Knowledge and Learning Objects, 3,* 57.
Reynolds, P. (2006). *Bloggers: An army of irregulars*. Retrieved from http://news.bbc.co.uk/2/hi/4696668.stm.
Richardson, W. (2006). *Blogs, wikis, podcasts and other powerful web tools for classrooms*. Thousand Oaks, CA: Corwin Press.
Salter, D. (2008). The challenge of feedback: Too little too late. *Ed-Media Conference, Association for the Advancement of Computing in Education*. June 30–July 4, 2008. Vienna, Austria.
Technorati. (n.d.). *About Technorati*. Retrieved from http://www.technorati.com/about/
Wikipedia. (n.d.). *Wikipedia: About*. Retrieved from http://en.wikipedia.org/wiki/Wikipedia:About

9. Mobile Technologies and Digital Resources for Learning

> **Learning Outcomes:**
>
> - Discuss affordances of mobile technology for teaching and learning;
> - Outline recommendations for the design of digital resources for learning on small screens of mobile devices;
> - Discuss the educational uses of iPads and other tables;
> - Integrate recommendations for the 'design for small screens' and 'learning use' when designing a digital resource for learning for mobile delivery; and
> - Design a digital learning environment by integrating the affordances of mobile technologies.

9.1 Introduction to Mobile Learning

This chapter explores affordances of mobile technology for learning, and emphasizes that emerging mobile technologies are effective platforms for the delivery of digital learning resources, anytime and anywhere. The central focus of this book is on digital resources for learning and their uses in learning-centered activities. In this sense, mobile technology is discussed in the context of its affordances to deliver such digital resources for learning, while these resources for learning are examined in the context of their design for such an application.

Mobile and handheld digital devices nowadays include Internet and wireless network connectivity, and extensions such as a mobile phone and network, Wi-Fi connectivity, Bluetooth connectivity, a camera, GPS connectivity, and a variety of add-on hardware and software. These devices have been referred to, in the past, as Personal Digital Assistants (PDAs), Pocket PCs, 'smartphones', 'wearables' (Sharples 2000), 'communicators' or 'mobile multimedia machines' (Attewell 2005), and more recently, slates, tabs and tablets. The number of mobile phones has almost exceeded the number of people in the world (see http://www.internetworldstats.com/mobile.htm). In some places, such as Hong Kong, for example, mobile phone penetrations have exceeded 200%, meaning that a significant number of people own two mobile phones or even more. Increasingly, more powerful tablet technology is becoming widely adopted, and the percentage of people who own such technology is increasing rapidly.

In education, the Horizon Report since 2011 has been emphasizing the importance of mobile technology, and adds that this technology coupled with cloud computing will have a strong impact on teaching and learning at all levels (see New Media Consortium 2011). As a number of these devices increases, this technology is becoming an inextricable part of the digital life for many individuals around the world (see Attewell 2005). The literature suggests mobile technologies have been positively accepted by students (Donaldson 2016) and teachers (Domingo and Gargante 2016), and that these tools have a productive effect on learning engagement, attitude and achievement (e.g., Churchill et al. 2014; Duprey et al. 2016; Fabian et al. 2016; Liaw et al. 2010). However, there is still a lack of recommendations in relation to the design of educational resources for mobile application. Significant investment is taking place in education around the world, universities and schools are increasingly purchasing mobile technology devices, setting up supporting infrastructure, and investing in the professional development of teachers, all with very limited, empirically developed guidelines on the effective integration of this technology in teaching and learning. Over the last few years, there has been a hugely increased number of Apps available. There are now more than 2 million Apps in the Android App Store and more than 2 million Apps in the Apple App Store (see Statista 2016). In 2014, there were almost 260 billion downloads of Apps across the major platforms, including iOS, Android, Blackberry and Windows (Statista 2016).

In relation to education, although there are more than 100,000 Apps under the education category available just in the App Store, the global download of these Apps accounts to 7% of total app downloads, or commerce that equates to almost a billion US dollars. Despite these statistics, the quality of many of those Apps is less than satisfactory. The same old thinking underlines the design of Apps, and there is widely spread naïve understanding of how this technology can support teaching and learning other than to present explicit multimedia content for learners to consume and remember. The use of education games via Apps is also wide spread, and these represent a step forward into a more productive direction, however, overall, there is a lot of work that needs to be done to improve the design of Apps in ways that support learning-centered practices. There is serious shortage of useful guidelines for the design of resources that give full attention to affordances of mobile technology, screen real estate, interaction and ways how this technology can be used in

9.1 Introduction to Mobile Learning

learning-centered activities. This chapter attempts to provide some ideas regarding the useful design aspects for resources for mobile technology application.

9.2 Affordances of Mobile Technology

Mobile technology offers a spectrum of tools for teachers, educational opportunities and new options for student-technology partnerships in learning. Empowered with interactive multimedia presentational capabilities, handheld technology permits the delivery of a range of multimedia material such as video, audio, graphics and integrated media. If appropriately designed for the context, educationally useful digital resources for learning can be effectively delivered via mobile technologies to students at any time, inside and outside of classrooms.

> **Important**
> Empowered with interactive multimedia presentational capabilities, handheld technology permits the delivery of a range of multimedia material such as video, audio, graphics and integrated media. If appropriately designed for the context, educationally useful digital resources for learning can be effectively delivered via mobile technologies to students at any time, inside and outside of classrooms.

Studies report a variety of issues in relation to the use of mobile technologies in education. Examples of issues reported include: use of mobile technology during classes, enabling teachers and students to share files (Ray 2002); allowing students to ask anonymous questions, answer polls, and give teachers feedback (Ratto et al. 2003); delivering an intelligent tutoring system (Kazi 2005); delivering quizzes (Segal et al. 2005); disseminating information and collecting data during field trips (So 2004) and outdoor educational activities (Churchill et al. 2010; Land and Zimmerman 2015); supporting students' inquiries (Sharples et al. 2002; Clyde 2004); supporting computer collaborative learning (Roschelle and Pea 2002; Zurita and Nussbaum 2004); improving literacy and numeracy for disadvantaged young adults (Attewell 2005); as a personal technology for lifelong learning (Sharples 2000); as personalized learning environments (e.g. Anderson and Blackwood 2004; Song and Fox 2008; Waycott and Kukulska-Hulme 2003), as an instructional tool and a replacement to laptops (e.g., Shen et al. 2009); as a tool for learning on the move (e.g., Seppälä and Alamäki 2003; Wong et al. 2011); as a mediating tool for ubiquitous, seamless and situated learning experiences (Looi et al. 2010; Wong and Looi 2011), and so on. Studies are emerging to report the benefits and adoption of mobile technologies in a number of subject domains, such as in science education (e.g., Burden and Kearney 2016; Zydney and Warner 2016), mathematics education (e.g., Borba et al. 2016; Bringula et al. 2017; Chiu 2016; Schuck 2016), geography education (e.g., Jarvis et al. 2016; Peirce 2016), language education, (e.g., Burston

2016; Lai 2016; Lindaman and Nolan 2016), medical education (e.g., Briz-Ponce et al. 2016; Wilkinson and Barter 2016) and psychology education (Diliberto-Macaluso and Hughes 2016).[1]

Affordance is a useful concept that can be applied to interpret how teachers engage technology in their practice. How mobile technology will be used in education depends largely on teachers' understandings of affordances of this technology. It includes actual uses native to the device and applications, and those uses that emerge in teachers' practice. Norman (1988) defines affordances as "the perceived and actual properties of the thing, primarily those fundamental properties that determine just how the thing could possibly be used" (p. 9). For Barnes (2000), a teacher's use of new technology in teaching and learning is carried out with a belief that this technology will afford learning in some way. Churchill and Churchill (2008) in their study, examined a teacher's use of mobile technology, and articulated the following five affordances of mobile technology:

- *Multimedia-access tool*—a variety of digital resources can be delivered via mobile technology, such as e-books, web pages, presentations, interactive resources, audio files and video segments. These resources can be accessed anytime, anywhere, by connecting to the Internet using 3G/4G or wireless network connections, from the memory of the device or storage card if the resources were previously downloaded, or through synchronization of the device with a computer. However, it is noted that merely moving resources from a computer to a mobile device might not lead to effective learning. Resources for mobile device uses must be designed with certain principles in mind. Churchill and Churchill (2008) suggest that a digital resource for learning consisting of a single interface, containing multimodal information that focuses on an important concept from a discipline (a conceptual representation resource), and which does not require long usage time, might be an effective resource for learning supported by mobile technology.
- *Connectivity tool*—mobile technology empowers students to connect to each other, facilitators and experts in the field, exchange ideas and files, collaboratively build understanding, manage activities and negotiate roles in their projects, etc. Connection might be established synchronously and asynchronously over mobile telephony and wireless networks that support voice and multimedia data transmission.
- *Capture tool*—mobile technology is equipped with capture capabilities that include the capture of video and still photographs. Students might, for example, photograph and videotape machines and people during their industry visits, or photograph diagrams from a book or catalogue. The capture affordance also includes audio capture. For example, students might interview experts and capture their own audio notes, or capture characteristic sounds of a faulty engine. There is a possibility for specially designed extensions and consoles to

---
[1]See Haßler et al. (2016), Liu et al. (2014) and Pimmer et al. (2016), for extensive reviews of studies investigating adoption of mobile technologies in education.

9.2 Affordances of Mobile Technology

be attached to a mobile device and used to capture, store and process other kinds of data such as, for example, recording the global positioning of certain air pollution sources or even operating a mini drone via iPhone to capture aerial photographs and videos (e.g., Drone Ace).
- *Representational tool*—mobile technology might be used by students to create representations that demonstrate their thinking and knowledge. These might be, for example, mind maps, presentations or captured and edited images and videos.
- *Analytical tool*—mobile technology might be used as an analytical tool to aid students' activities. For example, these might include standard, scientific and graphic calculators or specially designed analytical tools created by teachers to allow students to process certain data from the environment.

> **Important**
> How mobile technology will be used in education depends largely on teachers' understandings of the affordances of this technology.

There are a number of other studies that have investigated and report the affordances of mobile technology. For example, Klopfer and Squire (2005) describe five potential educational affordances of mobile technology: (a) portability, as handhelds can be taken to different locations; (b) social interactivity, as handhelds can be used to collaborate with other people; (c) context sensitivity, as handhelds can be used to gather real or simulated data; (d) connectivity, as handhelds enable connection to data collection devices, other handhelds, and to a network; and (e) individuality, as handhelds can provide scaffolding to the learners. Similarly, Patten et al. (2006) present a framework that consists of the following affordances of PDA technology: (a) administration, (b) referential, (c) interactive, (d) microworld, (e) data collection, (f) location awareness, and (g) collaboration. Furthermore, Liaw et al. (2010) suggest five affordances of mobile technology for education: (a) educational content and knowledge delivery, (b) adaptive learning applications, (c) interactive applications, (d) individual applications, and (e) collaborative applications. A summary of these various studies of affordances of mobile technology is presented in Table 9.1. These affordances from the literature are sorted into an emergent framework for understanding affordances for teaching and learning that include the following six categories: (a) resources tool, (b) connectivity tool, (c) collaborative tool, (d) capture tool, (e) analytic tool, and (f) representational tool.

> **Activity 9.1**
> *For each of the affordances of mobile technology explicated in this chapter (Resources, Connectivity, Collaborative, Capture, Analytical, Representational) attend to the following:*

Table 9.1 Affordances of mobile technology across the relevant studies

Klopfer and Squire (2005)	Patten et al. (2006)	Churchill and Churchill (2008)	Liaw et al. (2010)	Summary of affordances emerging from across the studies
• Social interactivity (3[a]) • Portability (1, 2) • Context sensitivity (4) • Connectivity (2, 3) • Individuality (1)	• Administration[b] • Referential (1) • Interactive resource (1) • Microworld environment (1, 6) • Data collection (4) • Location awareness (4) • Collaboration (3)	• Multimedia access (1) • Connectivity tool (2) • Capture tool (4) • Representational tool (6) • Analytical tool (5)	• Educational content and knowledge delivery (1) • Adaptive learning applications (1) • Interactive applications (3) • Individual applications (6) • Collaborative applications (3)	1. Resources 2. Connectivity 3. Collaborative 4. Capture 5. Analytical 6. Representational

[a]Corresponds to an affordance listed in the summary (final column)
[b]Considering that central interest of this book is teaching and learning, this affordance is left out from the summary

> - *Identify one mobile application (App); and*
> - *Describe how each of the affordance supports the integral parts of the RASE learning design (e.g., how connectivity supports Activity or Support, or how representational affordances support Evaluation).*

9.3 Digital Resources for Small Screens of Mobile Devices

As it can be seen from the discussion of the affordances of mobile technology for education, the 'resources' category emerges as one of the key affordances across different studies. Given the powerful multimedia capabilities of contemporary mobile technologies and increasing speed of Internet connectivity, all kinds of digital resources, including digital resources for learning, can be delivered via devices. Increasingly powerful mobile technology processors, growing internal and external memory spaces, fast Internet connection via 3G and 4D (and soon to come 5G) networks and retina screen resolution, make such devices able to serve as powerful multimedia delivery technology.

9.3 Digital Resources for Small Screens of Mobile Devices

> **Important**
> How mobile technology will be used in education depends largely on teachers' understandings of the affordances of this technology.

The design of resources for mobile technology application needs to pay attention to issues including at least the design for presentation via small screens and design for mobile learning uses. For most mobile technology devices, excluding today's powerful, large screen tablets, screen space represents a challenge for the delivery of digital resources for learning. In general, the literature is limited in terms of recommendations for the design of multimedia material for mobile learning, and overall, there is a lack of suitable guidelines to inform design and uses. Most of the previous studies have been focused on understanding issues such as text formatting, image resolution, scrolling and quality of other media, but overall, they fail short of providing sustainable recommendations for the design of specifically digital resources for learning.

In the study of design of digital resources for learning for small screen presentation, the author of this book arrived at a number of recommendations for design (see Churchill and Hedberg 2008). The study included interviews with educational professionals and observations of their interactions with mobile digital resources for learning, and the continuous redesign of a number of digital resources based on feedback from students and suggestions from teachers. Overall, greater use of other modalities (in particular visuals) and interactivity over text is recommended as a means of maximizing the amount of educationally useful information presented on a single small screen of a mobile device. The following seven recommendations emerged from this study.

- *Recommendation 1: Design for full screen presentation*—Throughout our study, all the participants indicated preference for full-screen presentation of information when accessing digital resources for learning via a mobile device. Full-screen presentation increases the amount of available space and this appears to create an improved user experience.
- *Recommendation 2: Design for landscape presentation*—Typically, a screen of a mobile device is presented in portrait layout, although recent devices support auto-rotation. This is different from most traditional devices, such as computers and television screens, and from many contemporary technologies such as screens in digital cameras and game consoles. Although the goal of a mobile device is to be comfortable to hold in a single hand (usually because it is reasonable for some devices to assume that the other hand is holding a stylus pen during interaction, or used to navigate with fingers, except in the context of the latest iPhone which is targeted to be used by a single hand), participants in our study were unanimous that presentation of digital resources for learning in a landscape position was preferred. From a design perspective, it appeared that the landscape screens also offered more flexibility to a design to arrange the screen and interactive elements more effectively.

- *Recommendation 3: Minimize scrolling*—The participants agreed with the literature and suggested that scrolling should be avoided or at least minimized. While several authors propose as an alternative, dragging the content presented on a screen (e.g., Albers and Kim 2001), in this study, the participants also treated this approach unfavorably. Some content that required dragging was presented to the participants who found this method of control uncomfortable. As emphasized earlier, learning objects should utilize visualization and interactivity and minimize the amount of text presented on a screen. Scrolling is largely a characteristic of navigation through text and long web pages. Contemporary devices even afford to eye-tracking based scrolling. Considering that digital resources for learning primarily utilize other kind of modalities, different methods should underline navigation, if any navigation is required. Often, a digital resource for learning is designed such that everything is squeezed into a single representation presented on a single screen (or portion if it). Design practices have shown that large amounts of information can be organized and effectively presented in this way. However, this study identified another method that allows visual and interactive content to extend beyond the limits of a single screen.
- *Recommendation 4: Design for short contacts and task centeredness*—A mobile device personally assists and supports an individual in his or her activities, e.g., conducting a business, making scientific inquiry, planning a trip, creating art, learning, and so on. Attention is often divided so that an individual might be undertaking some tasks simultaneously or in a variety of modalities when drawing on the assistance of a mobile device. This contact with a device is purposeful and usually short in terms of time (e.g., checking calendar and tasks, calculating, viewing latest news headlines or stock market movement, capturing an image, or making a personal note). Applying this thinking to the design of digital resources for learning, they should be designed in a way that provides for learning activity-centered information to be provided in a single action on a small screen requiring short contact time. One of the general concerns of the participants was the impact of the prolonged use of mobile-based digital resources for learning on their health and, in particular, to the possible eye-strain of students. This is real problem when mobile device users spend excessive amounts of time reading long texts and e-books. Reading a long text over a mobile device is an activity that is somewhat disconnected with any real-world task; it requires continuous and prolonged perception and concentration on a small screen area and rationally, this seems likely to cause problems. An audio podcast would seem a much better match with the task and the affordances of a handheld device. However, the digital resources for learning and their design should be based upon a consideration that these representations are to be task-oriented where the main perceptual and conceptual effort is directed at the activity rather than at the small screen or the device.
- *Recommendation 5: One step interaction*—The design goal for a digital resource for learning should be to provide through visualization and interactivity, all necessary information with a single display that fits the screen of the

9.3 Digital Resources for Small Screens of Mobile Devices

mobile device. Interactive elements (e.g., buttons, hot-spots, roll-overs, or sliders) when integrated in a digital resource for learning should provide immediate feedback to the learner. Single interactions, such as changing a position of a slider, should result in immediate updates on the screen presented in a way that is perceptually and immediately noticeable in response to a learner's action. This can be achieved by visual effects such as text formatting, use of contrasting colors, and the flashing of prompts that are exposed upon interaction. Audio effects can also capture the user's attention, although this might be less effective in noisy environments (unless we assume that the user has earphones). Visuals can also be adversely affected by environmental factors such as natural or artificial lighting, and reflections on the screen (although there are some devices and screen protectors that make the screen non-reflective). However, an average user is likely to tilt the device or cover the screen by their hand to prevent reflection and achieve better visual contact with the screen. Figure 9.1 shows an example of a digital resource for learning designed in the context of our study that demonstrates this principle of 'one step interaction'.

This digital resource for learning provides a concept representation of a circle. It can be reused in a variety of activities (developed by a teacher) that lead to the construction of a range of associated mathematical concepts from basic properties of a circle to more complex concepts. This resource allows a user to manipulate a diameter of the circle by dragging a corresponding slider. Manipulating the diameter of by the dragging of the slider will result in an immediate update to the

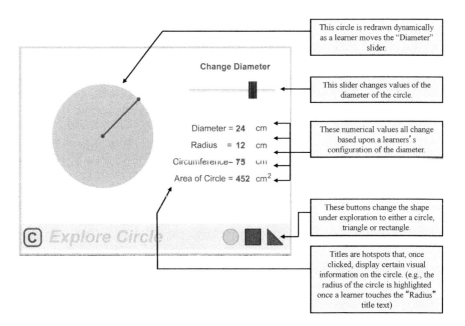

Fig. 9.1 'Shapes' digital resource for learning

display in multiple modalities: the circle will be redrawn in a corresponding size and the numerical information regarding associated parameters will be updated (such as the value of the circumference).

- *Recommendation 6: Zooming facility to enlarge the display beyond the physical limits of the screen*—Dragging of the screen has been seen based on the participants' feedback as more favourable and effective for a user than scrolling. In this study, we explored this possibility through the redesign and use of a digital resource for the learning title *"Pulley System"*. This digital resource for learning is a conceptual representation of the mechanical transfer of power through a pulley system. It allows students to manipulate a number of parameters (load, effort and the number of pulleys) to investigate the impact of the configuration on the pulley system. Exploring these relationships should lead to a deeper understanding of the key concepts encapsulated by the resource. The understanding in the long run might be supported by perceptual impressions and the individual's cognitive ability to recreate relationships in their mind through their imagination. In educational applications, a teacher might create an activity in which students are engaged in inquiry and exploration of the underlining relationships, generalization and application of their conclusions in problem-solving. Subsequently, this digital resource for learning might be a reference tool in further study.

A user can drag the two sliders in order to change the quantitative values of the load to be lifted and the effort to be exerted to lift this load, or vice versa. These values are represented as numbers on the screen and this information was purposefully formatted in a slightly smaller font size to require an average user to use the magnifier to read the information on the small screen.

Experimentation began by using a standard feature of the player that supports magnification of the display beyond the physical limits of the screen of the mobile device. If the stylus pen is held against the screen for few seconds, an option that allows magnifying is activated. On other devices, using two fingers and stretching the displayed content achieves magnification of the screen. The magnified display then becomes moveable with a stylus or a single finger. However, from casual demonstration and trailing with the participants, this possibility was not sufficiently explicit and was not employed by the average user. Thus, in design, it is more appropriate to make this function more explicit via an interactive element on the main screen interface. To enable this redesign, the new interface of the digital resource for learning included a button that would simply magnify the display to a larger size (see Fig. 9.2). This button also activated the feature that permits a user to drag the entire screen in any direction to access hidden areas of the display beyond the physical limits of the screen.

However, we discovered that this redesign was not optimal; participants did not always recognize the function so, in a third redesign, the button that previously magnified the screen, activated a moveable square that acted as a magnifying glass (see Fig. 9.3). The participants were able to move the rectangle to different areas of

9.3 Digital Resources for Small Screens of Mobile Devices

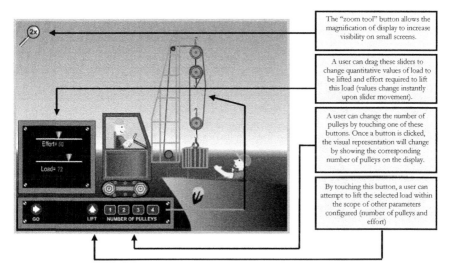

Fig. 9.2 *Pulley system* learning object with a button that magnifies the display

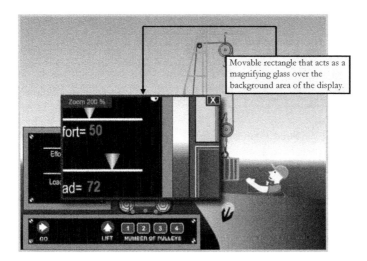

Fig. 9.3 Employing a moveable rectangle that acts as a magnifying glass

the display and to preview a magnified background of the area covered by it. In this new approach, the user was able to see the whole display and, at the same time, have access to magnification of the required information and this resulted in enthusiastic user endorsement.

However, this third approach solved only a limitation of the visual display but not aspects of the interactivity, such as the case when the user finds the sliders to be too small for effective manipulation. Interacting with the sliders inside of the

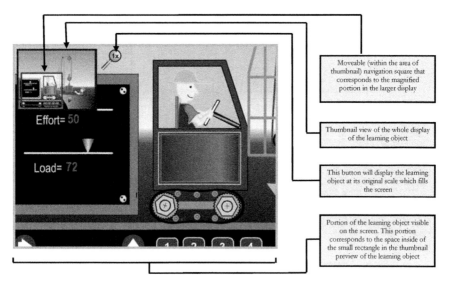

Fig. 9.4 Navigable thumbnail preview of the screen that allows focus on magnified areas

magnifying rectangle was not possible and if the participants wanted to reposition them, they had to close the magnifying rectangle, reposition the sliders, open the magnifying rectangle and move it until the desired magnified part of the display became visible. This design worked against the proposed principle of 'one step interaction', as a user was unable to see clearly and immediately the impact of their change of parameters.

This resulted in a fourth design which allowed the user to click on a button to magnify the displayed digital resource for learning beyond the limits of the physical screen while at the same time displaying a small thumbnail view of the whole display in the top-left corner (see Fig. 9.4). This thumbnail served as a navigation area that contained another smaller movable rectangle. Moving the rectangle within the thumbnail would result in the repositioning of the enlarged display. This final approach was selected as most favourable by the participants and accordingly, based on the study, it was proposed as a suitable design.

- *Recommendation 7: Movable, collapsible, overlapping, semitransparent interactive panels*—Our final effort concentrated on exploring design possibilities that utilize floating panels in order to maximize the amount of information presented on a display. This focus emerged from the involvement with the participants as they suggested in relation to the *Pulley System* learning object that the sliders and buttons could be presented within a floating panel. Rather than redesigning an existing digital resource, the researcher created a new digital resource for learning to increase the number available for potential further study. The final progressive result of the engagement was the *Parallel and Series Circuits* digital resource for learning presented in Fig. 9.5.

9.3 Digital Resources for Small Screens of Mobile Devices

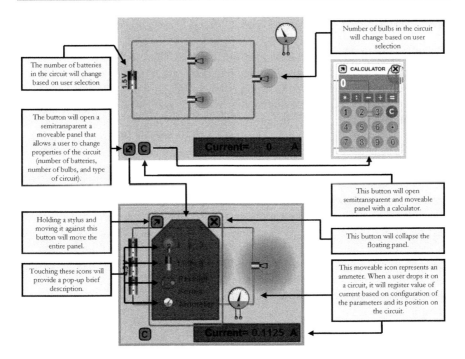

Fig. 9.5 A prototype of 'parallel and series circuit' digital resource for learning

The initial design contained a non-transparent floating panel that permitted a user to change the number of bulbs, number of batteries and type of circuit, and it also provided a very brief description of these properties. The participants demonstrated discomfort in having to frequently move the panel in other to see what changes had taken place on the circuit. Again, this design worked against the principle of 'one step interaction' as it was not always possible for a user to immediately 'see' the outcome of their interaction with an interface element. Thus, a design action taken at this stage was to make the floating panes semitransparent so that the learners had limited visual contact with the information on the background. These designs received greater support and matched the participants' experiences. At a later stage, the class teacher requested a panel with a calculator to enable the students to also analyse the values of parameters of their configurations.

Activity 9.2
Go back to the "Atmosphere" digital resource for learning you designed at the end of Chap. 2. Evaluate your design and explain what needs to be done to redesign it for a small screen of a mobile device. How can the seven recommendations for design for a small screen presented so far in this chapter assist you to redesign this resource for mobile delivery? Are there any challenges for redesigning the "Atmosphere" digital resource for learning?

9.4 Design for Learning Uses

In addition to these recommendations for the design for small screens of mobile technology devices, this book's author has been concentrating on exploring and developing recommendations for, what is labeled as 'design for learning uses' via mobile devices. In particular, attention is given to the design and use of concept representation resources as the most suitable form for application via mobile devices. The key idea here is that conceptual representations representing conceptual knowledge from a discipline, can be provided from outside, through the use of mobile technology, to learners anytime and anywhere when their activity demands use of that conceptual knowledge. In other words, if concepts are not available in a learner's knowledge when required by an activity, or are partly available, then external concept representations resources can serve to supplement this deficiency. In this sense, the external conceptual representation resources serve as tools that mediate the learner's activity, and their use will lead to the development of internal tools that can mediate future activities requiring that conceptual knowledge. Readers are reminded that concept representation resources should be designed to support a learning-centred activity, not as an instructional media, but as a mediating tool.

> **Important**
> Design of resources for mobile technology application needs to pay attention to issues including, at least, the design for presentation via small screens and design for mobile learning uses.

Overall, a concept representation resource design process requires a designer to have:

(a) ability to identify a suitable concept from a discipline for development into a conceptual representation resource, (b) deep knowledge of the concept, (c) understanding of pedagogically appropriate ways of representing the concept, (d) creativity in representing through interactive multimedia art, and (e) understanding of effective interactivity and interface design across delivery technologies. However, even the most effectively designed concept representation resource might not be effective unless properly integrated in a learning design. Pedagogically effective use of a concept representation must be driven by a learning activity. To plan the educational utility of a concept representation resource, teachers are required to understand its possible learning uses. The understanding of learning uses will, in turn, provide ideas for more the effective design of a concept representation resource. This understanding is useful to both (a) designers of a concept representation resource, and (b) teachers involved in development of a learning design where that resource is used. In relation to mobile devices, teachers need to be aware of the affordances of this technology and how to deploy these to support learning activities.

9.4 Design for Learning Uses

The author previously conducted a study to explicate a set of recommendations for the design of conceptual representation resources and their application via mobile technology (see Churchill 2013). That study developed recommendations based on the author's engagement in the design and explorative use of a particular concept representation resource with students and their Geography teachers from an international secondary school in Hong Kong. Initially, the author collaborated with the teachers to design a concept representation resource, observed the lessons in preparation for the fieldwork-based activity where this digital resource was to be used via mobile devices, and travelled to Northern Thailand with the participants to observe fieldwork uses of both mobile technology and the concept representation resource. During the fieldtrip, the students were required to conduct a study of a river—one of the key concepts in the secondary school Geography curriculum. This topic includes issues such as how a river changes downstream, how farming and various human settlements influence these changes, obtaining key measurements such as a river's width, depth, velocity and gradient, and examining other related parameters including discharge and hydraulic radius. Teaching and learning about these concepts requires time (in and out of the classroom), and it is a challenge for students to integrate all the elements into coherent conceptual knowledge. Such conceptual knowledge is essential to students in meeting the final demands of their curriculum assessment specified by the International Baccalaureate. Prior to the field trip, the students were briefed in the class about the rivers and their properties. During the field trip, they were equipped with mobile devices (the HP iPAQ rw6828 Multimedia Messenger). In addition, there was one notebook computer available per five-to-six students. Mobile devices were used mostly during fieldwork, and notebooks when the students returned from the field to their base-camp to summarize their day's learning as an ongoing report that would form the basis of their case study of the river. As well as recording collected data, capturing images and other tasks, the mobile devices were used to access a concept representation resource of a river that was designed by the author in collaboration with the participating teachers specifically for the purpose of this fieldtrip.

To understand learning uses of the concept representation resource and develop design recommendations, the author conducted observations in the class and during fieldwork, and administered interviews with the students and teachers. Images taken during the fieldwork were coded and used for the purpose of the stimulated recall interviewing as well. The participating students' work was also used as a source of data. Emerging understanding was triangulated using these multiple sources of data. The data were organized, with the participating teachers' help, in a set of internally homogenous and externally heterogeneous categories that resulted in understanding of, and recommendations for, learning uses of the concept representation resource via mobile technology. These learning uses were finally arranged in a set of emerging recommendations for the design (design for learning uses).

Prior to the trip, the author held a number of discussions with the two Geography teachers in relation to the content of the concept representation resource. The participating teachers were both experienced Geography educators and enthusiastic technology users. The two teachers identified the river as the critical concept in the students Geography knowledge. The discussions about the content of the concept representation resource, and the specific ways of representing its content, resulted in hand-drawn sketches, which essentially became a storyboard, or blueprint, for the production of the first version. The author then produced initial and subsequent versions of the concept representation resource using Adobe Flash authoring software. In the absence of appropriate design recommendations from the literature, the design process was guided by the author's multimedia design experience and interaction with the two teachers. The first version of the concept representation resource is presented in Fig. 9.6.

The concept representation resource contains information about a number of important river parameters, enables calculations of river discharge, presents the impact on flow rates of the shape of a riverbed, and allows identification of common bedrocks at different locations along the river. Various aspects of content are presented based on a student's interaction with the concept representation resource. A student can arrive at an understanding of the issues affecting the river through interaction and manipulation of specific parameters (e.g., how the cross-section of

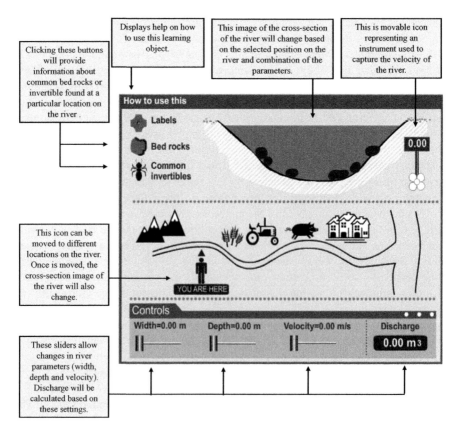

Fig. 9.6 The first version of the 'river' concept representation resource

9.4 Design for Learning Uses

the river changes as one moves down the river), and by systematic exploration of specific information (e.g., how river discharge is calculated based on values of width, depth and velocity).

Although the two participating teachers received the concept representation resource with enthusiasm, certain limitations emerged. The original intention was to design a concept representation resource for presentation via the small screens of mobile devices for use in the fieldwork. However, while the final product that emerged was suitable for presentation via computers and a projector, its design was less effective for presentation via mobile devices. The author installed the concept representation resource on a mobile device and asked the two teachers and two of their students to interact with its interface. These participants perceived the interface elements as too small, while some information was not easily readable.

The user feedback demonstrated the challenging nature of designing for presentation via mobile technology. It became clear at this point that much more consideration needed to be given to small screen design issues. Attention was given to the "movable, collapsible, overlapping, semitransparent interactive panels" design feature suggested by Churchill and Hedberg (2008). This recommendation suggests the utility of floating panels in order to maximize the information presented on a single display at one time. The content of the new design was organized into four groups presented in panels accessible by clicking relevant tabs, which allowed the students to easily navigate from one panel to another. The groups of content within the panels related to the main scenario of a river. As the author engaged in the process of redesigning and testing the different interface features based on the small screen design requirements, it became evident that revision of the content is needed. The participating teachers realized that additional content would be useful (e.g., hydraulic radius) while some previously included was determined unnecessary (e.g., common invertebrates). The process of redesigning the concept representation resource led the teachers to re-examine the content as well as their own knowledge. Redesign of the interface, simpler presentation, and improved utilization of the presentation area through groupings of elements, created the possibility for content to be more effectively arranged in the small screen space. The process of involving the teachers in the design was a productive activity for them, as they appeared to have been revising their own conceptual knowledge while pondering on the most suitable ways to present that knowledge to their students. At the same time, they increased their understanding of the affordances of technology for the presentation of educationally useful material. The final version of the concept representation resource is presented in Fig. 9.7.

Prior to the field trip, the participating teachers displayed the concept representation resource via a projector and used it as a visual aid when explaining the key concepts of a river (e.g., depth, velocity, discharge). They then distributed in their classes mobile devices with the final version of the concept representation resource, with which students were asked to interact while focusing on a few guiding questions (e.g., how bedrocks change as the river pursues its course). These questions led to class discussions on the key properties of a river. The teachers also

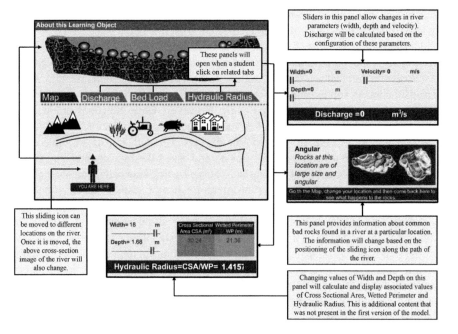

Fig. 9.7 The final version of the 'river' conceptual representation resource

made a connection between the content of the concept representation resource and other material available to students (e.g., the Geography textbook). Understanding of the key properties was required for students to effectively complete related fieldwork (e.g., collecting and comparing water discharge values at a number of points along the river, or describing with supporting evidence how the physical properties of the river changed along its path as it progressed downstream). In line with suggestions that the use of a concept representation resource might support development of some cognitive residue (see Mayer 1989; Norman 1983; Seel 2003), the concept representation resource in this inquiry allowed the participating students to develop some preliminary form of psychological tool based on the multimodal information and interaction presented. This tool was useful later as an aid for enabling the students to better visualize the key concepts when working on their fieldwork on the river or related activities (e.g., as some students suggested, when writing up the ongoing river case study report). The author is currently engaged in further study to investigate forms of cognitive residues and associated mind processes when these residues are used. It is hoped that such investigation will lead to further refining of the concept representation resource design recommendations, and provide outcomes that challenge, revise or further extend theoretical works such as Cognitive Theory of Multimedia Learning (e.g., Mayer 2003) and Cognitive Load Theory (Sweller 1994), and make more prominent links to ideas such as those held by Vygotsky (1962).

9.4 Design for Learning Uses

Once in the field, the students used the concept representation resource to support their tasks in any way they perceived as useful. After the fieldwork, the concept representation resource proved useful as a tool that facilitated reflections and writing up of the river case study report. The students were provided with a PowerPoint template, which they populated with their data, evidence and media from the field, before presenting their conclusions. During the fieldwork engagements, the students used handhelds to store measurements, collect images, capture video, take audio-recorded notes etc., and these were used as data, evidence and media for the report. The template was also embedded with the concept representation resource, along with relevant questions requiring the students to refer to the representation resource when developing their arguments in the report.

Throughout the implementation of the concept representation resource, the author engaged with the teachers and students involved, and observed uses in the class and the field. The data provided interesting information on various ways that the concept representation resource supported teaching and learning. During the data collection, images were taken of characteristic uses of the conceptual representation resource. The author often discussed emerging observations with the students, and after the completion of the outdoor learning, used some of the images in stimulated recall interviews with some selected students and the two teachers. These interviews explored experiences with the concept representation resource, and how it was used to assist in learning and work in the field with mobile technology. Units for analysis were located and extracted from the data, including interview transcripts and observations, and sorted into emerging categories reflecting uses of the concept representation resource. Data were also identified in the artefacts (reports written by the students). The categories of learning use emerging from the data included: preparation tool, collaboration tool, external cognitive supplement, aid to observations, decision-making tool, analytical tool, tool for inquiry, experimentation environment, tool for generalizing, tool for linking of theory and the world outside of the classroom, environment for articulation of components of knowledge, and a reflective tool. See Table 9.2 for examples of statements by the participating students representing units of data. The two participating teachers assisted the author in sorting the data into categories leading to the articulation of these learning uses. The author and teachers also collaborated on the coding of the collected images (see Fig. 9.8 for examples).

Overall, as mentioned, uses of the concept representation resource and involving the teachers and students in the study, resulted in a number of specific ideas about ways in which this resource supported learning (learning uses):

- *Preparation tool*—Prior to the field trip, the teachers presented the concept representation resource via a projector and used it as a visual aid when explaining the key concepts of a river (e.g., depth, velocity, discharge). The teachers also made a link between the content of the conceptual representation resource and that from the textbook used by the students. Further, prior to the trip, the students were issued with handheld devices to explore the concept

Table 9.2 Examples of statements (edited) by the participating students classified into categories of learning uses

Learning use	Example of statements by the students (units)—unedited
Preparation tool	With stuff like this [the conceptual representation resource] we can replace a lot of paper. Teachers can just send you stuff to your mobile before you go to the field. I could learn this material even on a school bus
Reflection tool	This resource makes more interesting to revise from, and to present to other people. It might make stuff easier to understand. After you finish the school day you can go home and use the learning resource, basically, you will summarize everything you done during the day
Collaboration tool	I can work on some data and he [a partner] can work on some data and then we can exchange our findings and other things from this resource
Analytical tool	All my data collection I done with help of the resource and mobile device. I did not even take any paper with me. In the resource, you can do all formulas so you do not have to calculate things in your head
Tool for inquiry	The interactive picture [the conceptual representation resource] helped us to find that the downstream changes you would expect would include an increase in discharge, a decrease in bed-load size and increase in roundness and with no change in water quality
Tool for generalizing	From the results, we have collected from this investigation, the velocity decreases as we go downstream of the river, therefore, erosion increases so the bed-load size decreases and gets more rounder. We are not 100% confident, as there may be errors during data collection. We checked our conclusions with pictogram [the conceptual representation resource] and it appears to be OK

representation resource and other functions. These enabled students to form some initial conceptual understanding before the field trip commenced.

- *Collaboration tool*—The students often showed each other various configurations of the concept representation resource, and discussed relevant issues. In addition, they used the concept representation resource in collaboratively working with the data. For example, one student collected measurements on the river and informed another student, who then entered these values in the concept representation resource in order to perform some associated calculations. The second student then passed these values to a third student, who recorded them in a spreadsheet. Following the data collection, the students used the conceptual representation resource to double-check the data that they had entered in the spreadsheet.
- *External cognitive supplement*—During the outdoor activity, the concept representation resource appeared to overcome some limitations in students' knowledge by supplementing it externally; that is, students were able to access representations of required concepts at any time they needed to do so.
- *Aid to observations*—The concept representation resource enabled the students to configure parameters according to their observation of the reality. For example, if they observed bedrocks of a certain shape in the river, they could configure the screen of the concept representation resource accordingly, and then identify other associated parameters not directly observable in the field.

9.4 Design for Learning Uses

Fig. 9.8 Examples of images captured during the field trip and analysed in the context of the study (faces are blurred to conceal the identities of the participants)

- *Decision-making tool*—The concept representation resource served as a tool to guide students' decision-making. The students were able to make their decisions, such as where to collect their next set of measurements, based on expectations developed through their interaction with the conceptual representation resource.
- *Analytical tool*—The conceptual representation resource enabled students to carry out certain calculations and analysis by configuring parameters according to data that they collected on the river (e.g., by entering values of width, depth and velocity of the river based on their measurements, they were able to obtain the value of discharge).
- *Tool for inquiry*—The students appeared to identify certain unknown parameters of the river through direct observation in the field, and then attempted to search for confirmation of their observations in the concept representation resource (or vice versa).
- *Experimentation environment*—The concept representation resource allowed students to experiment with the parameters from their observation and carry out certain predictions.
- *Tool for generalizing*—The concept representation resource supported the students easily moving between observations and conclusions and making generalizations from their observations and analysis of the collected data.

- *Tool for linking of theory and the world outside of the classroom*—During the outdoor activity, the students often compared aspects of their theoretical knowledge with what they observed in reality (e.g., shape of the river bed); they were able to do so because the concept representation resource provided them with a link. Thus, the resource enabled links between theoretical knowledge and reality, bridging learning in the class and the world outside the class.
- *Environment for articulation of components of knowledge*—The concept representation resource also enabled students to make connections between different parts of their knowledge and observations (as once they identified an element from their knowledge or observation in the concept representation resource, the resource presented other associated elements).
- *Reflective tool*—After the outdoor activity, the concept representation resource was used as a tool that facilitated reflection and possibly contributed to consolidation of newly acquired knowledge. It was also perceived as a useful revision tool, enabling students to check back on required conceptual knowledge when working on assignments or preparing for examination.

Activity 9.3
Look at the "Shapes" conceptual representation resource featured in Fig. 9.1. Think about and describe how this digital resource for learning can be used for each of the following purposes outlined above. Provide your explanation in the table below:

Specific uses	Explanation how the "shapes" resources can be used for the specific purpose
• Preparation tool	
• Collaboration tool	
• External cognitive supplement	
• Aid to observations	
• Decision-making tool	
• Analytical tool	
• Tool for inquiry	
• Experimentation environment	
• Tool for generalizing	
• Tool for linking of theory and the world outside of the classroom	
• Environment for articulation of components of knowledge	
• Reflective tool	

The final list of the categories of learning uses was discussed and ultimately confirmed with the participating teaches. An understanding of these possibilities for learning uses of a concept representation resource via mobile technology, as

9.4 Design for Learning Uses

Table 9.3 Recommendations for design for learning uses of concept representation resource via mobile technology

Design for learning uses recommendations	Learning uses identified during the fieldtrip
Design for observation	• Aid to observations • Tool for linking of theory and the world outside the classroom • Tool for inquiry
Design for analytical use	• Analytical tool
Design for experimentation	• Experimentation environment • Tool for generalizing
Design for thinking	• Environment of articulation of components of knowledge • External cognitive supplement • Decision-making tool
Design for reuse	• Preparation tool • Collaboration tool • Reflective tool

identified in the inquiry, is useful for teachers involved in planning the use of such representations in instruction. Furthermore, to create an optimal match between learning uses and features of a concept representation resource, a designer of a concept representation resource should consider design features that will support possible learning uses via mobile technology (by considering affordances of this technology when designed as a resource). In order to explicate a design for learning use recommendations, the specific learning uses identified in the inquiry were sorted into emerging categories. These categories represent recommendations on the design for learning uses and include the following: designs for observation, analytical use, experimentation, thinking, and reuse recommendations (see Table 9.3).

The following elaborates on each of these specific recommendations for design for learning uses:

- *Design for observation*—A concept representation resource should be designed in a way that supports learners to make links between the real world and represented properties of a concept. It should be designed so that learners can recognize properties from a real environment in the interface of a concept representation resource, as well as the converse. These representations of properties are not simply copies of the real world. Rather, designers should represent reality through illustrations, diagrammatical representations, analogies, metaphors, signs, cues, symbols, and icons.
- *Design for analytical use*—A concept representation resource should contain design features that allow learners to input data from the real environment for analytical processing (e.g., a special purpose calculator). Designers should use interactive features (e.g., sliders, dialers, hot-spot areas and text-input boxes) to enable input of parameters. Outcomes of interactions can be displayed in a

variety of formats such as numbers, graphs, audio, verbal/written statements, pictorial representations, and animation.

- *Design for experimentation*—A concept representation resource should enable learners to manipulate parameters and properties, and observe changes that result from such manipulations. Also, it might be useful to allow the manipulation of outcomes of analytical use to enable learners to examine how these changes affect related parameters. The changes should be highlighted to provide cues and encourage generalizing. A concept representation resource's design features should allow emergent generalizations to be tested in some way.
- *Design for thinking*—Designers should design a concept representation resource to include features that initiate and support thinking. This can be achieved by integrating triggers (e.g., signals and cues) to capture attention and initiate curiosity. Some design ideas from the Cognitive Theories of Multimedia Learning (Mayer 2001) could be useful, although the author of this book does not fully subscribe for these. For example, a concept representation resource design should support the cognitive activities of linking mental models (verbal and visual) developed through interaction with a concept representation resource.
- *Design for reuse*—The design of a concept representation resource for mobile devices should allow reuse in different environments and activities. For example, reuse might include a classroom presentation, or use by multiple learners as they collaborate. Other applications might require delivery via devices other than mobile technology, such as a computer, a projector or an interactive white board. The design of a concept representation resource needs to consider at least two issues for flexibility of reuse: (a) interactivity should be supported by a variety of devices, and (b) presentation of a concept representation resource on a large screen should not cause split attention problems (see Mayer 2001). In certain cases, it might be useful to provide features that allow data from a concept representation resource to be saved in an external file for reuse, sent to a specific Cloud-based space or for exchange between collaborating users (e.g., through the Internet or via mobile device connectivity affordance).

In addition to the two sets of recommendations, i.e., 'small screen design' and 'design for learning uses' recommendations, discussed in this chapter, the design of a concept representation resource for learning application via mobile technology, should give attention to the third set of 'design for presentation' recommendations, previously discussed in Chap. 3. Table 9.4 presents how the three sets of recommendations were applied in the design of the 'River conceptual representation resource.'

The author is currently exploring these recommendations in the context of redesigning a number of concept representation resources for application via mobile technology. In one case, the recommendations are applied to the design of a concept representation resource on a mechanical engineering course. This concept

9.4 Design for Learning Uses

Table 9.4 Design features of the 'River' conceptual representation resource (crr)

	Recommendations	Design features from the "River" conceptual representation resource (crr)
Design for presentation	• Present information visually	• Information in the crr is presented mostly visually (e.g., cross-section of the river and downstream changes). Text is used for buttons, labels, values and instruction
	• Design for interaction	• The crr allows a learner to manipulate parameters through sliders (e.g., position on the river). Outcomes of manipulations are presented visually and numerically (e.g., river cross-section and value of discharge)
	• Design a holistic scenario	• Elements such as cross-section of the river and the river path are arranged in a way that integrates them into a single scenario
	• Design for a single screen	• Content of the crr is presented in a single screen
	• Design for small space	• The crr is designed for effective presentation in a 320×240 pixel screen area
	• Use audio and video only if it is the only option	• No audio or video content is present in the crr. Although audio could add some realism (e.g., water flow), its presence is not necessary
	• Use colour in moderation	• Colour use is limited in the design. Colours include blue, white, black, brown, maroon and green
	• Avoid unnecessary decorative elements	• No decorative elements are used in the crr. All elements are related to essential content
	• Design with a single font	• Only Arial font is used in the crr.
	• Use frames to logically divide the screen area	• The screen is divided into functional areas. Top part of the screen presents the cross section of the river and its changes. Bottom part of the screen presents related content and interactive elements
Design for small screen	• Design for full-screen presentation	• When presented via handheld device, the crr is displayed in the full-screen mode
	• Design for landscape presentation	• The crr is displayed in landscape mode.
	• Minimize scrolling	• Content is designed in such a way that scrolling is not required
	• Design for short contacts and task-centeredness	• Content is presented visually to maximize amount of information that can be viewed in shortest time. The content displayed, such as numerical values, can support tasks like analysing real river parameters (e.g., parameters can be configured based on requirements pertaining to the real environment)

(continued)

Table 9.4 (continued)

Recommendations		Design features from the "River" conceptual representation resource (crr)
	• Design for one-step interaction	• Any single interaction will result in the immediate display on the screen of related information. Outcome of any interaction is immediately noticeable
	• Provide zooming facility	• Zooming has not been utilized in the crr. A redesigned version of the crr should contain this facility
	• Design movable, collapsible, overlapping, semi-transparent interactive panels	• Content is distributed in four panels, each containing content information and interactive features. Cross-section of the river remains displayed at all stages. The redesigned version of the crr will build further upon this recommendation by including features such as semi-transparent panels
Design for learning uses	• Design for observation	• Visual elements (e.g., illustrations) are designed in ways that are easily related to reality (e.g., rocks in the river bed or colour of water). Also, elements of reality (e.g., farm land) are easily related to visuals in the crr
	• Design for analytical use	• Interactive features allow the manipulation of parameters and calculation of associated outputs (e.g., changes in the river's width, depth and velocity will calculate and output value of discharge)
	• Design for experimentation	• The crr allows a learner to manipulate parameters and experiment with outputs (e.g., how hydraulic radius varies based on changes of the width and the height of the river)
	• Design for thinking	• Prominent colour and objects are used to highlight information such as how velocity is averaged across the river, or to highlight certain manifests in order to lead a learner to query and generalize
	• Design for reuse	• The crr is designed to be flexible and easily rescaled to fit larger screens and be displayed via computers and projectors. Interaction used (sliders and clickable spots) is supported across different devices. The crr can be embedded in other digital media environments such as PowerPoint slides or blogs

9.4 Design for Learning Uses

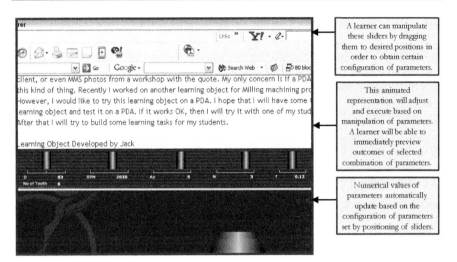

Fig. 9.9 'Machining (milling)' concept representation resource

representation resource represents the concept of machining parameters in machining (milling) process (see Fig. 9.9).

It allows a learner to: (a) manipulate parameters such as cutting speed and depth of cut to obtain values of other related parameters (design for analytical use), and (b) observe changes in visual representation of the machining process (design for observation). The design incorporates interactive features and arrangements of screen elements that connect analytical use with observation (design for experimentation). This allows experimentation with parameters and observable effects presented visually. Outcomes of interaction with the interface of the concept representation resource provide cues and signs that hint to links between certain content, e.g., a change to the colour red in a 'rotations per minute' parameter indicates that the input value exceeds the allowed range. These features were designed based on the design for thinking recommendation to help students note important information and cognitively link between representations. The design for reuse recommendation was also considered in the process. The design incorporated uses of overlapping panels in order to optimize presentation on a single small screen area, so that the conceptual representation resource might be used on a variety of devices. Mobile technology is, in particular, important in this context, as taking this concept representation resource to the workshop with real equipment, with provide students with an external conceptual supplement supporting their use of machines. This experience demonstrates the usefulness of the recommendation, and provides some further ideas about procedure for their application in the design process.

9.5 iPads and other Tables in Education

Tablet devices are increasingly becoming popular around the world. In 2015, there were 320 million tablets sold around the world, compared to almost 2 billion mobile phones. By 2018, this number is expected to approach almost 1.5 billion (eMarketer 2015). This means that the increasing number of individuals around the world will have access to this technology.

Education institutions around the world are increasing adopting this technology in teaching and learning. Apple iPad devices appear to be favoured by educational institutions and teachers, although price difference can make other tablets much more affordable to institutions that face limited budgets (e.g., in the developing world).

> **Important**
> Tablets are promising education technology and tools for the delivery of digital resources to learning-centred activities at anytime and anywhere.

The literature and cases of adoption of tablet technology are beginning to emerge. The Catholic Education-Diocese of Parramatta in Australia experimented with iPads in eight primary and three secondary schools (Catholic Education-Diocese of Parramatta 2010). This trial found that iPads were effective as: (a) support for learning in various settings due to portability and fit-for-task suitability, (b) support for student engagement and quick access to apps that students require for a particular learning task, and (c) students of all levels can use apps, especially for the reinforcement and rote learning of basic concepts. The 'Step Forward' pilot implementation of iPads at Trinity College of the University of Melbourne suggests this technology supports different learning styles and allows students to achieve their goals faster (Jennings et al. 2011). Furthermore, it is suggested that iPads are more effective than other computing technology such as laptops, and using this technology resulted in reduced printing and paper use. A survey of student and teacher experiences at Trinity College shows that iPads are overwhelmingly recommended for use (76.2% of staff and 80% of students). For Jennings et al. (2011), the advantages of iPads include educational flexibility and value, low cost, size and weight, battery life, low maintenance need, and touch screen. Furthermore, Murphy and Williams (2011) suggest iPads are effective technology for the presentation of class materials via multimedia systems. Other suggested advantages of iPads include size, battery life, instant on, transition between applications, multi-touch screen, cost, e-reader, multimedia support and playback, and connection to multimedia systems. Ostashewski and Reid (2010) add that the key advantage of iPads is that they can be used as a multimedia database. Other advantages suggested include ease of interaction via the touch screen, screen size, controllable multimedia playback, sound volume, and data collection capabilities. Forty teachers from a number of faculties at the University of San Francisco used iPads over six months in 2011 (Bansavich 2011). Implementation was monitored by the university's Centre for Instruction and Technology. It was noted that the key advantage of iPads for higher education include e-reader and electronic textbook capabilities, annotating and note taking for meeting and classroom features, multimedia viewing, interactivity, portability, design, ease of use, access to Apps, and speed of the device. Bansavich (2011) reports that iPads were found to be effective in language learning, clinical settings, and sciences (especially due to Apps). Also, it is suggested that iPads could be used in the contexts of student advising, lab setting, fieldwork, research and tutorial viewing. A similar pilot implementation of iPads at the University of Texas at Tyler suggests that this technology promotes greater communication between students and teachers (see Beebe 2011). Beebe (2011) writes that the participating students appeared to be more motivated to attend the class and turn in their assignments, and iPads lead students to be more responsible in their learning. It was also noted that students saved considerably by using e-books rather than purchasing physical books from the bookshop. Although tablets include many of the functions of a laptop and small screen mobile devices, essentially, this is a new platform for classroom computing (Walters 2011). For Walters (2011), the key advantage of an iPad is that it is a creation not just a consumption tool. Specifically, for teachers, Walters (2011) suggests an iPad can be used as a 'book in their pedagogical library' and a tool that allows easy experimentation with technology. Also, teachers can easily collect assignments. Walters (2011) suggests that portability and kinaesthetic interaction support students to develop visual and spatial skills, and achieve the level of 'Create' at the peak of Bloom's Taxonomy. The author of this book summarized reports of applications of iPads in education and positive features claimed in the literature in Table 9.5.

The author of this book conducted his own study (funded by the Hong Kong's Research Grants Council), building on the affordances of mobile technology, discussed previously in this book, and further exploring iPad tablet affordances as they emerge from teachers' efforts to understand and use this new technology. The study essentially explored how affordances of this tablet are utilized, how the participating teachers' private theories relate to the adoption of these affordances, and how the adoption of affordances leads to transformation in these teachers' private theories (see Churchill and Wang 2014). A group of nine teachers from different faculties from the University representing a range of disciplines from science, humanities and art, were included in the study over a period of 18 months. The study explicated patterns of private theories for each of the participants by interviewing them about a number of issues related to their teaching. A new iPad device was provided to each of the participants at the beginning of the study. Four sets of interviews were conducted: one focusing on private theories upon beginning of the study; the second (group) interview, several months later after iPads had been received, focusing on initial impressions, apps downloaded and used; the third interview at the beginning of the subsequent academic year focusing on the participants' plans for further uses, and any emerging issues; and the fourth sets of individual interviews to sum-up experience and register changes in private theories. At the same

Table 9.5 Summary of characteristics and educational uses of iPad devices from the literature

Features of iPads	Educational uses of iPads
• Design of the device • Size and weight • Multi-touch screen and interactivity • Long battery life • Speed of the device • Relatively low cost • Low maintenance need • Portability • Easy to use • Ease of connection to multimedia systems • Instant on • Quick transition between applications • E-reader and electronic textbook capabilities • Multimedia support and playback • Availability of Apps	• Presentation of class materials via multimedia systems (1)[a] • iPad provides access to multimedia databases and e-books (1) • Book in teachers pedagogical library (1) • Provides quick access to Apps that students might require for a particular learning task (1–7) • Students of all levels can use Apps, especially for reinforcement and rote learning of basic concepts (1) • Teachers can easily collect assignments (2) • Tool that allows teachers to easily experiment with technology (5) • A tool for creation, not just for consumption (6) • iPad provides annotating and note taking features for meeting and classrooms (6, 7) • Supports learning engagement in variety of settings due to portability and fit-for-task suitability (1–7) • Supports different learning styles (1–6) • Kinaesthetic and multi-touch interaction support students to develop visual and spatial skills (1–6) • Students can achieve their learning goals faster with appropriate use of iPads (1–6) • Students can achieve the level of "create" at the peak of the Bloom's taxonomy with appropriate use of iPads (1–6)

[a]Related to an affordance listed in the last column of Table 9.1

time, effort has been made to collect any further data through a social networking site (Edmodo.com) set-up to allow reflections and sharing amongst the people involved in the research.

The author examined Apps used by the participants, in order to develop categories of Apps found useful by teachers. The following categories of Apps emerged:

- Productivity Apps—These include tools such as word-processing, document annotation, creating of multimedia material tools. Specific Apps used include Mail, iAnnotate, Docs2PDF, Neu.Annotate, PDF Notes, Office2DH, iMovie and Dragon.
- Teaching Apps—These include tools that support classroom teaching, such as those that support connection to a projector, mark-book, presentation tools and classroom management tools. Examples of Apps used are Moodle, EdMondo, Clicker School, TeacherPal, Prezi Viewer, Slides Shark, LanSchool Teacher.
- Notes Apps—These are tools that enable note taking in combination with audio recording, drawing and typing. Examples of Apps are HansOn, Bamboo Paper, Penultimate, AudioNote, Draw Free and iPocketDraw.

- Communication (and Social Networking) Apps—These include tools that support communication and social networking. Some specific Apps include Facebook, Skype, Messages, FaceTime and MyPad.
- Drives—These include tools that allow connectivity to the Cloud, network drives and a computer. Some specific Apps include Air Shawing, FileBrowser, Dropbox, ZumoDrive, Air Drive and AirDisk.
- Blogging Apps—These tools allow convenient blogging via an iPad device. These Apps include Blogsy and Wordpress.
- Content Accessing Apps—These include tools such as e-books, multimedia material, digital resources for learning and video accessing tools. Some specific Apps include iBooks, Kindle, YouTube, Perfect Reader, iTunes and iTunesU.

Activity 9.4

Search AppStore and/or PlayStore for Apps, and identify at least one per each of the categories reported in this chapter. Describe the Apps selected, provide source(s) and explain how these might be useful to support the RASE learning design. Complete the following table:

App category	Description and source	How the App supports aspects of the RASE
• Productivity Apps		
• Teaching Apps		
• Notes Apps		
• Communication (and social networking) Apps		
• Drives		
• Blogging Apps		
• Content accessing Apps		

Furthermore, attempts were made to link these categories of Apps to specific areas of private theories and affordances of mobile technology. This has been done by identifying links between the categories of Apps and categories of affordances through the participant's private theories. The categories of private theories were those identified by a previous study and included theories about: students, learning, teacher roles, technology, lesson design, and education changes (see Churchill 2005). Data from interviews and observations were unitized and coded according to associations with three aspects: a Category of Apps, an Area of Private Theories, and an Affordance of Mobile Technology.

The explicated pattern of links between these three aspects is presented in Fig. 9.10. The figure shows links between areas of private theories (in the middle), categories of Apps (on the left), and affordance of mobile technology (on the right-hand side of the diagram). The numbers on links between any two connections (categories of apps and private theories, or private theories and affordances)

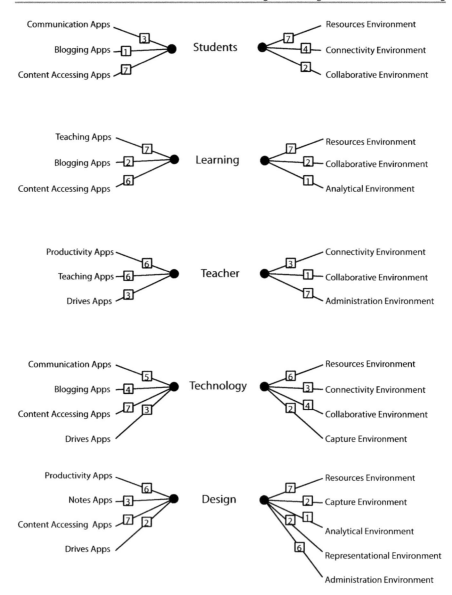

Fig. 9.10 Connections between categories of Apps, private theories and affordances of mobile technology

represents the number of participants whose data from the study indicates such a link. For example, three participants associated 'Communication Apps' with their 'Private Theories about Students,' while seven participants associated 'Private Theories about Students' with 'Resources Environment' affordance. The purpose of opting for such summary statistics as a mean of cross-case analysis was to

9.5 iPads and other Tables in Education

Table 9.6 Summary of connections

Categories of Apps used by the participants	No. of connections	Areas of the participants' private theories	No. of connections	Affordances of mobile technology from previous studies	No. of connections
Productivity Apps	12	Students	24	**Resources environment**	27
Teaching Apps	13	Learning	25	Connectivity environment	10
Notes Apps	3	**Teacher**	26	Collaborative environment	9
Communication Apps	8	Technology	34	Capture environment	4
Drives Apps	8	Design	36	Analytical environment	2
Blogging Apps	7	Educational changes[a]		Representational environment	2
Content accessing Apps	27			Administration environment	13
Total	78		145		67

[a]No data related to this area of private theories were analyzed

understand how adoption is taking place in general. Table 9.6 shows a summary of connections between 'Categories of Apps used by the Participants', 'Areas of the Participants' 'Private Theories', and 'Affordances of Mobile Technology from Previous Studies'.

These results expose the nature of adoption of tablet technology by the cases of teachers in the study. The following are observations relevant to digital resources for learning:

- The most used category of Apps was Content Accessing Apps (27 connections), while the most referred affordance was Resources (27 connections). This indicates a strong inclination of teachers to adopt iPads as a medium for access to resources such as web sites, YouTube videos, e-book, digital resources for learning, and articles.
- The most dominant theories were those about Design (36 connections). Private Theories about Design most strongly related to Content Accessing Apps on one side (7), and Resources affordance on the other (7). This shows that the participating teachers' instructional planning was strongly focusing on content.
- The second most dominant theories were about Technology (34 connections). Private Theories about Technology most strongly related to Content Accessing Apps on one side (7), and Resources affordance on the other (6). Similar to the previous observation, access to content resources played a central role in thinking about technology.

- Private Theories about Students most strongly related to Content Accessing Apps (7) and Resources affordance (7). Similarly, Private Theories about Learning most strongly related to Teaching (7) and Content Accessing Apps (6) on one side, and Resources affordance on the other (7). Content appears to dominate in both cases.

A strong focus on Content Accessing Apps and Resources affordances of mobile technology indicates that the participating teachers placed priority on an iPad to serve as a tool for access and delivery of content resources. This is confirmation that, as teachers' adoption of tablets is very much driven by resources, we need to pay considerable attention to issues of design of digital resources for learning with thus technology. However, there is a serious problem observed in the data from this study.

A previous study by Churchill (2005) informs that most desired outcomes in terms of embracing activity-based, learning-centred pedagogy is achieved when teachers make their instructional planning decisions and technology use based upon their private theories about 'Learning.' However, in the case of our study, 'Learning' was the second last most dominated category of theories. The most dominated were theories about 'Design' and 'Teacher,' indicating that the central issue on their instructional planning was, not what students will be doing to learn, but what they will be doing as teachers, and how technology will help them in the process or even take over teaching from them. Driven by initial enthusiasm, it was believed that tablets will have a positive transformative effect on teachers, enabling them to more closely focus on uses of affordances to support their private theories about 'Learning', and that his will lead to learning-centred practices. However, on the contrary, the results show that this has not occurred, and the participating teachers were using iPads in a way that reflects traditional, teacher-centred approaches, where the technology was considered as a medium for transfer of knowledge, rather than as a set of tools that support learning through activities. In this sense, resources were perceived as direct teaching tools, rather than tools that mediate learning activities.

In summary, tablets are perceived as effective tools for delivery of digital resources for learning, however, teachers are more likely to use these resources in more traditional, teacher-directed ways, rather than to plan their utility in learning-centered activities. Considering this, other affordances of tablet technology are less likely to be adopted in the way that reflects learning-centered practice.

9.6 A Case of Design of an App Resource: From a Small-Screen Mobile Device to a Tablet Version

Nevertheless, tablets are promising education technology and tools for the delivery of digital resources to learning-centred activities at anytime and anywhere. The digital resources for learning should be designed to fully leverage upon affordance of this technology, and in a way that reflects possible learning uses. The 'design for learning uses' recommendations identified previously in this book, fully apply to resources designed for application via tablets. Additional consideration needs to be given to the nature of interaction which is more intuitive, responsive and natural due to the large screen space, and supports not only single user and single click, but multiple users, gestures, and multi-touch that can be applied to enhance the design outcome. In addition, tablets create more opportunities for the integration of various affordances in a set of tolls and platforms for learning.

9.6.1 Development of a Resource for Mobile Learning

This part of the chapter describes a digital resource for learning designed and developed in the context of Chinese language learning (see Jie et al. 2014). In 2009, the author met an exceptional teacher of Chinese as a Foreign Language at the University of Hong Kong. The teacher was dedicated and keen to solve some fundamental problems in teaching Chinese as a foreign language she understood existed in the context of her practice. Over the years, she has encountered challenges the teaching of Chinese characters to non-Chinese students. Most of her students were exchange undergraduate students from foreign countries keen to learn the Chinese language.

The teacher understood that it is difficult for students to learn the order of strokes; they have to practice them multiple times in order to remember a single character, and there was absence of any system for them to remember such order, other than to practice each one repeatedly. In her current practice, she would write a character on the white board, explaining the stroke order and students would follow by completing exercises prescribed in their book. As for many Chinese language teachers, she was traditional in her approach, and was hardly familiar with the affordances of educational technology. However, she recognized her challenge and was open to new ideas.

During a number of meetings with this teacher, the author was featuring various digital resources for learning, and discussed how mobile technology might be used in her teaching. The teacher emphasized that one of the key challenges in her teaching was the teaching of fundamental Chinese characters and 'four tones' in pronunciation. Over time, a couple of small prototypes were developed by the author for the purpose of demonstrating possibilities that technology might offer (Fig. 9.11).

The prototype displayed a small set of five Chinese characters, and allowed a learner to play a sequence demonstrating how each of these was written. It also allowed the learner to listen to a recorded pronunciation of each character, access an English-equivalent meaning and 'Pinyin' (pronunciation written in alphabetical characters), preview history from its initial pictorial form, through traditional and simplified forms, and preview some examples where this character was used to form words and sentences. The teacher was told that it is even possible to design a feature that allows learners to practice writing characters by dragging a stylus or a

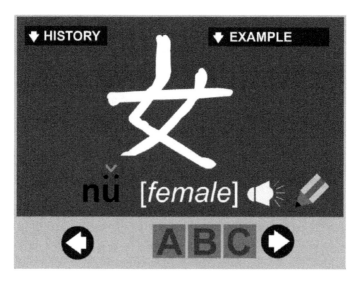

Fig. 9.11 A prototype of digital resources for learning developed to showcase design possibilities to the teacher in relation to challenges she raised in her practice

finger over the screen. She was also told that mobile technology would allow students to have access to such a resource anytime and anywhere, and use it in a variety of learning and practicing situations.

After seeing the prototype, the teacher almost immediately become enthusiastic about such possibilities offered to her for application via mobile technology. The agreement reached was to pursue funding opportunities in the future, to develop such projects and experiments with its use with Chinese as second language university students. An appropriate opportunity emerged when the university made a call for applications for Teaching Development Grants. An application was made, and it was successfully funded, and enabled the project to purchase some mobile devices, and secure a programmer and a multimedia designer to help in the development. The author of this book undertook instructional design of the digital resources and experimentation with learners, while the teacher provided essential content expertise. After several months of development, collaboration and explorations, a digital resource for learning via mobile technology titled 'Mobilese' was launched. The resource was made available for use via Pocket PC Windows Mobile devices and major mobile handsets at that time, such as Nokia and Sony. Key screens from this information display resource are presented in Fig. 9.12.

The Mobilese allows a learner to examine characters from a set of 200 Chinese simplified characters. At the home interface, a learner can select one of the displayed characters, or narrow down their choices by selecting one of the categories that classify characters according to a number of strokes required to write it. Alternatively, a student can search for a character according to Pinyin. The 200 characters were carefully selected and included in the Mobilese by the participating Chinese language expert, that is, the teacher.

9.6 A Case of Design of an App Resource: From a Small-Screen Mobile ...

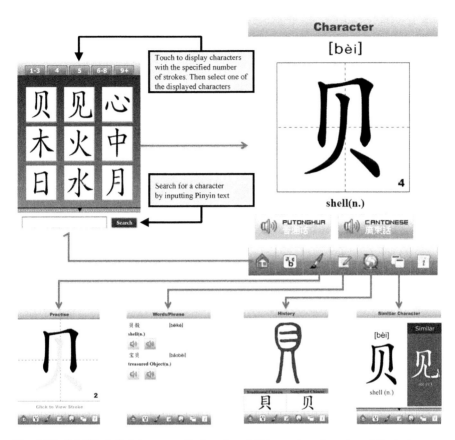

Fig. 9.12 'Mobilise' digital resource for learning of Chinese characters via mobile devices

Once a character is selected, it will be displayed on the interface and a set of functionalities will be made available. Now, a learner is able to preview a character, and practice writing it by recreating the correct stroke order. Unique to the approach is that a student cannot write a character in any incorrect order, that is, rather than receiving feedback for being incorrect, he or she must discover a proper sequence in his or her own way. Most of the other Chinese language resources reviewed by the author and the collaborating teacher approached this differently by proving learner feedback if they are wrong or correct, or showing the correct sequence. However, both the author and the teacher believed that it is much more effective to allow students to struggle with the complexity and work out the correct sequence in their own way. Another unique feature of this resource is that of 'similar characters'. The teacher, based on her almost 40 years of teaching experience, understood that her students often make mistakes and mix-up characters that are somehow similar. Such characters have been identified and a feature was created to allow students to preview similar characters, and focus on the specific aspects of these characters that cause mix-ups. An additional functionality allows a learner to examine the history of a specific character, listen to pronunciation in Putonghua and Cantonese versions, and explore examples of words in Putonghua and Cantonese that use that character.

The teacher and her colleagues at the University enthusiastically received the Mobilese. At the same time, as claimed by the teacher, students were quick in embracing this resource, and it was continuously used through a semester by them in a variety of situations: in a class, when studying independently, at home, in the library and even on the bus to or from the University to home. In the absence of any formal way of capturing improvements in students' learning, judged by the teachers' and students' claims collected at the time, the Mobilese helped them in their learning in new ways which were not possible without such technology before.

9.6.2 Development of iMobilese for iPod Delivery

The Mobilese was placed on the Internet at the site http://mobilese.cite.hku.hk/, and made available for download and use free-of-charge for anyone interested in it. Several thousand downloads were registered. However, by this stage, Apple iOS devices, such as iPhones and iPods begun to emerge, and many students were asking for the Mobilese in a version that would work on these platforms. The team begun to think about the redevelopment of the Mobilese into an iMobilese version for Apple iOS delivery. The iOS devices (e.g., iPods and iPhone) enable learners to effortlessly input and output information in a variety of formats to learn a language. Learners are not confined by fixed devices, and they can use a variety of tools supported by this mobile technology (e.g., camera features). The mobility of these devices enables learners to learn while walking around in the classroom, on their way home, or any other places, whenever they feel like learning. Computer-based digital resources require certain levels of technical competency to successfully accomplish learning tasks, such as typing with the keyboard and handling the mouse, which is challenging for lower-grade students (Wong et al. 2011). Writing with fingers on a tangible user interface of a mobile device is more intuitive, fun and close to handwriting experience. There is evidence that interaction with tangible user interfaces may reduce the cognitive load required for learning (Kim and Maher 2008).

An attempt was made to secure further funding for the project to be redeveloped. At these earlier stages of such technology, the standard funding bodies were not able to understand the importance of moving into this direction, and funding was not secured. Traditionally, education institutions are slow in embracing innovation even though there are enthusiastic members willing to explore. Nevertheless, public interest in the Mobilise grew, and soon there were a number of schools interested to use this digital resource in their context. In particular, an international school from Hong Kong become interested in Mobilese, however, they required certain modifications, and wanted it to be available for implementation via iPod Touch mobile devices. After a number of discussions, the author proposed a redevelopment of the Mobilese with the development of new features, and reorganization of the content according to the school's needs and in a way that was suitable for their early primary learners and the Chinese language curriculum. The school's principal, Chinese language curriculum leaders and technology coordinators favoured this proposal, and soon the school was ready to provide substantial funding and enter in the collaborative project agreement for the redevelopment of this digital resource for learning for application via iOS devices.

The team from the University was comprised of the author, as an expert on technology in education, the expert teacher who worked with the author on the initial version of the Mobilese as an adviser on Chinese language teaching, a professor from the Faculty of Engineering as an expert on computer science, a post-doctoral fellow leading the research component of the project, a research assistant who facilitated data collection and arrangements, and an iOS App programmer supported by a part-time graphics/multimedia designer. The team conducted classroom observations of the Chinese character lessons, observations of students' current iPod uses, review of the curriculum and teaching documentation and resources at the school, and interviews with the school's Chinese language teachers. This data informed subsequent redesign and development of new features of the 'iMobilese' digital resource for learning resulting from the project. The project team also explored how various affordances of mobile technology (in addition the 'resources' affordance) can contribute to the final product.

A considerable redesign was made from the initial version of the Mobilese, although the fundamental idea of character learning through visuals and interactivity remains the same in both digital resources for learning via mobile technology. The redesigned digital resources focused on traditional, rather than simplified characters according to the specific curriculum of the Chinese language at the school. Additional functionalities and arrangements were built in the resources in a way that reflect the recommendations from the school's teachers and the curriculum leader, advices of experts from the team, and a number of affordances of mobile technology.

The interface of the iMobilese resource was made more colorful and attractive, especially for early primary school learners. This is what teachers claimed is necessary to be included in the redesign. The team tested several different interface designs until finally, the one that appeared most attractive to learners and teachers, was finally determined. However, it must be noted that such selection was based upon preferences, rather than any empirical data that links various designs to the achievements of learning outcomes. Although the author's previous study led to a recommendation that resources for mobile application should be designed for landscape presentation, both Mobilese and iMobilese moved away from this recommendation, and followed the standard portrait presentation native to small screen mobile devices. Later on in our involvement with the development, again it emerged that landscape presentation could have been more effective and would provide more flexibility in designing the interface and arranging the content. However, the final resource was delivered in portrait orientation.

In the iMobilese, similar as in the previous design of the Mobilese, learners were able to select for learning a character from a list of 200 included in the resource.

These 200 characters were carefully selected and determined by the Chinese language teachers from the school, based on the school's curriculum and advices from the Chinese language expert from the University's team. The menu for selecting characters has taken a new approach. Characters on the menu are sorted by default according to a number of strokes in ascending order. However, a learner is able to rearrange these in alphabetical order according to Pinyin, or according to units predefined flexibly by teachers based on the school's curriculum program.

Exploring the characters in iMobilese is similar, in many ways, as is done in the Mobilese. Learners are able to preview how characters are written in a stroke-by-stroke order, examine similar characters, and explore words using those characters. However, there are a number of new features. Firstly, a learner is now able to mark a character he or she is exploring, as 'favourite,' 'need to learn,' or 'known' for ones that are learnt already. This information is then made available for easy reference at the main interface where learners select characters to explore. Then, a learner can quickly access a list of characters he or she marked as 'favourite,' 'need to learn' or 'already known'. This information is also saved and can be examined by a teacher or parents. The main interface of the iMobilese is shown in the Fig. 9.13.

An additional and new feature allows a learner to save their own attempt of the independent writing of characters. Practicing of writing a character in the original Mobiles was done only in one way—a learner writes a character in the only possible way according to specific stroke-by-stroke order, and cannot achieve it in any other way. In the iMobilese, the practicing of writing characters is done in three different ways (see Fig. 9.14). Firstly, scaffolded by emerging stars to be connected

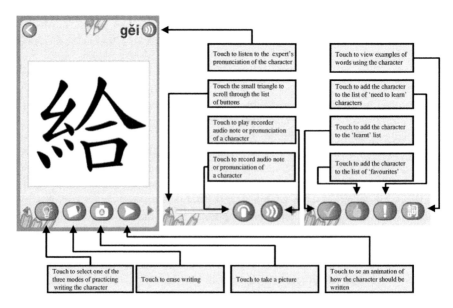

Fig. 9.13 Main screen of the 'iMobilese' for exploring individual characters

9.6 A Case of Design of an App Resource: From a Small-Screen Mobile ...

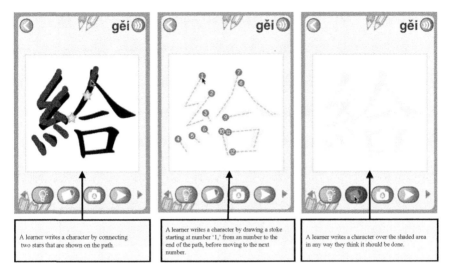

Fig. 9.14 Three ways for a learner to practice writing a character in the iMobilese

by strokes in a specific order. Secondly, by a skeleton that shows stroke order and paths, and requires a learner to complete the order in that specific sequence starting at number 1. Thirdly, by presenting a shade of a whole character and allowing a learner to complete that character in his or her own way. A learner's final writing of a character is saved in the system for later preview.

Further attempts in the redesign were made to integrate capture affordances of mobile technology. In the iMobilese, learners are able to record sounds and take photographs. While viewing a specific character, a learner can record his or her own voice for the purposes of comparing own pronunciation to recording of an expert available in the resource. In fact, by using this feature, a learner can capture any audio, such audio notes, or record a teacher or a class friend. Furthermore, a learner can take photographs of objects, people, book pages and scenes that he or she associates with a specific character. These audio recordings, photographs taken, as well as images of characters written by a learner, are all saved on the device. A learner can access these through a repository feature available in the iMobilese (see Fig. 9.15). There are two intentions and ideas for this. Firstly, these media files are saved for learners to use later in. For example, they might use these to share with other learners, or build a presentations and digital stories. Secondly, teachers and parents could preview these files to get ideas about learning progress and engagement. The plan was to integrate some kind of Cloud-based technology, such as, DropBox, where these files are uploaded from the system for learners and teachers to access. However, due to technical constraints, this was not implemented in this version of iMobilese. Currently, teachers are simply reviewing these files by accessing them on iPod devices assigned to learners. Any copying of files from an iPod is done manually by synching or by emails or multimedia messaging.

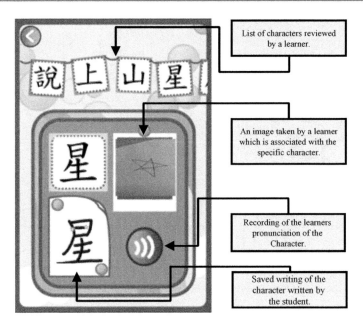

Fig. 9.15 Repository of saved media created by a learner

The iMobilese also includes three practice resources: 'Word Maker,' 'Pinyin Match,' and 'Hear and Match'. The participating teachers were keen to have such items included. They believed that such a resource would be productive for learning, and access learners' results would help them with ideas regarding their progress. In Word Maker, learners match characters to form words. Learners should make a maximum number of words within one minute. Pinyin Match is a practice resource that engages learners in associating characters with the correct Pinyin. Learners can match as many characters as they can with Pinyin during one minute. Hear and Match is a practice resource to reinforce listening skills. In this practice, students hear sounds and select matching characters in a one-minute time limit. All practice resources calculate the number of correct matches within one minute, and learners would strive to obtain higher scores by repeating the practice. Also, learners can compete with each other on scores received in the practices. Results of the practices are stored on the device and can be accessed by a teacher. The practices have been developed based on the worksheet exercise that teachers used in their teaching. These practice resources are shown in Fig. 9.16.

In fact, how iMobilese was developed, is that it has become more of an integrated set of digital resources for learning, rather than a stand-alone resource of one of the forms introduced in this book. However, although such an integrated digital resource for learning is possible to be developed, essentially, the resource would fall in one of the main categories discussed based on its primary purpose. In the case of iMobilese, it is still an information display resource, though, a large one that includes 200 characters. A digital resource for learning can be developed in a way,

9.6 A Case of Design of an App Resource: From a Small-Screen Mobile ...

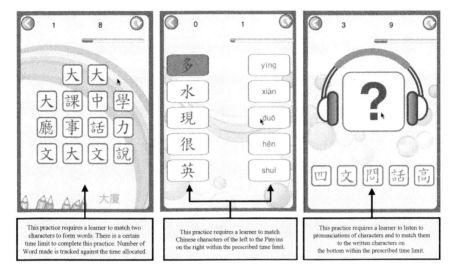

Fig. 9.16 Practice resources included in the iMobilese

not only to include various forms of resources integrated together, but also to include various affordances, such as is the case of integrating capture tools in iMobilese. These can support activities where digital resources are used, and might possibly support the development of new literacies and skills for 21st century.

The University team, led by the author of this book, interviewed four Chinese language teachers at the school, and observed twelve lessons, in order to understand how the iMobilese was integrated into teaching, and how learners used the App in their learning activities. Data shows that the App were used in four different ways (see Jie et al. 2014):

- The App was used in combination with workbooks as a tool for demonstration, practice, and reference. For example, learners used the iMobilese to watch demonstrations and practice writing in correct stroke order first (see Fig. 9.17A). Then, learners used the workbook to practice handwriting with pencils, while writing down a word constructed with the character. They referred to the iMobilese when encountering unknown characters.
- Learners used iMobilese to independently practice writing and speaking Learners in groups received a sheet listing the characters they needed to review and practice (see Fig. 9.17B). They took screenshots of their writing and recorded their speaking of a sentence constructed with the character. In most cases, learners played back their recorded speaking immediately. They learned independently and under the supervision of a teaching assistant. The teaching assistant assessed learners' learning performance by checking their captures.

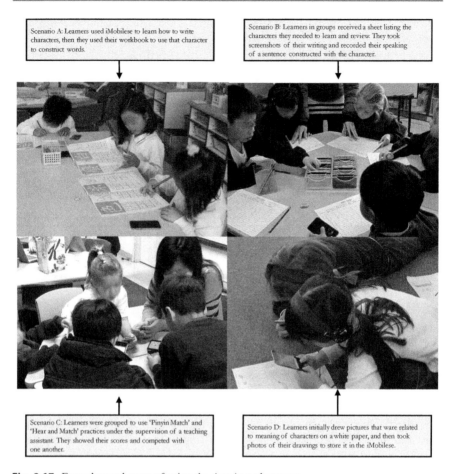

Fig. 9.17 Four observed ways of using the App in a classroom

- The App was used to support practice-based group learning for reinforcing Pinyin pronunciation and listening skills. In addition to practicing individually, students were grouped to use practice resources under the supervision of a teaching assistant (see Fig. 9.17C). They showed their scores and competed with one another. They appeared to be very excited in a positive way due to this competitive practice-based engagement.
- The App was used to facilitate characters' meaning making by taking photos of real-world objects. For example, in a class, students initially drew pictures on white paper that were related to the meaning of characters, and then took photos of their drawings to store it in the iMobilese (see Fig. 9.17D). In another example, learners took their iPod Touches home and captured photos of real-world objects that they associated with characters they were learning.

Jie et al. (2014) reporting on the research part of this project, informed that data from observations, showed that almost all students could fluently operate the iMobilese in their learning activities, and were engaged and responsive. The analysis of 17 students' learning artefacts supports the findings of the observations, including 259 screenshots of handwritings, 357 audio files, and 41 photos stored in the iPod Touches. The results indicated that with the assistance of the App, almost all students were capable of writing as well as pronouncing characters correctly; nearly two thirds of the photos taken by the students were related to the meanings of the characters. The teachers reported there were observable improvements in aspects of language learning, and students' interests and engagement in writing characters, especially for those with low levels of Chinese language ability. According to the interview data, the App was capable of satisfying the teachers' pedagogy by enriching group activities, accommodating a variety of learning abilities, and encouraging students input and output of language. All of the teachers felt that the App saved time previously spent on repeated demonstration; more importantly, it greatly engaged students by increasing their learning interests and confidence. It removed the barrier of limited vocabulary of primary school students, and allowed them to be more creative in sentence construction through speaking it out, rather than writing. The scaffolding offered by the App was considered particularly helpful for students with lower levels of Chinese language ability to master the correct procedure of writing a character. They further suggested that it was important that the App had a built-in capability that could adapt to, and challenge various levels of Chinese language abilities. Inspired by the iMobilese, the teachers were challenged to explore the new instructional methods and were willing to keep trying it. As the participating teachers from the school engaged with iMobilese, their demand for features grew. Their interest drew them to explore technology and applications in their classroom and, as a consequence, they have become more demanding and willing to see further development, such as connectivity with other tools (e.g., Twitter); screen-casting functionality for learners to showcase their work; uploading of learners' work in a Cloud-based space; development of an iPad version as iPod touch screen was too small; a feature to allow the teachers to check if students can follow the stroke order; a tool that promotes creativity with use of multimedia (e.g., a kind of presentation making tool with the iMobilese); and a portfolio for the management of evidences of continuing language learning. The results of the learners' interviews were generally consistent with that of teachers' interviews. Fifteen of the 17 learners stated that they enjoyed learning with the App because it made writing Chinese characters more engaging than with pencil and paper. The majority (13 out of 17) felt that their writing, reading, and speaking were improved with the help of the iMobilese. They felt a sense of success when they reviewed what they had achieved through their files. Two learners also mentioned that they were excited about sharing their writing and photos, stored within the iMobilese, with their parents and friends. All learners indicated that they would like to continue using the iMobilese App in their later studies.

9.6.3 Tablet Version of iMobilese Digital Resource for Learning

A logical progression for iMobilese was to develop in the Tablet/iPad version. By this stage of our research and development, iPad has become a popular piece of technology, and many schools around the world have begun to explore its uses. At the same time, a rapidly increasing number of Apps developed for iPads, have begun to emerge. Although both, small devices and tablets, essentially used variations of the same operating systems, and the same App can be delivered via both; the large screen size of iPads assures greater screen design possibilities, functionalities and integration of tools made possible by this powerful learning and information technology.

Recently, the author met a director of a technology company from Hong Kong who showed interest in the iMobilese approach to digital resources for learning. In idea explored the development of a commercial iPad App for learning of Chinese characters, that can be used by variety of audiences, such as school learners, independent learners across the Globe, language schools, corporate training, etc. Subsequently, the director made the decision to invest in the development of such a resource. From the author's perspective, having an unconstrained budget to develop and experiment with his ideas was an ideal situation and soon, a collaborative agreement was formalized and the design process begun.

The most immediate idea was to redesign iMobilese given the larger screen area possibilities and new form of interaction, and expand its content to include up to 1000 characters. However, further thinking lead the author to ambitiously pursue other possibilities, including, to develop this resource in a platform that makes possible a variety of activities, such as digital storytelling and social networking, and provides a tool for teachers to manage the processes of learning in their own way. Fundamental to this plan was to leverage upon possible affordances of mobile technology, in particular, resources, collaborative, capture and representational affordances. In this sense, a plan for a new generation of educational Apps for Tablets was born, and the particular product to be developed was the Chinese Learning Apps System, or the CLAS. The screen capture of the prototype of the CLAS is presented in Fig. 9.18.

As it can be seen in Fig. 9.18, the new interface is much more complex, and there are a variety of tools incorporated by build upon different affordances of mobile technology. Such an App is not only a digital resource for learning, but it incorporates the features of learning management, social networking and representational tools in a platform that supports learning activities. Such integration is made possible by the developments in mobile technology and opportunities that it creates for education.

In addition to the development of this app for Chinese language learning (which is in the prototype stage now), the author is engaged in designing a similar App for mathematics education. Rather than having a collection of characters such as in the

9.6 A Case of Design of an App Resource: From a Small-Screen Mobile ...

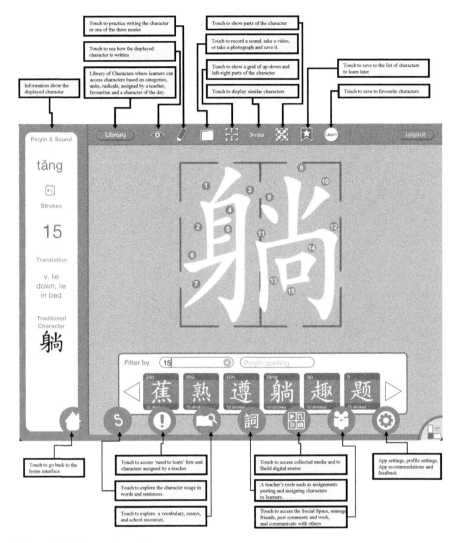

Fig. 9.18 Tablet version of the resource

CLASS, this App will contain a collection of conceptual representation resources for mathematics education. Learners will be able to explore these resources in various ways, engage with tools such as annotation, digital storytelling, concept mapping and social networking, while teachers will have an additional component that allows them to set up activities for students. This project is in a very early stage, however, some preliminary designs have already been put in place, and the author is waiting for a suitable funding opportunity to implement these ideas.

Activity 9.5
Look back at the "Season Change" digital resources you designed earlier at the end of Chap. 3. *Redesign the interface of this resource to be more effective for presentation* via *mobile devices. What principles have you used to guide your decision? Complete this form to indicate how you integrated the recommendations introduced in this chapter in your redesign (see* Table 9.3 *for an example).*

Recommendations	Description of how you integrated the recommendations in your design	
Design for presentation	• Present information visually	•
	• Design for interaction	•
	• Design a holistic scenario	•
	• Design for a single screen	•
	• Design for small space	•
	• Use audio and video only if it is the only option	•
	• Use color in moderation	•
	• Avoid unnecessary decorative elements	•
	• Design with a single font	•
	• Use frames to logically divide the screen area	•
		•
Design for small screen	• Design for full-screen presentation	•
	• Design for landscape presentation	•
	• Minimize scrolling	•
	• Design for short contacts and task-centeredness	•
	• Design for one-step interaction	•
	• Provide zooming facility	•
	• Design movable, collapsible, overlapping, semi-transparent interactive panels	•
Design for learning uses	• Design for observation	•
	• Design for analytical use	•
	• Design for experimentation	•
	• Design for thinking	•
	• Design for reuse	•

References

Albers, M., & Kim, L. (2001). Information design for the small-screen interface: an overview of web design issues for personal digital assistants. *Technical Communications, 49*(1), 45–60.

Anderson, P., & Blackwood, A. (2004). Mobile and PDA technologies and their future use in education. *JISC Technology and Standards Watch, 4*(3), 3–33.

References

Attewell, J. (2005). *Mobile technologies for learning*. London: Learning and Skills Development Agency.

Bansavich, J. C. (2011). *iPad study at USF*. Retrieved September 5, 2011 from http://ipad.wiki.usfca.edu/file/view/iPad+Study+at+USF+Report.pdf

Barnes, S. (2000). What does electronic conferencing afford distance education? *Distance Education, 21*(2), 236–247.

Beebe, A. (2011). *iPads in the college composition classroom: A pilot program at the University of Texas at Tyler*. Retrieved from http://conferences.cluteonline.com/index.php/IAC/2011NO/paper/view/177

Borba, M. C., Askar, P., Engelbrecht, J., Gadanidis, G., Llinares, S., & Aguilar, M. S. (2016). Blended learning, e-learning and mobile learning in mathematics education. *ZDM, 48*(5), 589–610.

Bringula, R. P., Alvarez, J. N., Evangelista, M. A., & So, R. B. (2017). Learner interface interactions with mobile-assisted learning in mathematics: Effects on and relationship with mathematics performance. *International Journal of Mobile and Blended Learning (IJMBL), 9*(1), 34–48.

Briz-Ponce, L., Juanes-Méndez, J. A., García-Peñalvo, F. J., & Pereira, A. (2016). Effects of mobile learning in medical education: A counterfactual evaluation. *Journal of Medical Systems, 40*(6), 1–6.

Burden, K., & Kearney, M. (2016). Future scenarios for mobile science learning. *Research in Science Education*, pp. 1–22.

Burston, J. (2016). Realizing the potential of mobile phone technology for language learning. *IALLT Journal of Language Learning Technologies, 41*(2).

Catholic Education-Diocese of Parramatta. (2010). *iPad in schools: Use testing*. Retrieved from http://learningwithipads.blogspot.com/2011_04_01_archive.html

Chiu, T. K. (2016). Effects of prior knowledge on mathematics different order thinking skills in mobile multimedia environments. In *Mobile learning design* (pp. 373–386). Singapore: Springer.

Churchill, D. (2005). Teachers' private theories and their design of technology-based learning. *British Journal of Educational Technology, 37*(4), 559–576.

Churchill, D. (2013). Conceptual model design and learning uses. *Interactive Learning Environments, 21*(1), 54–67.

Churchill, D., & Churchill, N. (2008). Educational affordances of PDAs: A study of a teacher's exploration of this technology. *Computers and Education, 50*(4), 1439–1450.

Churchill, D., & Hedberg, G. (2008). Learning object design considerations for small-screen handheld devices. *Computers and Education, 50*(3), 881–893.

Churchill, D., & Wang, T. (2014). Teacher's use of iPads in higher education. *Educational Media International, 51*(3), 214–225.

Churchill, D., Kennedy, D. M., Flint, D., & Cotton, N. (2010). Using handhelds to support students' outdoor educational activities. *International Journal of Continuing Engineering Education and Life-Long Learning, 20*(1), 54–72.

Churchill, D., Lu, J., & Chiu, K. F. T. (2014). Integrating mobile technologies, social media and learning design. *Educational Media International, 51*(3), 163–165.

Clyde, L. A. (2004). M-learning. *Teacher Librarian, 32*(1), 45–46.

Diliberto-Macaluso, K., & Hughes, A. (2016). The use of mobile apps to enhance student learning in introduction to psychology. *Teaching of Psychology, 43*(1), 48–52.

Domingo, M. G., & Gargante, A. B. (2016). Exploring the use of educational technology in primary education: Teachers' perception of mobile technology learning impacts and applications' use in the classroom. *Computers in Human Behavior, 56*, 21–28.

Donaldson, R. L. (2016). *Student acceptance of mobile learning*. Retrieved from http://diginole.lib.fsu.edu/islandora/object/fsu%3A168891

Duprey, M. D., Hutchings, A., & Mamishian, A. H. (2016). *Promoting student engagement through the use of mobile applications.* Retrieved from http://vhl.aws.openrepository.com/vhl/handle/10755/620612

Fabian, K., Topping, K. J., & Barron, I. G. (2016). Mobile technology and mathematics: Effects on students' attitudes, engagement, and achievement. *Journal of Computers in Education, 3*(1), 77–104.

Haßler, B., Major, L., & Hennessy, S. (2016). Tablet use in schools: A critical review of the evidence for learning outcomes. *Journal of Computer Assisted Learning, 32*(2), 139–156.

Jarvis, C., Tate, N., Dickie, J., & Brown, G. (2016). Mobile learning in a human geography field course. *Journal of Geography, 115*(2), 61–71.

Jennings, G., Anderson, T., Dorset, M., & Mitchell, J. (2011). *Report on the step forward iPad pilot project.* Retrieved from http://bit.ly/lddBoy

Jie, L., Churchill, D., Meng, S., Tam, V., & Chen, A. (2014). Learning Chinese characters via mobile technology in a primary school classroom. In D. Churchill, L. Jie, & M. King (Eds.), *Technology integration, social media, and learning design* (pp. 52–71). Hong Kong: CIHCD.

Kazi, S. A. (2005). *Vocatest: An intelligent tutoring system for vocabulary using m-learning approach.* Paper to be presented at the redesigning pedagogy: Research, policy, practice conference, 30 May–1 June 2005, Singapore.

Kim, M. J., & Maher, M. L. (2008). The impact of tangible user interfaces on spatial cognition during collaborative design. *Design Studies, 29*(3), 222–253.

Klopfer, E., & Squire, K. (2005). *Environmental detectives: The development of an augmented reality platform for environmental simulations.* Retrieved March 15, 2005 from http://website.education.wisc.edu/kdsquire/manuscripts/ETRD-handheld-Draft.doc

Lai, A. (2016). Mobile immersion: An experiment using mobile instant messenger to support second-language learning. *Interactive Learning Environments, 24*(2), 277–290.

Land, S. M., & Zimmerman, H. T. (2015). Socio-technical dimensions of an outdoor mobile learning environment: A three-phase design-based research investigation. *Educational Technology Research and Development, 63*(2), 229–255.

Liaw, S. S., Hatala, M., & Huang, H. M. (2010). Investigating acceptance toward mobile learning to assist individual knowledge management: Based on activity theory approach. *Computers and Education, 54*(2), 446–454.

Lindaman, D., & Nolan, D. (2016). Mobile-assisted language learning: Application development projects within reach for language teachers. *IALLT Journal of Language Learning Technologies, 45*(1), 1–22.

Liu, M., Scordino, R., Geurtz, R., Navarrete, C., Ko, Y., & Lim, M. (2014). A look at research on mobile learning in K–12 education from 2007 to the present. *Journal of research on Technology in Education, 46*(4), 325–372.

Looi, C. K., Seow, P., Zhang, B., So, H. J., Chen, W.-L., & Wong, L. H. (2010). Leveraging mobile technology for sustainable seamless learning. *British Journal of Educational Technology, 41*(2), 154–169.

Mayer, R. (2001). *Multimedia learning.* New York: Cambridge University Press.

Mayer, E. R. (2003). The promise of multimedia learning: Using the same instructional design methods across different media. *Learning and Instruction, 13,* 125–139.

Mayer, R. E. (1989). Models for understanding. *Review of Educational Research, 59*(1), 43–64.

Murphy, T., & Williams, C. (2011). *The iPad as a class presentation platform.* Retrieved from http://155.225.14.146/asee-se/proceedings/ASEE2011/Papers/FP2011mur183_199.PDF

New Media Consortium. (2011). *The NMC horizon report: 2011K–12 education.* Retrieved from https://www.nmc.org/pdf/2011-Horizon-Report-K12.pdf

Norman, D. A. (1983). Some observation on mental models. In D. Gentner & A. L. Stevens (Eds.), *Mental models* (pp. 7–14). Hillsdale, NJ: Erlbaum.

Norman, D. A. (1988). *The psychology of everyday things.* New York, NY: Basic Books.

Ostashewski, N., & Reid, D. (2010). iPod, iPhone, and now iPad: The evolution of multimedia access in a mobile teaching context. *Proceedings of world conference on educational* multimedia, hypermedia and telecommunications 2010 (pp. 2862–2864). Chesapeake, VA: AACE.

Patten, B., Sánches, I. A., & Tangney, B. (2006). Designing collaborative, constructivist and contextual applications for handheld devices. *Computers and Education, 46,* 294–308.

Peirce, S. (2016). Making learning mobile: Using mobile technologies to bring GIS into the geography classroom. *Teaching Innovation Projects, 6*(1). Retrieved from http://ir.lib.uwo.ca/cgi/viewcontent.cgi?article=1063&context=tips

Pimmer, C., Mateescu, M., & Gröhbiel, U. (2016). Mobile and ubiquitous learning in higher education settings. A systematic review of empirical studies. *Computers in Human Behavior, 63,* 490–501.

Ratto, M., Shapiro, R. B, Truong, T. M., & Griswold, W. G. (2003). *The active class project: Experiments in encouraging classroom participation.* Retrieved from http://www-cse.ucsd.edu/~wgg/Abstracts/activeclass-cscl03.pdf

Ray, B. (2002). PDAs in the classroom: Integration strategies for K-12 educators. *International Journal of Educational Technology, 3*(1). Retrieved from http://www.ao.uiuc.edu/ijet/v3n1/ray/index.html

Roschelle, J., & Pea, R. (2002). A walk on the WILD side: How wireless handhelds may change CSCL. *International Journal of Cognition and Technology, 1*(1), 145–168.

Schuck, S. (2016). Enhancing teacher education in primary mathematics with mobile technologies. *Australian Journal of Teacher Education, 41*(3), 126–139.

Seel, N. M. (2003). Model-centered learning and instruction. *Technology Instruction Cognition and Learning, 1*(1), 59–85.

Segall, N., Toni, L., Doolen, J., & Porter, D. (2005). A usability comparison of PDA-based quizzes and paper-and-pencil quizzes. *Computers and Education, 45*(4), 417–432.

Seppälä, P., & Alamäki, H. (2003). Mobile learning in teacher training. *Journal of Computer Assisted learning, 19,* 330–335.

Sharples, M. (2000). The design of personal mobile technologies for lifelong learning. *Computers and Education, 34*(3–4), 177–193.

Sharples, M., Corlett, D., & Westmancott, O. (2002). The design and implementation of a mobile learning resource. *Personal and Ubiquitous Computing, 6,* 220–234.

Shen, R., Wang, M., Gao, W., Novak, D., & Tang, L. (2009). Mobile learning in a large blended computer science classroom: System function, pedagogies, and their impact on learning. *IEEE Transaction on Education, 52*(4), 538–546.

So, K. K. T. (2004). Applying wireless technology in field trips: A Hong Kong experience. *Australian Educational Computing, 19*(2). Retrieved from http://www.cite.hku.hk/people/tkkso/Publications/2004/Applying%20Wireless%20Technology%20in%20Field%20Trips.doc

Song, Y., & Fox, R. (2008). Using PDA for undergraduate student incidental vocabulary testing. *ReCALL, 20*(3), 290–314.

Statista. (2016). *Number of apps available in leading app stores as of June 2016.* Retrieved from http://www.statista.com/statistics/276623/number-of-apps-available-in-leading-app-stores/

Sweller, J. (1994). Cognitive load theory, learning difficulty, and instructional design. *Learning and Instruction, 4*(4), 295–312.

Vygotsky, S. L. (1962). *Thoughts and language.* Cambridge, MA: The MIT Press.

Walters, E. A. (2011). *Will the iPad revolutionize education?* Retrieved September 5, 2011 from http://www.iste.org/Libraries/Leading_and_Learning_Docs/May-2011-Point-Counterpoint.sflb.ashx

Waycott, J., & Kukulska-Hulme, A. (2003). Students' experiences with PDAs for reading course materials. *Personal and Ubiquitous Computing, 7*(1), 30–43.

Wilkinson, K., & Barter, P. (2016). Do mobile learning devices enhance learning in higher education anatomy classrooms? *Journal of Pedagogic Development, 6*(1).

Wong, L. H., & Looi, C. K. (2011). What seams do we remove in mobile-assisted seamless learning? A critical review of the literature. Computers & Education, 57, 2364–2381.

Wong, L. H., Chai, C. S., & Gao, P. (2011). The Chinese input challenges for Chinese as second language learners in computer-mediated writing: An exploratory study. *Turkish Online Journal of Educational Technology, 10*(3).

Zurita, G., & Nussbaum, M. (2004). Computer supported collaborative learning using wirelessly interconnected handheld computers. Computers & Education, 42, 289–314.

Zydney, J. M., & Warner, Z. (2016). Mobile apps for science learning: Review of research. *Computers and Education, 94*, 1–17.

Emerging Possibilities for Design of Digital Resources for Learning

Learning Outcomes:

- Discuss emerging representation technologies and how these might empower design possibilities;
- Analyze emerging forms of interactivity and possibilities these create for design of digital resources for learning; and
- Design a digital resource for learning to incorporate emerging representational and interactive possibilities.

10.1 New and Emerging Developments

This final chapter will make note of some of the latest and emerging interactive and representational technologies, and provide arguments how these might influence design, developments and delivery of digital resources for learning in the near future. However, considering that this is the final chapter in this book, in the last section, we will look back at the key points made so far.

A digital resource for learning is an interactive and multimodal representation that integrates text, visuals, sound, motion media formats and various forms of interactivity in an educationally-useful product. It is designed to facilitate the development of specific curriculum knowledge by serving as a mediating tool in a learning activity. Although visuals are the primary mode of representation, most often in such resources, other modalities can play an important role when integrated in their design. The two key terms in this definition are visual and interactive representational affordances. Driven by ever-increasing processing and storage capacities, capabilities of authoring, programming and design platforms, increased speed of Internet connectivity and access to big data, virtual intelligence, new possibilities of electronics, and so on, there have been significant developments in representational and interactive affordances. In addition, there has been a growth of emerging Internet-enabled devices. These developments in representation, interactivity and delivery technologies create new possibilities for the design and delivery of digital resources for learning. In this chapter, note is made about some of the most interesting emerging technologies and their possibilities for design and delivery of digital resources for learning.

10.1.1 Emerging Representation Technologies

Developments in representational affordances of technology have been increasingly focusing on 3-dimensional media as a way of: (a) escaping flatness of the screen, and (b) increasing realism of presentation, while allowing (c) access to content details in more intuitive and natural sensory and interactive ways. At the same time, there have been important developments in interactive possibilities, making interaction more intuitive, natural and device independent. In parallel with 3D representational possibilities, the development in devices capable of presenting such resources and supporting new forms of interactivity has been occurring. The most interesting developments and emerging possibilities for design and delivery of representations are noted bellow.

- *Holographic Technology*—this technology uses a set of projected lights (usually lasers or light-emitting diodes) and sensors for identifying interaction, to display an image in 3D view in the physical space. Techniques, such as the Spatial Augmented Reality, make possible to project graphical information into physical objects. Some advanced possibilities of this technology include that a learner can interact with the displayed 3D objects, resize, rotate and cross section objects to examine its internal components (e.g., dissecting a heart in interactive medical holography, such as the Real View Imaging), interact with an interface of a software, or visit distant places and people. Imagine a possibility where an image of a teacher in 3D can be teleported via network at different places across the world. For example, a teacher might hold a lecture on a stage in one location, while multiple cameras and assisted by special scanners, mirrors and sensors, record him or her from different angles. Then, laser beam projectors reassemble an image of that teacher on a stage at a different location anywhere in the world. Soon, we might have such technology radially available in lecture theatres. Lately, there has been attempt to make holographic imagery more accessible an affordable, as well as, available to mobile devices. For example, the Ostendo Quantum Photonic Imager being developed by Ostendo Technologies combines an image-processing chip with miniaturized light-emitting diodes (LEDs) capable of projecting small 3D images off mobile devices. Another example is a concept phone known as 'iHolo'. However, even

10.1 New and Emerging Developments

simpler solutions are proposed by some developers, such as TVK Entertainment, where users construct their own pyramid-shaped display unit out of transparent plastic sheets, and placing them on the screen surface of a mobile device, to view holographic images delivered with Vyomy 3D Hologram Projector App. Now, imagine a design possibility where we will not be bound to a screen of a device and can develop digital resources for learning where content is displayed in a physical space in front of us, either with, or without the use of wearable devices such as glasses and haptic accessories. The technologies are here, however, it might be sometime before we truly have these readily available to us in a very affordable way.

- *Augmented Reality*—This is a representational (and interactive) technology where a view of the reality is overlaid, supplemented or augmented by computer-generated content, such as, videos and images, for viewing through a screen of a device. Most often, Augmented Reality uses a head-mounted display that displays images of the physical and virtual worlds into the same field of view. Currently, the most powerful Augmented Reality technology, available commercially, is Microsoft's HoloLens. HoloLens is a holographic computing set from Microsoft that includes wearable glasses with transparent lenses and an integrated visual display, a processor and input device, a variety of sensors (either built in the HoloLens glasses, or external such as AR Bluetooth controller and Kinect), that lets you view, hear and interact with holograms within, what appears to be to your senses, an integrated experiential environment (your real environment overloaded with computer based content). With this technology, it is possible for a teacher to deliver a presentation at any location for learners, or for a learner to communicate with other learners, teachers and experts by having them being presented in 3D in an augmented space, such as at their homes, classrooms or elsewhere. This is already possible with HoloLens and such a communication/conferencing technique is known as 'holoportation'. A variety of applications are being explored at the moment, such as, for example, virtual traveling, one-to-one tutoring, sport coaching, construction industry, product previews in commerce, industrial design, navigation, and a doctor meeting patients at distance in medicine. A number of companies are exploring the development of wearable devices and Augmented reality technology for industrial application, e.g., Atheerair, Meta and APX. More lately, there have been interesting developments of contact lenses that display Augmented Reality. Such bionic devices are foreseen to contain circuitry, an antenna for wireless connectivity and communication, and some form of display embedded in. It is believed that Samsung is developing such technology to include a camera and interaction based on a blinking pattern. Developments of this kind of technology are also happening at Google.

Augmented Reality has become very popular via mobile devices, due to possibilities created by emerging features including various sensors (e.g., acceleration, GPS, and solid state compass), high resolution displays, fast processors and integrated cameras. There are now a variety of Augmented Reality Apps available for download and use (e.g., Augment, SkyView, Augmented Drawing and Anatomy 4D). Most of these Apps utilize camera affordance available to mobile devices, and overlie its screen with 3D visual content or other kinds of information that pops-up once the software identifies markers in the physical environment corresponding to internal triggers. For example, when a camera is pointed at a specific star in a clear sky evening, information about specific star constellation identified will be displayed on the screen. One educationally effective application includes the integration of Augmented Reality affordance with traditional textbook material. For example, in a Mathematics textbook, when a learner accesses a page with graphics of polyhedral objects, placing a mobile device camera over that page will display these objects in 3D on the screen, allowing a learner to explore these in more details (e.g., Pearson AR or EECD AR Apps). Or, if a learner places a camera over a page of a biology textbook with a diagram of human skeletal system, a 3D model pops-up on the screen. Typically, Augmented Reality in such Apps take two-dimensional images (and text) from paper, and turn these into 3D images on the screen of a mobile device. The camera on a device is configured to recognize certain properties in an image, or certain words in a block of text from a page, and produce a 3D image, replacing the flat 2-D image seen by the camera. Besides 3D images, Augmented Reality might trigger videos and other media (Augmented Media). Fundamental interaction in Augmented Reality usually includes rotation of a displayed 3D objects, zooming and repositioning, while emerging technologies such as HoloLens create numerous possibilities for interaction that go well beyond the fundamentals.

New possibilities are emerging very fast. For example, The University of Washington's Human Interface Technology Laboratory is developing a technique known as a virtual retinal display (also known as a retinal scan display or retinal projector) that projects images directly onto the retina of an eye. Magic Leap is developing an interesting and novel Augmented Reality commercial possibility based on this idea, and use of a special projector that shines light into a user's eyes. Light from this projector blends in with the light a user is receiving from the real world, creating an Augmented Reality effect (or Cinematic Reality as Magic Leap calls it). Imagine a possibility to watch a movie with characters appearing right in front of a user in 3D format. This is what Magic leap is trying to achieve. Another company, DAQRI, is developing a Smart Helmet based on functionalities that integrate Virtual and Augmented Reality and emerging forms of mind-machine interactivity.

- *Virtual Reality*—This technological possibility, also called Immersive Multimedia, involves a special set of wearable equipment that immerses a learner into a virtual world (imaginary, computer generated, or captured reality). Usually, a user wears a special helmet or glasses that isolate his or her view from the physical environment and immerses into the virtual world, and presents information to his or her senses via an integrated display. In addition to a wearable visual display unit which represent the core of the virtual reality option, other equipment can be utilized to increase interactivity and add realism. These might include speakers and earphones producing realistic audio effects (e.g., 3D audio); hardware attached to a user's body parts (a special set of sensors and hardware capable of interpreting body movements and actions, and even conducting eye tracking and iris recognition) that allow interaction with presented virtual scenarios; a glove, a special chair or a standing platform (e.g., omnidirectional treadmill such as Virtuix Omni) producing real physical effects (e.g., shaking ground, going around curves, and collisions); or other special equipment producing physical effects to senses, such as air blowing, temperature change, water spraying or releasing particular odour. However, such complex hardware and software systems can be extremely expensive and affordable only to special agencies requiring sophisticated training (e.g., airline industry, medical field, military and space exploration).

Nevertheless, simpler and much less expensive options are emerging. These are beginning to be accessible and affordable to educators, and make possible for designers to develop digital resources for virtual reality presentations and interaction. One simplest option is the Google Cardboard viewer. This is a foldable cardboard kit containing two lenses and a slot for an Android-based mobile device to be inserted in front of these lenses. There are various cardboard options in different colors and design, and a corresponding, slightly more expensive, plastic option. In addition to the viewer, there is an emerging set of Apps designed for this purpose, such as The Official Cardboard App, Cardboard Camera, YouTube 360 viewer, Hidden Temple, Proton Pulse, and Tilt Brush Gallery. An additional option from Google includes Jump Wheel that can be used with a Hero GoPro or similar cameras to capture stereoscopic videos and images for later use with the Google Cardboard. Some Apps are available that support capturing 3D objects and sceneries in 360° (e.g., Autodesk 123Catch or SCANN3D) which can be used to generate a model to be fed in another App for viewing via VR viewers. Technologies such as drones equipped with a Bubl camera might be handy for content capture. Other technologies can be used as well, such as various medical scanners to provide images for integration in Virtual Reality resources, 3D scanners and 3D modelling environments. Recently, HP released a very interesting technology called Sprout. It includes a computer preloaded with 3D image editing and 3D printing software, and a large touch pad called a Touch Mat with a rotational stand for 3D scanning of real objects. These 3D images can then be used in Virtual and Augmented Realities. Furthermore, in the near future, current 2D cameras on personal computers might be replaced with 3D cameras capable of recognizing objects and even measuring distances between them.

More expensive options than Google Cardboard, include devices projected to work together with computers, mobile devices, Interactive TVs and/or game consoles, such as: Samsung Gear VR, HTC Vive, Sony's PlayStation VR and Facebook's own Oculus Rift. Why would Facebook be interested in Virtual Reality Technology? The main reason is in the possibility it creates for combining immersive reality with social networking, teleconferencing, online shopping, films and social gaming. These devices, in addition to wide-angle field of view, include sensors such as Gyro angular velocity sensors, accelerometer and proximity meter, and a corresponding in-built or a handheld controller. For example, they track in real-time the movement of your head, allowing you to explore anything from the sky to the floor just as you do in reality. The possibility for integrated voice command, face recognition and even brain-machine interface is being explored, with some exceptional interactive possibilities emerging. At this stage, most of the content available via these devices include games, virtual tours and some application tools, although the possibilities for the delivery of digital resources for learning leveraging on affordances of this technology is very promising.

10.1.2 New Forms of Interactivity

In addition to the new representational possibilities, which largely focus on 3D media, there have been significant developments in interactive affordances of emerging technologies. In general, research and development focuses on interactions that utilize intuitive functionalities of human physiological and psychological systems. Some new forms of interactions are noted in the previous discussion of emerging forms of representations, e.g., HoloLens Augmented Reality Device and Google Cardboard Virtual Reality headsets. These emerging interactive possibilities often utilize sensors that allow a user to use body movements and voice commands for interaction, as well as other possibilities, such as, via haptic devices such as exoskeletons, gloves, wearables, point-sources, locomotive interfaces, force feedback devices and tactile displays (e.g., Oculus Touch, Gloveone, CyberGrasp, CyberForce, CyberGlove, CyberTouch, KOR-FX, PHANTOM Omni, Stompz, Teslasuit and Woojer, some of which not only allow you to move around a virtual space, but also feel forces and touch and manipulate objects in your hands), face recognition (e.g., Apps such as NameTag and KeyLemon) and brain machine interfacing (e.g., iFocusBand and Melon Headband). Here is a brief discussion of some interesting emerging developments at this stage.

- *Microsoft Kinect and similar technologies*—This is a natural user interface and motion sensing input device and software architecture developed by Microsoft, initially as a part of game consoles, but later for Windows-based computers. Now, Kinect includes software development kit (SDK) that allows developers to integrate this technology in the development of their applications. Kinect system is able to interpret specific body gestures, making possible hands-free control of electronic devices. It uses an infrared projector and depth sensor, camera, microphones, a special microprocessor and software, to track the movement of objects and individuals in physical 3D dimensional spaces. It also might include facial and voice recognition capabilities, as well as the so-called Force Feedback signal (e.g., feeling vibration of a hand-held controller). This technology is

10.1 New and Emerging Developments

capable of simultaneously tracking two or more people. Researchers have been active in integrating this technology in innovative applications and solutions. Examples of projects include the development of an application to interact hands-free with a web browser, PDF and PowerPoint presentations, integration with projectors to allow touchscreen-like capabilities on various surfaces, and hands-free review of medical imaging, allowing a surgeon to access the information without contamination. Developers of digital resources for learning are beginning to explore affordances of this technology. In addition to Microsoft, other companies have been active in the development of hands fee interactive technologies (e.g., Sony PlayStation Camera and PlayStation Eye). Certain models of mobile phones, as for example, Samsung Galaxy Note, support the interaction between human eye and the screen, enabling this so-called 'Smart Scroll', that is, scrolling within text such as web pages and long email messages by eye movement, or triggering certain functions, for example, by shaking the device or bringing it close to the mouth or ear. As mobile devices integrate more sensory hardware and features, we are likely to see some interesting interactive possibilities emerging in the near future.

- *Myo Gesture Control Armband Wearable Technology*—This is a less expensive, but limited alternative to Kinect technology, and an innovative product developed by a start-up company by engineering students from the University of Waterloo. This device, which is slipped on an arm, is capable of reading electrical activity of a user's hand muscles and the motion of arm, and use these to wirelessly control devices with hand gestures. The device includes software that allows a user to customize controls. Also, it includes an open application programming interface (API) and software development kit (SDK) enabling developers to develop their own applications to control, for example, home electronics, drones, computer games, and Augmented and Virtual Reality.
- *Voice Recognition*—Recently, there have been significant developments in voice recognition technology, thanks to impressive advancements in machine learning and artificial intelligence. Almost all leaders in IT industry have embarked on ventures to bring voice recognition interaction capabilities to their technologies, such as, for example, Apple Siri, Android Assistant, and Windows Cortana. Applications such as Naunce's Dragon Naturally Speaking and Speech-to-Text in Google Docs, allow hands-free document composition. Not just for spoken English language, but also other languages are catching up, e.g., Baidu's Deep Speech Chinese speech recognition. Speech recognition is being adopted as an effective strategy for interaction with devices, such as, mobile phones, wearable devices, Google glasses, Virtual Reality devices, game consoles, GPS devices, cars, motorcycle helmets, and music players. Although the recognition of complicates spoken phrases is still very challenging for machines, very good results have been already achieved. With fast advances in machine learning, voice interaction is becoming more reliable and practical. Very soon, voice recognition and interaction will be sufficiently reliable to be used for interacting with all sorts of electronic and computing devices in our environment. In the future, we might not be only able to effectively issue commands to devices, rather, we will be able

to have conversation with technology. Remember the futuristic 'Knowledge Navigator' video developed by Apple in 1987? It has almost became true.

- *Interactive Surfaces*—The development of curved and flexible screens and projectors makes it possible for any shape of surface to be converted into a visual display unit. Such screens can be highly interactive as well. One example of such technology is PufferShere, where the entire surface of a large sphere is an interactive visual display unit that allows multiple users to interact with the content and tools displayed. Today, multi-touch displays can be as a small as the screen of a mobile device, or as large as a dining table or even an entire wall (e.g., Data Arena at the University of Technology Sydney). Furthermore, not just an expensive screen, but the simpler use of special projectors can make it possible to turn any surface into an interactive display (e.g., Magic Box Interactive Floor for schools). Advanced display unit support interaction, not only between a screen and users, but also with devices, such as, mobile phones and tablets (e.g., placing a device on a surface, creates connection and allows integration of data, information and applications between these two technologies). Other biometric possibilities are emerging, such as face recognition and detecting human emotions.
- *Brain-Machine Interface (or Mind-Machine Interface)*—This kind of interaction includes controlling and interacting with devices using our thoughts. Although this sounds very futuristic, and it is yet some time before we will see any commercial application being possible on a wide scale, some serious research and development around the world has been taking place. At the same time, some simpler solutions are already available (as mentioned earlier, Apps such as iFocusBand and Melon Headband). Most of this research focuses on investigating, mapping, assisting, augmenting, or repairing human cognitive or sensory-motor functions by the utility of implants in brain or other areas of the human nervous system, and the use of devices corresponding to these. Ultimately, most of the current research aims to help disabled individuals (e.g., use of electrodes implanted in the hippocampus area of the brain to detect and prevent seizures in patients affected by epilepsy). Nevertheless, there is a growing research effort to develop more generic applications involving human interaction with personal computers and devices. For some pioneering developments, check out the work of researchers such as Theodore Berger from the University of Southern California, Kevin Warwick from Coventry University and Miguel Nicolelis from Duke University.

10.1.3 Other Relevant Technological Developments

In addition to those emerging developments related to representational and interactive affordances, the following are worth mentioning.

- *Smartwatches*—Lately, that has been an increased technological innovation, commercialization and availability of various wearable devices, largely dominated by smartwatches. The smartwatch idea emerged from a talented industrial design student at Delft University of Technology, Eric Migicovsky, who wanted to create a wearable device that would grab information from his phone and make his bicycle ride safer. This device became the Pebble smartwatch. Usually, smartwatch technology is designed to complement smart phones (e.g., Apple Watch, Android Wear or Samsung Gear), bringing certain aspects of information, functionalities and communication directly to such devices. Thus, Smartwatches, most often, today are not a replacement, but an extension of digital devices. According to emerging statistics, there are tens of millions of Smartwatch devices sold around the world. More recently, and very likely in the near future, Smartwatches will not be just extensions to smartphones but will become wearable computer technology capable of communications, notifications, applications, and numerous other affordances in its own. Currently, there are a number of operating systems for this kind of technology, such as Apple's watchOS, Android Wear, Pebble, and Tizen. A number of Apps available for Smartwatches is growing rapidly, while further possibilities exist for the utility of this technology as a haptic supplement to Augmented and Virtual Reality technologies. Examples of apps are: Google Keep for note keeping and managing of to-do-lists, Wear Audio Recorder for recording audio notes, Endomondo fitness App, Evernote App for notes and reminders, Video for Android Wear and YouTube for accessing YouTube content and viewing videos, Tweechip! for Twittering, PixtoCam that turns a Smartwatch into a viewer and control for a smartphone camera, Wear Phone for controlling phone features and contacts, Google Maps companion and navigation App, Watch Hailo for ordering a taxi drive, XE Currency currency exchange information App, 1Password passwords management, iTranslate translation App, BBC News App, Fantastical 2 calendar App, PCalc calculator, Drafts 4 for writing text through dictation, and Sky Guide sky and constellation guide.
- *Google Glass*—This technology is a wearable device that provides an innovative way to access tools and resources from the Internet and elsewhere, post media to blog sites and social networks, obtain just-in-time information, engage in interaction and communication with others, etc. This device creates new possibilities for interacting with technology (e.g., sound recognition, head movement, blinking patterns and interactive features on the side of the glasses), integration with other devices (e.g., smartphones), and delivers content and applications that can seamlessly integrate one's information and communication activities in the world. Some examples of Apps for Google Glass include: wpForGlass App that allows integration with Worpress, LynxFit fitness assistant, WhatsGlass WhatsApp App for communication, DriveSafe4Glass App that assists a car driver, Homework 4 Glass App that assists students to manage their activities and keep track of assignments, Glossaic social networking app for sharing videos and pictures, Glassware Media Manager that assists the management of media content, Glassentation that supports the presentation of slides,

CNN News Alerts for subscription and access to news topics, Blogger App that allows the syncing of information to blogger.com blogs and posting of images and voice text, Viddy Eye App for the capture, creating and sharing of videos, and Evercam App for exploring CCTV cameras. The Google Glass project has been officially closed, most likely due to strong competition from HoloLens that has emerged superior at this stage. However, this idea has set some ground breaking work for further development in such technology. Rather than completely closing this project, the Google Glass team (renamed to Project Aura) is more likely at the moment to keep it 'underground', far from exposure to corporate competitors, and to develop the next generation of wearable devices unmatched in the marketplace. At the same time, Google has set up the 'Google at Work' program that includes partnerships with a number of companies to develop customized enterprise applications of the Google Glass technology (e.g., Augmedix, Crowdoptic, GuidiGO and Parsable (formerly Wearable Intelligence).

- *Smart TV devices*—Television has become an interactive experience. It does not only include changing channels and watching video content as it has been in the past. TV now is a fully interactive device, integrated with the Internet, providing Apps, on-demand content delivery, e-commerce, interactive entertainment, and communication. With the large screen area of Smart TV devices, content can be presented effectively and interactively, however, the context for consumption and interaction is not anywhere as is the case with devices, rather, anytime in the comfort of our own houses (a critical factor to be considered for the design of digital resources for learning for this technology). There are a number of operating systems for Smart TVs, developed by alliances of TV manufacturing companies and technology leaders. However, the most popular these days are AndroidTV/Google TV and Samsung's Tizen. Smart TV's connect wirelessly with other devices, such smartphones, making the interaction and streaming of content between devices possible. There are a variety of App and options related to the Smart TV, such as YouTube, NetFlix, Skype, Opera Browser, Samsung Voice, Pandora, and TuneInRadio.
- *Big Data*—It is projected that in the near future, there will be tens of billions of devices, from industrial machines, scientific equipment, consumer electronics to everyday household and personal items, connected to the *Internet of Things*. These are already beginning to produce huge amounts of data, and have the ability to adjust performance based on 'learning' from data from other sources (e.g., your smart watch learns about your sleeping pattern, or patterns of similar people based on data from Cloud, and sends a decision algorithm to a coffee machine). It is projected that such an ecology of Internet-connected and data-producing devices will have important implications on multiple areas, from businesses, government services, education to individual lives. These technologies, together with other devices such as business and personal computing, wearable and mobile technologies, social networking posts, blogs, twits, data from learning analytics, communication etc., will all produce an unimaginable amount of data (Big Data). At the same time, an increased ability of technology

and artificial intelligence to analyze data in real-time at the speed of light means that highly relevant, contextualized and strategic information can be made available of the Cloud as demanded by specific contexts and tasks. How can we make use of such a huge volume of data from numerous sources? That will depend on the artificial intelligence that constantly looks for patterns in this data, matches it to specific requirements and profiles of users, and displays customized content and suggestion decisions just-in-time when required. Imagine a learning management infrastructure that constantly tracks data emerging from numerous sources, including scientific research, innovative design, publications, content repositories, discussion forums, social media, Internet of things lab and classroom equipment, sensors build into devices, etc., analyzes the indicators of learners' learning patterns and performances, and determines contextualized learning experiences and customized digital resources for specific learning requirements. Very interesting developments that can make this possible are in the branch of Artificial Intelligence called Deep Learning. Deep Learning focuses on the development of software technology that models activities of a human brain (more precisely, those of neurones and their networks) and create advanced possibilities for artificial intelligence to learn to interpret, analyze and recognize patterns in all sorts of data and representations (including images, natural language and sounds. Another venture worth mentioning is the European Human Brain Project and U.S. BRAIN projects, which are attempting to create artificial intelligence and simulation of the human brain that would leverage on massive amounts of computational powered available to learn, understand natural language, recognize images, analyze Big Data, think and make decisions. Will all these technologies and developments bring about new opportunities to education? Technically, many fantastic possibilities are out there, however, it is yet to see sound implementation as things are moving slowly in education. One of the most pioneering attempts to leverage upon strategies for the analysis of huge volumes of data in education is emerging under the umbrella term of *Learning Analytics*.

10.2 Emerging Developments and Digital Resources for Learning?

What do all these developments mean for the design and use/reuse of digital resources for learning? Literature is beginning to report cases of the adoption of emerging technologies in education, such as holographic technology (e.g., Sawant et al. 2016), virtual reality (e.g., Brown and Green 2016), augmented reality (e.g., Huang et al. 2016; Yilmaz 2016), big data and learning analytics (e.g., Dede 2016; Lawson et al. 2016; Merceron et al. 2016), and Kinect technology (Hsiao and Chen 2016; Faisal et al. 2016). One thing that is imminent is that the emerging representational and interactive affordances of technologies will introduce new possibilities for the design of resources and experiences for learning in a way that has never been possible until now. For example, designing content in 3D format for holographic delivery will allow escaping the flatness of a screen of a device, while this will lead to the increased realism of presentation and allow access to content details in more intuitive and natural sensory ways (perceptually experiencing digital resources almost as we experience real objects). With such technology, learners will be able to experience concepts in interactive way right in front of them augmenting their physical environment. For example, learners will be able to examine body organs, such as a heart, rotate and zoom on it to examine details, dissect it to examine its inner structure and functionalities, simulate its operation and manipulate parameters in search of relationships. Textbooks, traditional classroom displays and physical environments could be enhanced through the integration of augmented reality options that provide highly interactive experiences, with concept representations popping-up on learners' devices for exploration. Virtual reality will provide advanced options for creating immersive experiences where learners explore digital resources for learning in the context of a virtual world, for example, not just seeing the effect of forces or acceleration as a number changing on their screen, but also being exposed to the effects of acceleration in realistic ways. Overall, these will create a possibility for digital resources for learning to escape limitations of a single screen and the physical properties of a device, and increase realism, thus, leading to more immersive engagement and experiences. In fact, in the near future, we might be witnessing a whole new ecology of representational technologies supplementing and augmenting each other in the context of a learning activity.

In relation to the interactivity, digital resources for learning might integrate a variety of more intuitive and natural options for engagement. These might include various hands-free, natural interactivities such as through the use of sound recognition, hands, head and body movements, and the movements of eyes (or even using thoughts as more distinct possibility). In fact, new opportunities for the design of resources will impose a need for designers to leverage on emerging interactive options. So will other affordances of emerging devices, such as wearables, googles, VR headsets and emerging mobile handsets. Nevertheless, these emerging devices will impose certain design practices, in many ways enhancing design possibilities, but in some ways limiting current design practices. Thus, in some sense, we might refer to these as to 'disruptive representational design technologies' which demand designers to remain flexible and open to new possibilities.

Other further relevant and emerging possibilities must be noted. Certain digital resources for learning will likely be emerging based on social content generated by communities of experts and enhanced dynamically by new knowledge being generated by the communities of scientists, practitioners and enthusiasts. Social webs have equipped scientists, teachers, journalists, other professionals, students and everyone who is digitally connected with a set of tools for active participation in the production and dissemination of digital information. At almost every moment, new pieces of digital information are being added to the Internet, be it a professional news article, an academic content, business report, a blog post, YouTube video or Flickr image. Harvesting and extracting, and then repackaging information from all of these is yet largely theoretical, but increasingly appearing to be feasible [e.g., mashing methods make possible to integrate algorithms and harvest and extract data and information from API-enabled (Application Programming Interface) sources, such as blogs, Google maps and weather information, for integration into a new digital resource]. Although many readers might disregard social content and think of it as problematic in terms of truth and validity, trustworthiness of a source and in many instances, potentially damaging for young people, intelligent techniques for automated analysis and harvesting are beginning to emerge. As scientists articulate optimal formulas for extracting useful information based on certain topics and parameters, education scientists and designers of educational content should engage in developing methods for the automated articulation of digital resources for learning based on such dynamic and emerging information. Current extraordinary growth of Big Data and Internet of Things, analytical frameworks and ongoing scientific efforts are likely to significantly empower methods for automated construction and the redevelopment of digital resources for learning. This is not only about extracting useful and up-to-date information and data, but also leveraging upon multiple intelligences existing in the space of internet networks.

We might safely say that once a digital resource for learning has been developed and placed in an online repository system, it has only just begun its life. Human knowledge, and its representations are, as we know, under constant socio-cultural development and, therefore, such methods will be exceptionally useful to ensure that up-to-date resources are made available. Furthermore, analytic methods will make possible for digital resources for learning to 'learn' to be redeveloped based on their use, as well from interactions with other digital resources. It might emerge as possible that different digital resources for learning will be able to merge into new representations, delivering new resources. So-called future 'Intelligent Digital Resources for Learning' might be able to be learned by interacting with other resources. Also, these resources might be designed in a way that makes it possible for them to be learned from their user's use patterns, experiences, needs, preferences and profiles. Such possibilities have been used widely in other domains, such as online sales via Amazon.com where the system tracks users, and deploys predictive models to allocate further marketing opportunities. In addition to the intelligent digital resources for learning, we are likely to witness new and powerful forms of repositories and 'Smart Learning Management Systems'; ones that will begin to look and operate more like Amazon, Google and Facebook, for example, and equipped with powerful data analytics and prediction engines.

At the same time, representation development tools are becoming both, more powerful, intuitive and easier to use, thus, enabling more disciplinary experts to create representations to share their knowledge and research. Major digital literacy initiatives, such as US-based "Computer Science for All" will ensure that the future generations of designers, teachers and other professionals will be equipped with skills to effectively deploy technology to communicate information, knowledge and ideas. These will lead to much greater and more productive participation in the development of social content.

Finally, we need to acknowledge the emergency of new technologies that might give us new insight into how people learn and interact with devices and digital resources. For example, eye tracking technologies (e.g., Tobii), allow us to study how learners might interact with the content of a screen of devices, tract the movement of eyes over the screen display and understand the time spent on various areas of displayed content and interface elements. Emerging techniques and technologies and methods such as Functional neuroimaging (e.g., Functional Magnetic Resonance Imaging, or fMRI such as Nordic Neuro Lab equipment), might provide more information regarding brain activities, leading to the articulation of design possibilities that are optimized to support learning. Although this kind of research is still at an infant stage, some significant results are beginning to emerge.

10.3 Summary of Main Ideas from This Book

The central and organizing idea in this book is that, there is an unavoidable transformation of teaching and learning, influenced by broader changes and needs of contemporary societies. Therefore, we need to think differently about the design and use of digital resources for learning than has been done so far in the context of traditional teaching and learning. Speed and form of learning achieved in traditional educational practices that many of us are deeply familiar with, simply are no longer sufficient to enable individuals and societies to be in line with the developments and demands. The traditional, teaching-directed practices, where goals of teaching are to transfer curriculum content to learners, and where learners are to be prepared to score highly on examinations and develop knowledge in a specific discipline that they would use and practice throughout their life, are no longer holding their ground. Societies for today and the future need people who have deep conceptual foundations of disciplinary knowledge required for them to make sense of developments but, at the same time, they need to prepare them for lifelong learning and the challenges that emerge in front of all of us. Therefore, the goals of education should be that learners accumulate a lifelong lasting knowledge base (conceptual foundation) and skills needed to utilize these in successfully dealing with challenges (e.g., in continuous learning, problem solving, innovation, and emerging literacies). Teaching and learning practices, in this context, must focus on activities, not on information transmission from a teacher and resources, which equip students with dispositions and abilities to develop such capacity. Hence, activities must be central to learning, and teachers' primary roles should be the design and facilitation of such experiences for learners.

Important
Design of a learning experience should focus on an activity (e.g., problem solving, projects and inquiries) that engages learners in knowledge construction through the intellectual uses of knowledge content resources serving as mediating tools.

10.3 Summary of Main Ideas from This Book

In this book, we started with an argument that there is a need for the curriculum to embrace a new approach, not the traditional one focusing on information and a single dimension of what will learners know, but a multidimensional approach that integrates all aspects of knowledge development, knowledge use and emerging literacies and skills. Without an appropriate curriculum in place that emphasizes important components, there will not be any changes in traditional teaching and learning. The proposed model for the modern curriculum in this book, emphasizes three components, or directions:

- *Knowledge content dimensions*—where, in addition to (a) declarative and (b) procedural knowledge, more attention is to be given to the development of (c) conceptual knowledge shaping disciplinary specific theoretical thinking.
- *Knowledge use dimension*—disposition to make intellectual uses of knowledge content to solve problem, continuously learn and create innovation, and
- *New literacies and skills dimension*—which create conditions for effective participation in intellectual activities and engagements, and use of modern tools in the contemporary world.

Hence, three components have been emphasized and this proposed approach to the curriculum design is called the '3D curriculum'.

The traditional classroom practices are insufficient to achieve curriculum outcomes integrating these three dimensions. The traditional practices focus primarily on the content knowledge dimension, while knowledge use is given attention to a limited extent. However, even in this context of learning of curriculum knowledge content, the traditional practices are limited, as they are effective mostly with the learning of declarative and procedural aspects of content knowledge, while the development of conceptual knowledge is left to happen spontaneously. Traditional teachers naively equate knowledge with information to be transferred, and mostly are unaware, or lack understanding of the importance and meaning of conceptual knowledge. Information transfer can hardly achieve conceptual knowledge, and intellectually challenging activities are essential for deep thinking, generalizing, abstracting and conceptual changes to occur. Traditional practices need to be replaced with 'learning-centred' practices that focus on activities engaging learners in knowledge content development, knowledge use and the development of new literacies and skills.

Furthermore, in this book, a specific learning design model is introduced as a means for implementation of the 3D curriculum. That learning design model is called the 'RASE', on the basis that it includes four key components: resources (R), activity (A), support (S) and evaluation (E). Design of a learning experience should focus on an activity (e.g., problem solving, projects and inquiries) that engages learners in knowledge construction through intellectual uses of knowledge content resources serving as mediating tools. A teacher's role during the implementation of an activity is that of a facilitator supporting learners. Outcomes of an activity produced by learners must be formatively evaluated, and recommendations for improvements integrated in their final learning outcomes.

> **Important**
> Digital resources for learning are classified based on forms of curriculum knowledge content their designers intended to facilitate developing through learning activities, and accordingly, five distinct forms are explicated, including: information displays, presentation resources, practice resources, concept representations and data displays.

Traditionally, digital resources for learning have been designed as a replacement to a teacher in the context of information transfer. At best, such resources can support the learning of declarative and procedural knowledge, however, their effectiveness for the development of conceptual knowledge is limited and, if occurring, it is incidental rather than intentional. We need to think of a suitable design and structure of digital resources that would support conceptual knowledge development, as well as activities where knowledge is used, and where new literacies and skills are developed. Thus, this book expands the traditional conception of digital resources, and includes categories supporting the propositions of the 3D curriculum, enabling knowledge use, as well as, the development of new literacies and skills. In this context, digital resources for learning are classified based on forms of curriculum knowledge content their designers intended to facilitate developing through learning activities primarily, and accordingly, five distinct forms are explicated, including: information displays, presentation resources, practice resources, concept representations and data displays. Each of these digital resources has been discussed separately in various parts of this book. It has been emphasized that their design should enable effective learning within learning-centred activities where, in addition to the learning of knowledge content enabled by these resources, knowledge use and the development of new literacies and skills is made possible.

Another important proposition that emerges from these claims, is a call for an engagement by relevant agencies to develop systematic collections of digital resources for learning covering key disciplines. Current production effort is limited to endeavours of individual designers developing resources for specific topics without any deep and systematic analysis of disciplines and articulation of the entire collection of representations to cover important concepts. Educational authorities at a local, and perhaps agencies such as UNESCO at an international level, should invest in the development of systematic collections to be provided for teachers and learners. Such collections, in addition to serving as an important catalyst for advancement and transformation of teaching and learning, would serve as one of the important socio-cultural carriers of knowledge accumulated and distributed for equality of access to education for benefits of humanity. In this final chapter, emphasis was placed on emerging technological possibilities and opportunities. We are at the beginning of a very exciting time and new emerging possibilities for the design and delivery of digital resources for learning. We still need to remain, and perhaps increase our creative edge, coupled that with emerging technological possibilities, and resulting innovation will lead to new heights in education science.

> **Activity 10.1**
> *Let's think creatively about a possible design of a digital resource for learning that utilizes one or more of the representational and interactive affordances of emerging technologies. Select either Kinect or HoloLens, and prepare a small presentation of one or two slides to present an idea for design of a digital resource for learning that utilizes the affordances of that technology. You can sketch how this resource might look like and explain its interactive features.*

References

Brown, A., & Green, T. (2016). Virtual reality: Low-cost tools and resources for the classroom. *TechTrends, 60*(5), 517–519.

Dede, C. J. (2016). *Next steps for "Big Data" in education: Utilizing data-intensive research.* Retrieved from https://dash.harvard.edu/handle/1/28265473

Faisal, N., Usman, M., Pirzada, P., & Hassan, A. (2016). Innovating e-learning concepts in special education by Gesture Recognition Using Kinect. *Asian Journal of Engineering, Sciences and Technology,* Special Issue, 44–49.

Hsiao, H. S., & Chen, J. C. (2016). Using a gesture interactive game-based learning approach to improve preschool children's learning performance and motor skills. *Computers & Education, 95,* 151–162.

Huang, T. C., Chen, C. C., & Chou, Y. W. (2016). Animating eco-education: To see, feel, and discover in an augmented reality-based experiential learning environment. *Computers & Education, 96,* 72–82.

Lawson, C., Beer, C., Rossi, D., Moore, T., & Fleming, J. (2016). Identification of 'at risk' students using learning analytics: The ethical dilemmas of intervention strategies in a higher education institution. *Educational Technology Research and Development, 64*(5), 957–968.

Merceron, A., Blikstein, P., & Siemens, G. (2016). Learning analytics: From big data to meaningful data. *Journal of Learning Analytics, 2*(3), 4–8.

Sawant, P., Vagal, N., & Gupta, N. (2016). Holographic technology: From science fiction to reality. *Imperial Journal of Interdisciplinary Research, 2*(10).

Yilmaz, R. M. (2016). Educational magic toys developed with augmented reality technology for early childhood education. *Computers in Human Behavior, 54,* 240–248.

Internet Resources

In this Chapter, numerous technologies and resources are mentioned. Here is a list of these, sorted alphabetically, for readers to access. Note that these links might change through time, so it is advisable to use a search engine to locate a correct link in case it cannot be accessed based on the information provided below.

1Password, https://play.google.com/store/apps/details?id=com.agilebits.onepassword&hl=en

Anatomy 4D, https://play.google.com/store/apps/details?id=com.daqri.d4DAnatomy
Android Assistant, https://play.google.com/store/apps/details?id=com.speaktoit.assistant&hl=en
Android Wear, https://www.android.com/wear/
Apple Siri, http://www.apple.com/ios/siri/
Apple Watch, http://www.apple.com/watch/
Apple watchOS, http://www.apple.com/watch/
APX, https://apx-labs.com/
Atheerair, http://atheerair.com/
Augmedix, http://www.augmedix.com/
Augment, http://www.augment.com/
Augmented Drawing, https://play.google.com/store/apps/details?id=com.lyen.tracingpaper_full
Autodesk 123Catch, http://www.123dapp.com/catch
Baidu's Deep Speech, http://usa.baidu.com/tag/deep-speech/
BBC News, https://play.google.com/store/apps/details?id=bbc.mobile.news.ww
Blogger App for Glass, http://glass-apps.org/blogger-google-glass-app
Bubl camera, https://www.bublcam.com/
Cardboard Camera, https://play.google.com/store/apps/details?id=com.google.vr.cyclops&hl=en
CNN News Alerts for Glass, http://bits.blogs.nytimes.com/2013/05/16/new-apps-arrive-on-google-glass/?_r=0
Computer Science for All https://www.whitehouse.gov/blog/2016/01/30/computer-science-all
Crowdoptic, http://www.crowdoptic.com/
CyberForce, http://www.cyberglovesystems.com/cyberforce/
CyberGlove, http://www.cyberglovesystems.com/cyberglove-iii/
CyberGrasp, http://www.cyberglovesystems.com/cybergrasp/
CyberTouch, http://www.cyberglovesystems.com/cybertouch2/
DAQRI, http://daqri.com/
Data Arena at the University of Technology Sydney, http://www.uts.edu.au/partners-and-community/initiatives/data-arena/overview
Drafts 4, http://agiletortoise.com/drafts/
DriveSafe4Glass, http://glass-apps.org/drivesafe4glass-google-glass-app
EECD AR, https://play.google.com/store/apps/details?id=com.EECD.EECDAR
Endomondo, https://www.endomondo.com/
European Human Brain Project, https://www.humanbrainproject.eu/
Evercam for Glass, http://www.glassappsource.com/listing/evercam
Evernote, https://play.google.com/store/apps/details?id=com.evernote.wear
Fantastical, https://itunes.apple.com/gb/app/fantastical-2-for-iphone-calendar/id718043190?mt=8
Glassentation, http://glassentation.azurewebsites.net/
Glassware Media Manager, http://www.glassappsource.com/listing/media-gallery
Glossaic, http://www.glossaic.com/
Gloveone, https://www.gloveonevr.com/
Google Cardboard, https://www.google.com/get/cardboard/
Google/Android TV, http://www.android.com/tv/
Google Keep, http://www.google.com/keep/
Google Maps https://www.google.com/maps
GuidiGO, https://www.guidigo.com/
Hero GoPro, https://gopro.com/
Hidden Temple, https://play.google.com/store/apps/details?id=com.hg.hiddentemple&hl=en
Homework 4 for Glass, http://www.googleglassfans.com/archives/2543/my-homework-4-glass-is-a-new-way-to-manage-daily-tasks-for-a-busy-lifestyle
HP Sprout, http://www8.hp.com/us/en/sprout/home.html
HTC Vive, https://www.htcvive.com/us/
iFocusBand, http://www.ifocusband.com/
iHolo, http://www.fonearena.com/blog/23410/iholo-concept-phone.html

iTranslate, https://play.google.com/store/apps/details?id=at.nk.tools.iTranslate&hl=en
Jump Wheel, http://vrscout.com/projects/google-cardboard-jump-vr-google-io/
Kevin Warwick from the Coventry University, http://www.kevinwarwick.com/
KeyLemon, https://www.keylemon.com/
Knowledge Navigator, https://youtu.be/-jiBLQyUi38
KOR-FX, http://korfx.com/
LynxFit, http://lynxfit.launchrock.com/
Magic Box Interactive Floor, https://www.magibox.com.au/
Magic Leap, https://www.technologyreview.com/s/534971/magic-leap/
Melon Headband, http://www.thinkmelon.com/
Meta, https://www.metavision.com/
Microsoft HoloLens, https://www.microsoft.com/microsoft-hololens/en-us
Microsoft Kinect, https://developer.microsoft.com/en-us/windows/kinect?navV3Index=1
Miguel Nicolelis from the Duke University, http://www.nicolelislab.net/
Myo Gesture Control Armband, https://www.myo.com/
NameTag, http://www.nametag.ws/
Naunce's Dragon Naturally Speaking, http://www.nuance.com/dragon/index.htm
NetFlix for smart TV, https://play.google.com/store/apps/details?id=com.netflix.ninja
Nordic Neuro Lab http://www.nordicneurolab.com/products/
Oculus Rift, https://www.oculus.com/en-us/
Oculus Touch, https://www.oculus.com/en-us/touch/
Opera Browser for smart TV App, http://www.operasoftware.com/products/tv/tv-browser
Ostendo Quantum Photonic Imager, http://ostendo.com/
Pandora Smart TV App, https://tv.pandora.com/
Parsable, http://parsable.com/
PCalc, http://www.pcalc.com/iphone/index.html
Pearson AR, https://play.google.com/store/apps/details?id=com.pearson.pearsonar
Pebble, https://www.pebble.com/
PHANTOM Omni, http://www.dentsable.com/haptic-phantom-omni.htm
PixtoCam, https://play.google.com/store/apps/details?id=com.pixtogram.wear.zicam&hl=en
Playstation Eye, http://www.sony.co.in/local/product/playstation+eye
Proton Pulse, https://play.google.com/store/apps/details?id=com.ZeroTransform.ProtonPulse&hl=en
PufferShere, http://www.pufferfishdisplays.co.uk/
Real View Imaging, http://www.realviewimaging.com/
Samsung Galaxy Note, http://www.samsung.com/au/consumer/mobile-phone/galaxy-note/
Samsung Gear VR, http://www.samsung.com/global/galaxy/wearables/gear-vr/
Samsung Gear, http://www.samsung.com/global/galaxy/wearables/gear-vr/
Samsung Voice for smart TV, http://www.samsung.com/ph/smarttv/voice_control.html
SCANN3D, http://scann3d.smartmobilevision.com/
Sky Guide, https://itunes.apple.com/us/app/sky-guide-view-stars-night/id576588894?mt=8
Skype for smart TV, https://www.skype.com/en/download-skype/skype-for-tv/
SkyView, https://play.google.com/store/apps/details?id=com.t11.skyview&hl=en
Sony PlayStation Camera, https://www.playstation.com/en-us/explore/accessories/playstation-camera-ps4/
Sony's PlayStation VR, https://www.playstation.com/en-au/explore/playstation-vr/
Speech-to-Text in Google Docs, https://support.google.com/docs/answer/4492226?hl=en
Stompz, http://www.stompzvr.com/
Teslasuit, http://www.teslastudios.co.uk/teslasuit
The Official Cardboard App, https://play.google.com/store/apps/details?id=com.google.samples. apps.cardboarddemo&hl=en
The University of Washington Human Interface Technology Laboratory, https://www.hitl. washington.edu/home/

Theodore Berger from the University of Southern California, http://ngp.usc.edu/faculty/profile/?fid=23
Tilt Brush Gallery, http://www.tiltbrush.com/
Tizen, https://www.tizen.org/
Tobbi eye tracking http://www.tobii.com/
TuneInRadio for mart TV App, https://tunein.com/get-tunein/
TVK Vyomy 3D Hologram Projector, https://play.google.com/store/apps/details?id=com.vyom.hologramprojector
Tweechip!, https://play.google.com/store/search?q=Tweechip!&c=apps&hl=en
U.S. BRAIN, http://www.braininitiative.nih.gov/
Viddy Eye App, http://glassappz.com/apps/viddy-eye/
Video for Android Wear & YouTube, https://play.google.com/store/apps/details?id=com.appfour.weartube&hl=en
Virtuix Omni, http://www.virtuix.com/
Watch Hailo, https://play.google.com/store/apps/details?id=com.hailocab.consumer&hl=en
Wear Audio Recorder, https://play.google.com/store/apps/details?id=com.rimidalv.dictaphone&hl=en
Wear Phone, https://play.google.com/store/apps/details?id=com.mohammadag.wearphone&hl=en
WhatsGlass, http://www.glassappsource.com/listing/whats-glass-glass-app
Windows Cortana, http://windows.microsoft.com/en-us/windows-10/getstarted-what-is-cortana
Woojer, http://www.woojer.com/
wpForGlass, http://labs.webershandwick.com/wpforglass/2013/10/27/introducing-wpforglass/
XE Currency, https://play.google.com/store/apps/details?id=com.xe.currencypro&hl=en
YouTube 360 viewer, https://play.google.com/store/apps/details?id=com.VR_3DD.tube360&hl=en
YouTube for smart TV App, http://www.youtube.com/tv/

Printed by Printforce, the Netherlands